LOVE BEYOND *your* DREAMS

RIANA MILNE

*Break Free of Toxic Relationships
to Have the Love You Deserve*

LOVE BEYOND *your* DREAMS

RIANA MILNE
Creator of the Watch Me!™ Motivational Mindset

By the Sea Books Publishing Company

Love Beyond Your Dreams
Break Free of Toxic Relationships
to Have the Love You Deserve

Terriana (Riana) Milne, MA, LPC, LMHC, Cert. Relationship and Life Coach
NJ Licenses; LPC: 37PC00049500; LCADC: 37PC00091200
Florida Licenses: LMHC: MH-12148 ; CAP: 5808

By the Sea Books, LLC
Copyright © 2014

Editor: Irene Kavanagh
Cover Design: Gwyn Snider of GKS Creative
Author's Photographs: Alexi Panos and Stephana Ferrell
All rights reserved. Except as permitted under the United States Copyright Act, no parts of this publication may be reproduced or distributed in any form or by any means, or stored in a database retrieval system, without prior written consent from By the Sea Books, LLC and/or Terriana (Riana) Milne, unless otherwise indicated.

Send all inquiries to:
BytheSeaBookPublishing@gmail.com
Phone: 201-281-7887
Author's Website: www.RianaMilne.com
Facebook: Coach Riana Milne; LinkedIn, Twitter: Riana Milne
App: My Relationship Coach

By the Sea Books, LLC
ISBN 13: 978-0-9785965-6-9   SAN: 851-0784

Publisher's Cataloging-in-Publication
(Provided by Quality Books, Inc.)

Milne, Riana.
 Love beyond your dreams : break free of toxic relationships to have the love you deserve / Riana Milne. -- First edition.
   pages cm -- (Beyond your dreams relationships ; 2nd)
   Includes bibliographical references.
 LCCN 2013914786
 ISBN 978-0-9785965-6-9
 ISBN 978-0-9785965-9-0

  1. Mate selection. 2. Couples. 3. Intimacy (Psychology) 4. Love.   I. Title. II. Series: Milne, Riana. Beyond your dreams relationships ; 2nd.

HQ801.M55 2013   306.7
                QBI13-600199

Library of Congress Control Number: 2013914786

Published in the United States of America. All information and examples involving clients, students, or celebrities are based on actual events, but names have been changed or omitted to protect the privacy of the people involved.

Dedication

I dedicate this book to all those on a journey to learn how to find love by giving from their hearts and souls without losing themselves in the process.

To all those determined to unearth the good from the bad, to learn from all of life's lessons and become a kinder, more loving and empathetic soul because of them.

For all the life learners who view every relationship as having an opportunity for a lesson to be discovered, and to enjoy each one without judgment. When heartache or challenges appear, may our spiritual wisdom help us with the art of forgiveness.

For those who have faith that there is a more rewarding and compassionate way to love ourselves and others; who are tired of feeling hurt, battered, lied to, disrespected, disappointed, and without worth, who continually ask themselves, *"Why do I keep falling for partners like this?"* Feel confident that when you can identify and break free from toxic relationships, there exists the promise to have love beyond your dreams.

And, finally, I dedicate this book to "my Forever Love," the one who brought me the most intense love I've ever known along with the most pain I've ever endured. It inspired me to seek the answers I needed to understand, heal and move on to experience a wonderful, mutually healthy love, while continuing to live my higher purpose of helping others.

Partial proceeds from this book will go to various women's empowerment programs.

> "'Tis better to have loved and lost –
> Than never to have loved at all."
>
> – Alfred Tennyson, *In Memoriam*

Acknowledgments

I BECAME IMPASSIONED WITH the topic of love relationships because of my own life experiences. I have loved many who have hurt me without understanding why. I believed that if I did the right things in a relationship – remain honorable, true, loving, dedicated, romantic, passionate, affectionate and honest – I would naturally receive the same in return. It wasn't that I didn't love properly, but more that my boundaries were weak, or my expectations too high. I was either choosing the wrong partner or letting my own childhood fears and adolescent rejection issues get in the way of unconditional love and a relationship that was evolved.

Now that I'm older, I look back at my romantic relationships with gratitude and a warm heart. I don't harbor anger, for those men have been my life's greatest teachers. I had an enormous amount of romantic fun, and a ton of heartache! But in the end, I survived and my experiences taught me to have a great deal of compassion for them and for others. I feel a great deal of empathy towards those suffering in relationship pain, and it encouraged me to seek the knowledge I needed in order to love in a healthier, spiritual and more selective way. It is this knowledge that I share here.

I thank all of the fun, beautiful men I've known for helping me get to the path of a higher consciousness of love and wisdom through spirituality and deep faith. I'm grateful that our experiences pushed me to study, to receive relationship counseling and coaching, and to find a way to love myself more, which has led me to love beyond my dreams. I have stronger personal boundaries while loving others unconditionally.

Ultimately, they gave me the strength to say, "Goodbye, good luck and God bless" when the relationship had run its course and the lessons were learned, leaving me with an appreciative smile for our fabulous memories.

I would like to thank all those who worked so hard on my behalf to produce this work of love: cover design by Gwyn Snider of GKS Creative; editing by Irene Kavanagh; and back cover copy by Graham Van Dixhorn of Write To Your Market.

Thank you to my test readers, whose loving suggestions, additions, and edits help me to reach others with compassion and understanding: Michael Logston, MA, LPC, LCADC; Annamarie Germanio, Bobbi Milne; Jamie Siracusa; Stephana Ferrell, Lisa Spengler and Sybil Jerkins-Blanding.

To my daughters Stephana and Alexi, my sister Bobbi, and my dear friends, Jacqui, Michael, Sybil, and Annamarie, your honest suggestions inspired me to be authentic in my writing. Please know that your encouraging, loving dedication helped me immensely in my hours of sorrow and recovery. I cannot thank you all enough, but please know that your effort to help me inspired me to write this book, which will assist so many others who also experienced a toxic love relationship.

Disclaimer

THIS BOOK IS DESIGNED to provide information on different strategies to better your life. It aims to educate you on various motivational and spiritual approaches to a mind-set that helps you reach your relationship goals and overcome your challenges.

It is sold with the understanding that the publisher and author are not engaged in rendering legal, psychological, counseling, or other professional services in this book. If medical, legal, or other expert assistance is required, the services of a competent professional should be sought. If you are depressed, feel suicidal, or need immediate mental health care, please call 911 or go to your local hospital emergency room.

It is not the purpose of this book to reprint all the information that is otherwise available to authors and/or publishers, but instead to complement, amplify, and supplement other texts. You are urged to read all the available referenced material, learn as much as possible about this topic, and tailor the information to your individual needs. For more information, see the many resources provided in the back of this book.

Every effort has been made to make this book as accurate as possible. However, there may be mistakes, both typographical and in content. Therefore, this text should be used only as a general educational guide and not as the ultimate source of self-help information. Furthermore, this book contains information that is current only up to the printing date.

The purpose of this book is to educate and entertain. The author, Riana Milne, and By the Sea Book Publishing shall have neither liability nor responsibility to any person or entity with respect to any loss or damage caused, or alleged to have been caused, directly or indirectly, by the information contained in this book or other related information, eBooks and audio products.

If you do not wish to be bound by the above, you may return this book to the publisher for a full refund.

Contents

Introduction: *Love Yourself More*	1
Section One	
How to Spot the Emotional Manipulator or Toxic Person	13
1) What Is a Toxic Partner?	23
2) Why Are You Attracting Toxic Partners?	33
3) The Warning Signs When Dating	45
4) Types of Toxic People	53
A) The Emotional Manipulators: Narcissistic, Borderline, and Bipolar Personality Disorders	53
B) The Charming Con Artist: Antisocial Personality Disorder, Sociopaths and Psychopaths	64
C) The Addicted and Types of Addiction	72
D) The ACOA Personality Type	92
E) The Chronic Cheater, Emotional and Sexual Affairs	105
F) The Jealous and Controlling, Paranoid	110

G)	The Passive-Aggressive, Poor Communicators	116
H)	The Angry and Critical, Mood Disorders	121
I)	The Dramatic Histrionic	123
J)	The Avoidant, Commitment Phobic	125
K)	The Perfectionistic, Obsessive-Compulsive	138
L)	The Habitual Liar	142
M)	Abusive Partners	144
N)	The Overly Anxious	151
O)	Peter Pan Syndrome, the Mama's Boy, and the Mother Hater	157

Section Two
Stop the Cycle of Dysfunction — **167**

5) Should I Stay or Should I Go? — 169
6) Try Coaching and Couples Counseling — 193
7) Are You Codependent? — 205
8) Are You a Love Addict? — 213

Section Three
Save Yourself – The Path to Healing — **223**

9) Dealing with the Lost Dreams, Anger and Pain — 225
10) How to Move On — 231
11) Building Support Systems — 243
12) Use the "Watch Me!" Mind-set for Change — 247
13) Creating New Goals for a New Life — 251
14) Learning to Be Alone — 263

Contents

15)	Relapse and Return to the Love Object	269
16)	Healing through Spirituality and Reinventing Yourself	277
17)	Letting Go – Forgiveness and the Goodbye Letter	287

Section Four
Having Love Beyond Your Dreams — **291**

18)	What Is an Evolved Relationship?	293
19)	How to Meet a Healthy Partner	303
20)	Defining Qualities, Needs and Requirements	327
21)	The Law of Attraction for Love	341
22)	Learning to Love Unconditionally	347
23)	Relationship Rules of Success	351

Conclusion
Love Yourself More! Facing Your Future Boldly — 359

Poems of Love and Emotion — 369

Riana and her daughters, Stephana Ferrell and Alexi Panos, share thoughts of love to contemplate, inspire and motivate.

References and Recommended Reading — 375

About the Author

Riana Milne has a three-part master's degree in applied clinical and counseling psychology and is a licensed professional counselor (LPC/NJ), a licensed clinical alcohol and drug counselor (LCADC/NJ), a Florida Licensed Mental Health Counselor (LMHC) and Certified Addictions Professional (CAP), and a Certified Relationship Coach for individuals, couples, and families. She has her own practice, Therapy by the Sea, LLC in Egg Harbor Township, NJ and Delray Beach FL. Her app, "My Relationship Coach," offers convenient coaching for her clients around the world. Riana served as a student-assistance counselor (SAC) within schools, helping students with emotional and relationship issues from grades kindergarten through college.

She is also an interfaith minister and uses spiritual concepts with her inspirational and motivational coaching and therapy style. Clients are helped to overcome pain and fear and encouraged to learn and practice holistic change for personal growth in mind, body, and spirit. The Watch Me! mind-set as discussed in her first book of this series, *Live Beyond Your Dreams – from Fear and Doubt to Personal Power, Purpose and Success,* is an instructional, motivational program for personal power, purpose and success that she has taught for over thirty years.

Now she brings this inspirational system to love relationships, coaching those who have experienced significant relationship anguish to enjoy healthy, lifelong love. Riana is a professional speaker, has had various radio shows, and has appeared on many TV shows. Her relationship coaching clients are men and women of all ages from teens to seniors, as well as singles, couples, and families. *Love Beyond Your Dreams* will inspire you to change the way you love and give you the confidence not to settle for less. Visit Riana's web site, www.RianaMilne.com for more articles on relationships.

Introduction

Love Yourself More

*Every part of your life involves relationships;
when they are peaceful, loving and happy
you will personally feel the same.* – Riana Milne

THIS BOOK HAS BEEN WRITTEN primarily for women of any age, culture, race or background, straight or gay, single or married, who have been hurt by a destructive partner. It speaks as well to partners in current abusive relationships, whether emotional, verbal, or physical. It is for all who live with constant anxiety or depression from being lied to, belittled, put down, hurt, or isolated from any sense of worth as a priority in their partner's life. Many of the concepts are equally viable for men in toxic relationships, but for ease of writing, I address mainly the female gender.

It is for every person seeking to understand that we're all God's children and in our humanness lies the truth that we all make mistakes. Because of our childhood wounds, abuse and experiences, we can act out impulsively from deep pain, fear, anxiety, lack of self-love or feelings of abandonment. In doing so, we often choose partners who ultimately are unhealthy for us.

Sigmund Freud believed that people are the product of their past and that the first five or six years of life shape their character in adult relationships. Parental influence in early developmental years is deeply integrated into adult mental and emotional health. Emotional manipulators have deep childhood wounds that stem from abuse, neglect, loneliness, deprivation and other major traumas. As adults they feel anger, shame, anxiety and insecurity and project these emotions onto their partner. They are fiercely attracted to romantic, giving, honest, kind and often codependent partners who accept their narcissism. These people are experts at hiding their toxic personalities by pretending to be loving, attentive, sacrificial and generous. A codependent adult is attracted to the manipulator who reminds them of an emotionally absent, distant, toxic or narcissistic parent. In childhood, the codependent would have been held to particularly high standards to earn parental love and acceptance.

Throughout my adult life, I found myself immediately attracted to charming, good-looking men, and with these partners I had an extremely satisfying romantic, sexual life. However, the men I chose to commit to were emotional manipulators, sociopathic liars, controlling, toxic, angry, selfish and passive-aggressive. During the good times, it was the best! But they were unable to maintain a long-lasting relationship of integrity because of their addictions, deception, lies and emotional shortcomings due to their own childhood wounds. I became determined to research and discover why this kept happening to me – a very kind, loving, helpful and honorable woman.

After several years of investigation, and taking thousands of hours of classes to become a certified coach, I began to write

Introduction: Love Yourself More

this book with the purpose of helping myself and others. What I needed to know about the toxic personality types who broke my heart became crystal clear when I started dating again. I could spot the emotional manipulator on the first or second date. I figured I would make my relationship pain worth something and help others avoid despair.

Looking back, I was a young girl who adored her handsome, charming, affectionate and outgoing father who was rarely home. When he was home, he was amazingly loving, affectionate and tons of fun, and he taught me many valuable life lessons. However, unbeknown to us, he was a CIA and FBI agent; and due to this work, we never knew where he was or when he would be home. He also was an official at many track and field events all over the country, which removed him from our family. I remember always asking, "When is Daddy coming home?" and being given promises that were not often kept by him. Many birthday parties, modeling shows, and other special events for me went by without my father in attendance. However, he did attend the swim meets in which I and all my siblings took part, and we had a treasured two-week family vacation each Christmas to Key West, Florida.

At the impressionable age of ten, I discovered with my older brother that our dad had a secret life – one that we had to hold as a sworn secret for many years from my mother and siblings. His absences upset and overwhelmed my mom who had five kids to care for. She often seemed lonely and depressed but took great joy in raising us and was quite a perfectionist, insisting that we do well. She was an extremely smart, accomplished woman in Real Estate and worked hard to give us kids a good life.

I was the fourth of five children, and was quiet and introspective. I loved the arts and wrote my feelings in poetry form in several journals. My first crush in seventh grade was on a handsome boy named Joe who never quite returned my love for him, but we were friends. I loved him for three years, often feeling rejected and not good enough. At age twelve, I started modeling for major department stores in Philadelphia and, at fourteen, got hired as a promotional model to work with top entertainers and musicians for WFIL "famous 56" radio in Philadelphia. My modeling and talent jobs saved me and I finally gained the self-confidence I needed as a teenager. I attended seven proms and had a great boyfriend by grade 10.

Still, between the no-fault abandonment of my loving father with his secret life (whom I know now was clearly ACOA [Adult Child of an Alcoholic; or of other family traumas], having traumatically lost his own father at the age of twelve), the unfulfilled love for Joe in key female developmental teen years, and never feeling good enough compared to my successfully athletic brothers (who I adore to this day), I see as an adult how these early situations caused me to be codependent in my love relationships. Early circumstances had hard-wired me into loving handsome, aloof, charming and romantic men. I became determined to break this personal pattern, and with knowledge, came power.

My goal now is to help you gain the ability to save yourself from risky personality types. I want you to learn as much as possible and break free from toxic relationships for good. You deserve a healthy love life!

Love Beyond Your Dreams – Break Free of Toxic Relationships to Have the Love You Deserve is a psychological educational system that will help you choose a healthier and more peaceful path in both life and your relationships.

It begins with knowledge. You can't change what you don't understand. This book combines the knowledge of personal experience with my training as a certified relationship coach and licensed

Introduction: Love Yourself More

psychotherapist. Examples are taken from the fourteen years in my marriage-and-family private counseling practice, Therapy by the Sea, LLC (with all names changed and situations altered for confidentiality). I also discuss relationship and life-coaching techniques (for singles and couples) acquired throughout many years of reading and self-study as well as from my training and certification with *Relationship Coaching International*.

As a certified relationship coach, I help to improve your odds for success in finding the right partner so that you can have the love you deserve and the relationship beyond your dreams. We first discuss childhood trauma or destructive patterns that have led to toxic love partners. By investing the time and effort now, you'll avoid future emotional despair by making smarter choices in a mate. I will teach you to swiftly move on from a person not right for you, to stop destructive habits that push good partners away, and to attract a healthy love partner into your life.

Please understand that this book is not meant to diagnose any specific person or disorder, or to suggest any treatments for those with mental health disorders, or to recommend specific treatments for readers or their partners. It has been written mainly to educate, inform and suggest avenues to try for better emotional health, healing and recovery from toxic relationships.

I also have gathered many excellent resources and references from top authors in the subjects discussed. I wholeheartedly believe in bibliotherapy, in which I recommend to clients books from experts on topics pertinent to them while they are engaged in coaching or counseling. This exercise helps widen their growth and understanding of topics and situations they currently are experiencing. Please take a moment to review the reference list and see which books could be helpful to your own particular situation.

This book contains four sections: How to SPOT the Emotional Manipulator or Toxic Person; How to STOP the Cycle of Dysfunction; SAVE Yourself – The Path to Healing; and Having Love Beyond Your Dreams.

Section One, *How to Spot the Emotional Manipulator or Toxic Person,* describes the warning signs and clues you need to know when meeting a potential partner.

Chapter 1 presents an overview: "What Is a Toxic Partner?" See what defines a healthy, loving and evolving relationship, and understand what a toxic relationship feels like. I also touched on this topic in Chapter 8 of my last book, *"Live Beyond Your Dreams."*

Chapter 2: "Why Are You Attracting Toxic Partners?" will help to clarify as well as analyze toxic situations and what can be done about them. One of the most common questions I hear is, "Why do I always end up getting hurt?" The chapter explores childhood wounds that linger throughout adult life, leading to unhealthy adult relationship choices and attraction to dysfunctional partners based on "chemistry."

Chapter 3: "The Warning Signs When Dating" identifies the red flags you should look for. Dating with a healthy sense of awareness by consciously living "in the now" and carefully listening and watching what your date says and does, as well as understanding dysfunctional behavioral patterns, will help you easily spot a potentially harmful mate.

Chapter 4: "Types of Toxic People" describes in plain language the most common personality disorders. Many traits don't necessarily make for "bad people," but might be wrong particularly for you in a healthy love relationship. Many personality disorders do not emerge right away, but knowing about them keeps you on the lookout for traits and behaviors that can give you clues to something more dysfunctional or dangerous. We all have the

Introduction: Love Yourself More

capacity to transform negative childhood programming with a true desire to change and the help of counseling. This chapter briefly explains the sixteen types of toxic personality behaviors to watch for.

Section Two, entitled *Stop the Cycle of Dysfunction*, helps you decide whether your relationship is worth saving or is so dysfunctional that it's in your best interest to leave it. Each partner must be invested in the change process, whether seeking couples counseling or individual coaching, or better yet, agreeing to both.

Chapter 5 addresses the choice: "Should I Stay or Should I Go?" Discussion centers on knowing when enough is enough and on defining and acknowledging your ultimate deal breakers. Learn about therapeutic separation, when to forgive and fight for the relationship before giving up too quickly, how to create relationship renewal or when to simply move on, protect and love yourself more.

Chapter 6: "Try Individual Coaching and Couples Counseling" explains the importance of both before making rash decisions. Coaching will help you work on individual concerns, negative habits, and personal needs that will make you a better partner. Couples counseling will teach you the communication skills necessary to speak openly and honestly about your needs, and, at the same time, really hear your partner's desires. It helps you examine your own baggage that you bring into your adult relationships and how to handle your "past demons" when they emerge.

Chapter 7 asks, "Are You Codependent?" and explores the underlying nature of this personality issue. Discover if you are codependent and learn the options you have to realize a fuller, more self-confident life controlled only by you.

Chapter 8: "Are You a Love Addict?" examines another personal behavior pattern you may have and must be willing to face.

It is critical to know what love addiction means. People with this syndrome often attract toxic love-avoidant partners by creating chemistry brought on by lust. Once recognized, you will know what to do to stop this harmful pattern.

Section Three, *Save Yourself – The Path to Healing*, offers nine chapters to help you through the healing process of a painful or unexpected breakup. Often, one partner thinks everything is fine until discovering the other partner's extramarital affair, an addiction, or a secret life of lies. This section focuses on a step-by-step strategy for regaining self-esteem, overall health and personal recovery.

Chapter 9: "Dealing with the Lost Dreams, Anger and Pain" explains how to function normally following the first shock of discovery or the breakup of your relationship. Not every suggestion will be right for you, but many should be considered for the fastest therapeutic change and getting you back to center.

Chapter 10: "How to Move On" explores the time needed to mourn the pain of lost dreams. Shock contains its own healing process: the progression of reaction is shock, fear, numbness/depression, anger and long-term sadness. Understanding this process, and knowing what to do through each stage, will help to speed your recovery.

Chapter 11: "Building Support Systems" is essential. Find a therapist to help you through the initial trauma while you expel the details and history of the relationship. Trust only one or two friends during this time. Surprisingly, family may turn against you, taking the other person's side. This chapter elaborates on support and how to handle rude and insensitive comments.

Chapter 12: "Use the Watch Me! Mind-set for Change" will guide you through the highlights of the first book in this series, *Live Beyond Your Dreams – from Fear and Doubt to Personal Power,*

Introduction: Love Yourself More

Purpose and Success. Learn to reset your goals for new dreams and a higher purpose through an amazingly effective motivational thought system. Discover ways to break lifelong negative messages from childhood.

Chapter 13: "Creating New Goals for a New Life" explores how all too often, a person becomes so obsessively attached that their goals and dreams are focused only on the love object and their life together. Following a breakup there is a sudden and overwhelming sense of emptiness along with extraordinary loss and fear of the future. This chapter helps you to put the focus back on you and your future.

Chapter 14: "Learning to be Alone" illustrates why solitude seems so frightening for many people. Women especially find it hard to journey out alone, and men often retreat into nights of mindless TV or trying to score with every woman they meet. Learn to create a healthy and successful single life.

Chapter 15: "Relapse and Return to The Love Object" explains this common occurrence. Although the behavior acted out against you may have been horrific, and your rational mind believes "I am done," the intensity of love addiction holds you emotionally captive. It may feel near impossible to stop wanting your partner back, but there are things you can do to stop this obsessive desire and prevent relapsing back to your toxic relationship.

Chapter 16: "Healing Through Spirituality and Reinventing Yourself" illustrates how a sense of faith will help you move through the change process and is crucial before considering dating again. Time is needed following a breakup to process your anger and to learn valuable lessons from the relationship. Learn to rebuild your self-esteem and confidence levels so that you can date from a place of strength and happiness, rather than desperation and pain.

Chapter 17: "Letting Go – Forgiveness and the Goodbye Letter" deals with the importance of timing. Eventually, you may want to write a goodbye letter to forgive your partner and find closure and value in the relationship, but think twice before sending it. Initially, it could be full of anger, blame, hurt and pain. Allow yourself enough time and space to heal and develop a spiritual mindfulness before sending a final letter.

Section Four, *Having Love Beyond Your Dreams*, demonstrates the promise of a wonderful love relationship when you free yourself from your toxic partner and follow new goals. The "love-yourself-more" philosophy includes embracing a higher and healthier spiritual consciousness towards life, leading to giving and accepting unconditional love for yourself and others. This will help you attract love into your life without forcing, controlling, rushing, or fearing the process of falling in love.

Chapter 18: "What Is an Evolved Relationship?" describes what qualities and traits are necessary to have within yourself and your partner and emphasizes its importance to a lifetime of love and happiness with one partner.

Chapter 19: "How to Meet a Healthy Partner" talks about the challenge of meeting an ideal partner who has accomplished similar spiritual growth and is able to be a responsible partner in the healthy, evolved love relationship. Nothing works if only one person is honorable and trustworthy.

Chapter 20: "Defining Qualities, Needs and Requirements." By now, your list hopefully will not include "hot, rich and handsome." This chapter focuses on qualities needed in a partner that best match your own positive traits and characteristics. Know exactly what you're looking for before you begin your search. Get ready to meet a lot of people – and slow down the passionate romance and the desire to become intimate or exclusive until you are friends first.

Chapter 21: "The Law of Attraction for Love" explains basic laws of attraction and how to use them. By living as your best self, by meeting your own emotional needs, by owning your core values and purpose, you will effortlessly radiate irresistible energy to attract healthy love into your life.

Chapter 22: "Learning to Love Unconditionally" will keep you open to possibilities as you date many and build new friendships. If, in time, you discover any toxic personality traits within a suitor, keep this person on a friendship level, and avoid progressing into a full-blown, intimate relationship. Remain friends as you continue to search for your evolved life partner.

Chapter 23: "Relationship Rules of Success" will expand on all these tips and more to help guide you into a healthy, more peaceful and rewarding love partnership.

Welcome to the *Love Beyond Your Dreams* system to learn to *break free of toxic relationships to find the love that you deserve!*

Wishing you Great Love,
Riana

Section One

How to Spot the Emotional Manipulator or Toxic Person

People with high self-esteem have it because they have overcome their failures. They have been put to the test of life, overcome the problems and grown.

– David Jensen

*I*T HAPPENS IN AN INSTANT. Something is said or done and you look at your partner or date and ask, *"Who is this person?"* and *"Why did I not see this sooner?"*

What you have uncovered is described as a "Dr. Jekyll and Mr. Hyde" personality type or a person the world sees as charming, outgoing, fun, affectionate and kindhearted, someone to emulate, and who is usually quite charismatic and attractive. This would be Dr. Jekyll.

Mr. Hyde is the complete opposite – the person the world rarely sees. This is the hidden person, one who is negative and deceiving and who possesses an evil, conning dark side. He seduces and charms his prey into a web of deceit. This is referred to as the "Lucifer effect," named after God's fallen angel.

Before realizing what has happened, the victim is immersed in a world very different from what they could have imagined. They lose themselves completely while trying to pick up the pieces of their once familiar life. The emotional manipulator has taken control while the victim consistently tries to please and placate the one who has slyly and systematically destroyed them.

How can you spot this toxic person sooner and protect yourself from an artful web of deception? It is difficult at best, but you must recognize the warning signs before you start dating. If you know what to look for and refer back to this book when you intuitively feel there could be trouble, you can stop yourself before getting too emotionally and sexually involved.

While falling in love, you get caught up in the euphoria of romantic lust and affection. You feel adored and catered to by a charming, giving, and accommodating person who appears to be perfect. You surrender so completely to the chemistry of intense attraction that you're willing to brush aside or ignore any warning signs you may feel. This book plainly lays out the signs you must not ignore, enabling you to spot toxic personality types and stop the relationship early on. If you ignore the signs and continue to date the emotional manipulator, you will be forced to reckon with the devastating aftermath for months or years after their destruction.

When the whirlwind courtship slowly settles into an exclusive, committed relationship, very often after a marriage, purchasing a home together, or having children, something monumental happens that catapults you into the reality of living with a "hidden" toxic person.

You may discover something that shocks you to the point of physical illness. You're unable to sleep, can't eat, and feel numb within your body. Your world becomes blurred and unnatural as you move through the pain of trying to make sense of his punishing behavior aimed directly at you. How is it possible that the one you cherish most could be so coldly and selfishly destroying your relationship?

You feel emotionally bludgeoned and your response involves extreme fear, helplessness, and horror. This distressing situation can cause recurrent and troubling flashbacks or dreams that revisit the hurtful experience. All these emotional and physical effects are signs of Post-Traumatic Stress Disorder (PTSD).

If you discover photos or videos of your partner's lover, or have personally seen your partner in the company of the person they are cheating with, these visual images may be relived in your mind for many months or years. Anything you witness, or have been confronted with, that involved a threatening feeling to yourself or others could lead to PTSD. It is essential that you get immediate therapeutic counseling support.

According to the DSM-IV-TR (*Diagnostic and Statistical Manual of Mental Disorders*), other signs of PTSD, lasting for the duration of at least one month, include irritability or explosions of anger, hyper-vigilance, lack of concentration, being easily startled, and difficulty in falling or staying asleep. You may also be affected significantly in important life spheres, like finding it difficult or impossible to function at work or in social situations.

Whatever reminds you of the traumatic event or person, whether thoughts, feelings, places, music, food, friends, or certain activities that instantly bring you to tears, can close down your emotions so that you feel nothing, not even love for your children.

Your partner may have created a situation so embarrassing that you choose to isolate yourself from others, losing interest in friends and social activities you had always enjoyed. Listening to music that you shared can trigger high emotions and tears, leaving you distraught.

When dreams and goals are unexpectedly shattered, you may find yourself no longer excited about your life, career, children, marriage or retirement plans. Once so alive, you now survive moment by moment, terrified of your partner and dealing with the choice of trying once more to keep everything together or deciding to take the brave step to love yourself more, end it and move on.

When you love someone, and you practice the art of spiritual forgiveness, you may decide to give your partner another chance to exhibit honesty and integrity. However, it takes a long time to rebuild shattered trust.

In my counseling center, I share a formula:

$$\text{Trust} = \frac{\text{Consistency}}{\text{Time}}$$

This means the person who caused the infraction must constantly show over a long period of time that their words and actions can be trusted again. They must show on a daily basis that they can be dependable, reliable, and honest. They must be willing to share their activities and whereabouts with their partner. It is essential that they keep their computers and phones open to their partner without passwords, proving over time that they have nothing to hide. Within six months to a year, trust can move towards being rebuilt.

Sometimes, for the sake of your vows, or to keep your family together, you're willing to ride the emotional rollercoaster for a while. As trust continues to be rebuilt over time, you start to relax and begin to enjoy the anticipation of the ride together again. You feel excited as you take off on a new journey with new promises and goals; often, the romance-and-flowers stage can be rekindled within both partners.

You experience the new rush and the fantastic highs, but slowly you begin to sense a sharp turn in the path. There are signs of increasing dissatisfaction, emotional distancing or negativity from your partner and you begin to feel uneasy, as though approaching a sudden and steep descent. You try to ignore any anxiety and intuitive warnings that foreshadow another emotional catastrophe.

Then, it happens again! Your toxic lover pulls another horrific stunt that crushes you to the core, often much worse than the first time.

Your world stops and you feel terrified. With furious and frightening speed, you fall in a downward spiral, descending and

Section One: How to Spot the Emotional Manipulator or Toxic Person

crashing to the bottom of your emotional pit. You're left dazed and wondering if you're able to recover from yet another horrific and dramatic rollercoaster ride with your partner.

You swear this episode is the last time. This had been the last ride, his last chance. After all, you've forgiven him a hundred times. You did everything to prove your perfect love over and over, and still, there is blame, criticism, and a total lack of respect, concern or remorse for you or his actions taken against you. Once again, there are more broken promises, more deceit and unending lies.

Your friends and family ask, "Why do you stay?" and you constantly hear the words, "You deserve better!" And, deep down, you know that you do. Your partner begs for your forgiveness after another demonstration of his lack of integrity, breaking your trust with even more lies. He will attempt to be the perfect partner for days or weeks after his infraction so that you will forgive him and stay in the relationship.

The early days of this relationship were phenomenal. Hanging on to the memories of an incredible, whirlwind, "romantic movie" type of courtship, you try again to convince yourself of his potential to be wonderful and his ability to change. You keep trying different ways to fix him, his problems, and the relationship, none of which appear to interest him.

"If only we could get back to how he was and how our relationship was in the beginning" is often the sobbing plea of a therapy client who shows up without her man. "He couldn't come today; there was something more important," she'd try calmly to explain, holding back her tears. Again, she would defend her partner, not seeing that once more he made her a distant second to his own selfish agenda.

No one is immune to the devastating emotional pain that accompanies the discovery of a deceitful or toxic loved one. It could be that they have been engaging in emotional or physical affairs or have been caught lying, conning, using or abusing you. Your partner may also have mental health issues as a result of childhood trauma, such as emotional, physical or sexual abuse, severe neglect, or parental abandonment. There also could be a biological, inherited component to their behavior, such as Bipolar or borderline personality disorder.

This book will give you simple and easy-to-understand definitions of major personality disorders. Lists will help summarize what to watch for, so you can spot toxic behavior as you start dating a prospective partner. If you are currently married to, or involved with, a toxic partner and are trying to identify what is wrong and whether you can fix it – read on. You will learn the facts and a deeper understanding of your current partner's Dr.-Jekyll-and-Mr.-Hyde personality.

As a licensed mental health and addictions counselor and relationship coach, I will explain, with love and compassion, the various mental illnesses and personality disorders. But this is not a substitute for getting your own therapy to further your understanding of the situation or to help you recover from the emotional damage created by a toxic person. Know that there is help for your partner that involves long-term therapy and medication management, if needed, for those with personality disorders.

My heart goes out to men and women of all ages who have unknowingly fallen in love with someone having a toxic personality disorder. I know your pain and pray for your healing and recovery. Not only do I understand, but I too have experienced this tragic, distressing type of love.

My empathy is deep, and my soul remembers the intense pain I experienced as my clients' own touching, tragic stories are too often told. It was my own shattering discovery of the deception

Section One: How to Spot the Emotional Manipulator or Toxic Person

of a loved one that put me on an urgent and spiritual quest to write this book. No one is immune to toxic love; it can happen to anybody. I survived it, became a better person because of it, and so can you!

I have dedicated this time in my life to doing the research, offering the references, and sharing the lists of the toxic personality warning signs so you will know what to watch for. Once you know what to spot in someone who is emotionally destructive, you will also know how to find a healthy partner and have the love you deserve.

I want to teach you how to spot, stop and save yourself from the emotional manipulator, and to inspire you to say "No!" to all the cheap drama.

I want you to choose to love yourself more.

Chapter 1

What Is a Toxic Partner?

So many men, so little time, how can I choose?
Don't want true love; just give me their bodies tonight....
– The Weather Girls, *It's Raining Men* (1982)

A TOXIC PARTNER IS ANYONE WHO makes you emotionally or physically ill by the way that they act or treat you. It is a person who is deceitful, makes his partner feel "not good enough" or bad about herself, is controlling and unsupportive, and he doesn't treat you right. You find yourself experiencing negative feelings that affect your behavior and lower your self-esteem. A toxic partner can make you feel guilty, ashamed, jealous, sad and angry.

The toxic person often displays some or all of the following behaviors:

- He puts you down, embarrasses you, or is sarcastic.
- He tries to control what you wear, act, do or say.

- He constantly blames or accuses you when you have done nothing wrong.
- He holds back affection or sex, or is financially stingy or controlling with money.
- He competes with you or sabotages your business.
- He makes you feel anxious and emotionally void.
- His bad behavior obliges you to apologize and defend him.
- You feel ashamed or embarrassed by his choices or actions.

The following questions offer further insights into toxic behavior and its effects on you:

- Does he zap your energy because he's overly needy and greedy for your time and attention?
- Do you feel relief when you are not with him?
- Have you lost your sense of self?
- Does he demonstrate extreme outbursts of anger toward you but act charming and kind to others?
- Does he ignore or dismiss your feelings or offer suggestions that make your ideas seem worthless?
- Does he isolate you from friends, family and a social life or activities outside the home?
- Does he have financial issues, create scams, or present ideas for which he borrows money from you but never pays you back?

Communication Issues

- He gives you the silent treatment when he is mad.
- He yells, curses or talks down to you.
- He often lectures, screams at, interrupts, ignores, or talks over you.
- He ignores your phone calls and texts but always expects to reach you.
- He is secretive and withholds information, ignoring your questions and making you feel crazy for asking him where he is.
- He refuses to talk about his feelings, clamming up or not talking to you for days.
- He is cold, condescending and critical in his words.
- He selfishly talks about himself, ignores your concerns, and never asks about your day.
- His vocal tones are nasty and often sound annoyed.
- He verbally changes stories to put blame on you.
- His words are sarcastic, cruel and belittling, and he often starts fights over little things.

Dishonesty and Lies

- There is repetitive lying and storytelling.
- He has a secret life or hidden addiction.

- There are long absences that aren't accounted for during which he refuses to answer his phone.
- He withholds important information for his own benefit or changes details with lies or omissions.
- You have found money missing that he took without asking you.
- He cheated on you more than once.
- You suspect shady behavior in his business practices.
- You find yourself lying to others to cover his drug, alcohol, or other addiction problems.

In Chapter 8 of my first book written for the public, *Watch Me!*, I give this description of being involved with a toxic partner:

Your entire physical, emotional, and mental well-being is disturbed. These circumstances can be defined as "walking on eggshells," or describing your partner as "Dr. Jekyll and Mr. Hyde" – you never know WHO you're going to get! If you feel fear when your partner walks through the door; if you wonder if he'll drink and ignore you all night – or worse – scream and lash out in anger, ridicule or blame; then you are in a toxic relationship.

Prolonged negative stress releases toxins throughout our bodies. When we are being emotionally or physically abused, our bodies go into a fight-or-flight mode. Eventually, the immune system wears down, making it difficult to fight off colds, flu, and other diseases, which could bring imbedded viruses to the surface, or create new ones, such as Epstein-Barr virus (chronic fatigue syndrome).

What Is a Toxic Partner?

Other physical ailments you may experience include migraines, stomachaches, and extreme fatigue. One's mental health could suffer with symptoms of depression, anxiety, panic attacks, emotional withdrawal, and low self-esteem. Toxic people and relationships can make you physically and emotionally sick. These issues then affect your ability to perform intellectually, socially, and professionally in the workplace.

An example of a toxic and conflicting relationship is one with a commitment-phobe. Initially very charming, romantic, and pleasing, the moment he feels too emotionally connected or gets engaged or married, he panics and starts sabotaging the relationship with irrational fighting or passive-aggressive behaviors such as cheating or watching porn – or he flees altogether. He soon resurfaces and begs for forgiveness using tears, flowers, and other niceties to win you back. It is a vicious cycle that the innocent partner never wins.

The once-sound mentally healthy partner often becomes obsessed and anxiety-ridden – analyzing what she did wrong, how to improve herself, how to make her emotionally manipulative partner less angry – and then tries anything to regain the addictive sexual passion these relationships have initially.

Can the toxic partner be fixed? With dedication and a commitment to intensive therapy, and sometimes with necessary medication, most but not all these dynamics can be helped and altered. But the toxic person (not his partner) must want the help for himself and be willing to invest in a long period of time in therapy. The problem is most of these personality types think nothing is wrong with them and that it's more their partner's issues that must be fixed. Their selfish, narcissistic and grandiose thinking doesn't allow them to admit something is wrong within them.

The toxic partner brings many dynamics from the past into a relationship. For example, childhood trauma that could consist of being a child of an alcoholic or drug user (ACOA) or whether he had been neglected, abandoned, or emotionally and/or physically abused by his parents can cause faulty coping mechanisms and adult mental health issues. All these problems can play a part in making up the ACOA or other personality types. It would benefit the abusive partner to enter into psychotherapy to examine his past and learn what he must do to overcome dysfunctional habits that began as childhood coping methods.

Not all toxic people have mental health challenges, but most of them do. Too often, though, the toxic partner refuses counseling because he won't believe he does anything wrong. This denial is strong and can last throughout adult life. He may enter counseling for a brief period of time, if only to win the partner back after an affair or other infraction. However, rarely will the toxic partner change his basic abusive tendencies, and the dysfunction is bound to cycle again.

The originally healthy partner who now feels she is going insane has two choices – enter into therapy herself to learn appropriate ways to deal with her abusive partner; or ideally, become strong enough to move on to a new, healthier, more peaceful and loving relationship.

An ideal relationship is one where both partners have a full life of their own; one is not overly dependent on the other for their source of happiness. Codependence means looking to the other partner for happiness. A sense of self-esteem and personal happiness can only come from within. Spiritual faith, personal purpose, and gratifying work to perpetuate that purpose must all be developed and nurtured.

It is important to be one another's best friend, to share hopes and dreams to celebrate accomplishments, and to discuss fears during difficult times. But do NOT look to him to solve your

What Is a Toxic Partner?

troubles, take away your challenges, control your decisions, tell you what you can or cannot do, or rescue you from your own unhappiness. That is *your* responsibility and if you need help from a life coach, get it.

Where do you find such an evolved partner? Let me be the first to tell you, it's very difficult! The spiritual world says, "Become the person who you want to attract in life, and when you become that person, your partner will come." In the process of your own personal growth, you will find that many suitors aren't "quite right" for you, so you must be patient. During this time, date freely and find the joy in extending unconditional friendship to each person without pushing for a steady relationship. The perfect relationship opportunity will eventually present itself. Get involved at your place of worship, and perhaps you will meet someone with similar spiritual ideals. This still won't guarantee success, but do try to frequent seminars, retreats, events, clubs or organizations that you have a genuine interest in and that encourages the presence and attendance of other like-minded people.

The bottom line remains: Don't suffer in a toxic relationship! You must love yourself more!

It is important to be able to spot the slick, emotional manipulator as soon as possible to save yourself from getting hurt or involved too fast. They know exactly what to do to initiate romance and passion, dazzle you with affection and attention and get you interested and committed quickly. That is your first warning sign!

As with anyone, start first as friends. Build a solid foundation of friendship before becoming intimate. Be careful of becoming sexually involved without regular dating and exclusivity. These charmers move fast and are looking for something from you – sex, money, a home, or other items of worth – so if they ask to move in with you or want to marry you quickly (six months or less), run as fast as you can! This kind of attention isn't something to feel flattered by; see it as a red flag for trouble ahead.

You need to understand "the ninety-day rule." Everyone initially dons the mask that shows their best personality traits. But it is likely that within the first three months, true character will start to emerge. It is important to live mindfully; in other words, watch and listen for all the clues that will be presented to you. You may see a small sign of deceit or uncover a lie if the person is predisposed to this behavior. Be careful not to "brush things off" because the chemistry is so intense or because you feel that you're falling in love. New passion can easily blind you to your new partner's infractions. This is a common and dangerous mistake. Let yourself see what must be seen.

I had a client who allowed her boyfriend of two months to move in with her after he asked her to be exclusive. He did profess he loved her, and talked of a future together, so she felt comfortable in allowing it. Within two weeks, she found her Last Will and Testament, and all the account numbers of her investments, on his computer. He had to physically go into her computer, download information, and upload it onto his. This was a grave infraction, and she should have kicked him out at that moment. Instead, because she loved him so much, she chose to forgive him, accepted his lousy excuse, and married him years later. He left their marriage after only five months, saying he felt unhappy because he didn't get half her house due to her prenup. He was clearly a fraud and married her for what she had worked so hard to acquire for herself over many years. Thank God, as her therapist, I advised her to have a prenup; otherwise, he could have gotten half of all her possessions with marriage.

If you can wait three to six months, or at least after twelve to fifteen dates, to become sexually involved (I know – this seems like an eternity), then you'll begin to see the real character and not be totally swayed by lust. Why become intimate with someone you barely know, only to later discover a personality disorder (think of the behavior of Glenn Close's character in *Fatal Attraction*)?

Usually within the first three months, a person with one or more of the top toxic personality traits will say or do something that leaves you feeling uncomfortable. If you're not sure whether the words or action are a deal breaker, seek advice from a relationship coach. It is imperative that you get an outside opinion because your heart may already be invested and you may not want to recognize the severity of the infraction. Keep in mind that your instincts are generally right when you feel the need to be concerned.

This first section is the most important of the four. If you can spot the emotional manipulator early on, you will not get too involved in the relationship, thus saving yourself a lot of emotional pain. You cannot love someone enough to make him change a fundamentally flawed personality or character traits shaped in childhood. Memorize the warning signs so that you stop the relationship as soon as you spot any of the toxic traits. Come back often to this section while you're dating and meeting people. Take the time needed to build your self-confidence and feel fully trusting towards your partner before moving on to exclusivity.

Chapter 2

Why Are You Attracting Toxic Partners?

If you depend on someone for your happiness you are becoming a slave, you are becoming dependent, you are creating bondage. And you depend on so many people; they all become subtle masters, they all exploit you in return. – Bhagwan Shree Rajneesh

---

THE VICTIMS OF AN EMOTIONAL MANIPULATOR are often exceptionally kind, forgiving, generous, caring, honest, hardworking, spiritually based, intelligent, socially confident and accomplished people. They help anyone in a pinch and make a loyal, lifelong friend. They could also be considered codependent, selfless, giving, people pleasing and compromising, all as a result of childhood relationships and the way they chose to cope within their family situation.

The emotional manipulator, who is selfish, controlling, distant and self-centered, loves this type of person and is immediately drawn to them. According to Ross Rosenberg, M.Ed., LCPC, researcher and author of *The Human Magnet Syndrome: The Lure of Dysfunctional*

Relationships, this irresistible attraction to the emotional manipulator compels the codependent to fall in love with someone appearing to be a perfect psychological and physical match, but who later becomes abusive, self-centered, demeaning and dishonest.

This attraction is so strong that both partners feel addicted to each other and stay in the relationship no matter what the cost. The seductive, lust-filled, romance movie type of courtship falls way to a painful pattern of unhealthy love, deceit, dysfunction, rekindled hope and passion, and then further disappointment. The pair is seen as a "dream couple" when other people witness their intense love, attraction, and affection for one another. Few realize that the dream-like stages of this apparently perfect relationship will soon segue into cheap drama, heartbreak and failure.

Both partners, in the course of their lives, may have endured a dysfunctional family pattern that included some form of neglect, abuse, or abandonment. The toxic partner may have one of three personality disorders: Antisocial, Borderline, or Narcissistic. He or she is often addicted to cheap drama, sex, drugs, alcohol, seductive romantic love, and spending money or gambling. A relationship that was once a sexual high full of lust, emotional validation and excitement for the toxic partner, suddenly feels restrictive. This leaves the toxic partner with a desperate need to escape when the relationship faces any of the difficult challenges of daily living. He acts impulsively or destructively to sabotage the relationship so that it ends suddenly. Once out, he then misses and craves the emotional connection and attention that the codependent offered, leading him back to the same partner and the seduction phase begins again.

These unhealthy patterns are the direct result of early childhood traumas causing repetitive, lifelong relationships that are painful and dysfunctional. What once served as both an unconscious and conscious means to survive early childhood traumas, later develops into habitual behavior and attraction blueprints that are very difficult to change.

The person drawn to a toxic partner frequently has deep-seated feelings about love and routinely chooses harmful partners despite their conscious desires not to do so. It's almost as if they were forced against their will to be wildly attracted to the same type, time after time, that will only bring them despair. Their unconscious mind rules this "insanity" and creates an irresistible attraction towards a certain type of partner. Without the knowledge of why they do what they do, they will live a life of brief, whirlwind, romantic excitement and sexual highs that lead to unfulfilled love and painful couplings.

The codependent person's love patterns include the following characteristics:

- She falls in love with what she believed to be the toxic partner's potential and she thinks she can fix him.
- She is lonely and settles for the toxic person despite sensing that something is wrong.
- She believes her partner's intensity or jealousy shows care and love.
- She loves the drama of the chase or seduction; it feels like a high to her.
- She is afraid to speak up; instead, she avoids conflict and lets her partner take control.
- She feels sorry for her partner's horrible childhood.
- She doesn't trust her own instincts and stays in a toxic relationship after discovering deception.

- She loves a few traits about her partner but ignores the red flags of several toxic behaviors.

- She believes she can tame her wild partner and thinks he will settle down once they are married.

- She believes that just because her toxic partner cheated on past lovers, their own relationship will be different and that he'll act honorably this time.

Remember that you can never change another person. It is essential to discuss background histories during the first or second date. If you discover signs of cheating or toxic behavior, believing that this love relationship will be any different becomes wishful thinking. The "player" mentality rarely changes. The major reason you feel so addicted to the toxic person is that he does have some positive qualities. He can be extremely romantic; tell you how different you are from any other woman; and make you feel cherished, beautiful, and wanted. You can see that he's strongly attracted to you. These are the reasons you hang in there so long. But you need to love yourself more. You need to think and feel, to the bottom of your core, that you deserve to receive a healthy, stable, loving partner.

Toxic people have a specific pattern of repeating the same poor behaviors in each relationship and then blaming their partner. Their immature conduct is selfish, rude, deceitful, manipulative, cold, controlling and passive-aggressive. If indeed they do have a mental illness never addressed through long-term intensive therapy, medication and/or behavior modification, the toxic behavior will likely repeat itself. Only they can institute positive behavioral change; however, the possibility of this occurring after a lifetime of abuse is low.

For example, a womanizing man will not be faithful for long in an exclusive relationship even though his partner is devoted, beautiful, and sexually attractive. Don't believe stories that his wife would never have sex with him or that they have "an arrangement" or "open marriage." He'll try to convince you that he cheated only because his wife was nasty, cold and impossible. But the saying is most often true: "once a cheater always a cheater." A man who chronically cheats does so to boost his own ego.

If you are being pursued by an unavailable man (who is married, engaged, or in an exclusive relationship), it will be only a matter of time before he strays again. Never marry "the affair." If you do marry someone you cheated with, the trust levels are already at zero. You will likely feel jealous and insecure each time the toxic person goes out the door.

Many toxic people lie about their relationship status, claiming they're single when, in fact, they're married. Unfortunately, this if often discovered after developing strong feelings for the person. This situation can occur with online dating. It's worth the forty-dollar background check if after the first or second date you want to spend more time with this person. If you find negative results, end the relationship and cut your losses early.

If you discover the person has adverse legal issues, discuss whether these are past or present. If he has three martinis on your first date, or had several DUI's then there may be an alcohol problem.

Dating consciously means being aware enough to look for anything and everything that is a warning sign. Ask a lot of questions and listen intently as you watch your date's body language and facial expressions. Inquire about his family background, birth order, his relationship with his parents and siblings, and where he was raised. If you grew up in an aristocratic or upscale environment, be wary of those from a lower economic status searching for "the good life" from you.

Emotional manipulators who grew up in meager or unfortunate circumstances often are looking for a rich person to marry in order to reap a financial reward. If you own your own home, have a well-paying job, have or will be inheriting money, or simply are of financial means, do not marry anyone, no matter how wonderful, without drawing up a prenuptial agreement! Toxic partners typically flee after the wedding and could take half of everything you own, which leads to an expensive divorce situation. Unfortunately, in today's world, you must plan for a worst-case scenario to protect yourself and your children.

It is common that successful, high-powered people who are in caregiver professions can become victims of the emotional manipulator because they believe in the ability to change. Such professionals include doctors, counselors, teachers, nurses, clergy, and lawyers. Professional women, who have made their way to the top while overcoming significant obstacles, may believe that changing a person is easily accomplished in comparison to what they do in the job market. So why not take the handsome, unemployed, romantic man and help him reach his potential? Because he won't. He'll only live off you financially, taking advantage of your generosity, hard work and success.

Don't feel sorry for him or believe his stories of why he can't find work. Don't be quick to let him move in. I heard a story of a successful female judge having been romantically pursued for close to a year before letting her attractive beau move into her gorgeous estate. Within a week he moved everything out of her home while she was at work. This included all her jewelry, art, and expensive custom furniture. None of it was ever found.

Don't try to save or rescue these toxic people. Money and sex are key motivators behind their seduction and they will play the part as long as it takes to score. This includes giving you expensive

Why Are You Attracting Toxic Partners?

gifts and making sure everyone knows about it. No matter what the story is, never, under any circumstances, give your new partner money. You won't get it back. These men lie about their status or talk about a high-paying job about to begin in an impressive position. They will swear it's a short-term loan to be paid back with their next paycheck. Don't do it! Look them up on a Google search, buy a background check, and question why this man would need your money if he's so successful. Some women now ask for a photo ID (license) before accepting a date. I suggest you exchange business cards and confirm his employment and full name through an Internet search.

These con men and women are slick. Have them sign a cohabitation agreement before deciding to live together in your home. Don't wait to complete the agreement until after they've moved in. They will hesitate, try to talk you out of it and make you feel guilty or hold it against you. Look seriously at any guy who needs to move in with you because he is at his mother's house or living with a roommate.

If you feel anxiety for any reason, trust your intuition and stop the relationship. So many clients, both men and women, admit to having seen small signs or ignoring one to two lies in the early romance stage. They turned a blind eye because they didn't want to stop the thrill of the sexual rush and falling in love.

Your state of anxiety is telling you to stop the relationship. Your body will indicate warning signs: stomachaches, headaches, lack of sleep, and addictive urges such as drinking alcohol, taking prescription pills, or engaging in other destructive behaviors to hide the pain of knowing that something is wrong. Follow your gut reaction!

Men who are overprotective or come across as jealous are full of cheap drama. An overly emotional, controlling or violent man is not a rush. Be careful – you could be attracted or addicted to the drama you may have grown up with, and it's not a sign of love. Consciously, you wouldn't choose a man who would abuse you, but unconsciously, you may choose exactly the toxic partner you say you would never want to be with.

Why would you do that? The information here is vitally important for you to understand. Psychology explains two reasons: First, you choose what you're used to, what was normal for you as a child. If you had a verbally and physically abusive, alcoholic father, this is what you now know as "normal." You repeat your childhood pattern and unconsciously choose that type of man. Consciously, though, you would never want a man who resembled your dysfunctional father.

Secondly, you unconsciously choose this type of man to "fix" your childhood drama; if you can fix it as an adult, it's finally healed in your unconscious mind and heart. Because you grew up with drama, you have a hard time finding the "chemistry of connection" with a healthier type of man. You may find him boring, unattractive and not sexy. Actually, that is *exactly* the type of man you need for a lasting, healthy relationship in which to feel cherished and truly loved.

Feelings of abandonment may occur in a woman who had a father come and go as she was being raised. Even though her father may have legitimately needed to be away from home due to his career, his work may have absented him from the home for days or weeks at a time. A young girl could be left with feelings of abandonment, always waiting and wondering, "When will Daddy be home?" Her father may have been very loving and affectionate towards her at home, but this uncertainty imprinted the type of man she is attracted to as an adult. This also applies to a woman who may have been adopted, lived in foster care, never knew her father, or never or rarely saw him after a divorce. Later in life she is deeply and dangerously attracted to the man who emotionally or physically distances himself. The man representing love and attraction for her (the love avoidant or one who abandons) will ultimately break her heart when he leaves her.

The childhood feeling of yearning for a love that remained uncertain and unreliable creates an anxiety that is the basis for later attraction to a certain type of man. You will feel a fierce, chemical attraction to a man who is aloof, hard to get, comes and goes as he pleases, doesn't answer questions, is often mentally and emotionally abusive (a "bad boy") and tends to have a secret life. You feel high when you try to catch such a man because your pattern has been to have Dad's loving attention once he was home. This imprints a pattern of falling in love with a man who creates a similarly dramatic yearning in you.

If you win him over, and he falls madly in love with you, he may in time become aloof, emotionally abusive or absent. This type of man will eventually become passive-aggressive, lash out and abandon you. When this happens, it leaves behind a long-lasting and emotionally debilitating pain.

Your childhood traumas or family dynamic and the relationships you had with each parent (or lack thereof) will fuel your attraction to the partner types you seek as an adult. Exploring your past issues and discussing your pattern of partners with a therapist can help you avoid a love relationship with a toxic partner. With knowledge comes power. With consistent study, and the ability to recognize early signs of a partner's problems, you'll stop pursuing the toxic mate and experiencing the subsequent pain.

The "curse" that pulls you towards the wrong type of partner is strong. It is essential to educate yourself on the nature of unhealthy, toxic people and the behaviors that ruin relationships. Early recognition of dysfunctional traits will empower you to save yourself from grief.

While dating, don't get romantically involved too soon; you need time to see if any toxic behavior or pattern emerges. It is human nature to desire love, sexual pleasure, connection, excitement and mutual understanding with your dream partner. It is also best to wait until you know who you're giving yourself to.

If one is strong and psychologically healthy, a similarly healthy lover can give everlasting love and help fulfill shared dreams. The key is to understand that negative attraction patterns can be altered by taking the time to slowly get to know a potential partner in an intelligent and informed manner.

As an aware, evolved and psychologically healthy person, you can recognize the right partner. A relationship can develop into a lifelong, nurturing, supportive and loving journey.

Dr. Seth Meyers, Psy.D, and author of the book, *Dr. Seth's Love Prescription*, talks about ways to overcome and break the cycle of Relationship Repetition Syndrome (RRS). RRS is a repetitive behavioral cycle that leads to the sabotaging of love relationships. You either idealize a partner externally, try to save wounded men, sacrifice yourself to prove your worthiness, or chase your desired partner. You are attracted to men who never meet your emotional needs, and only later, realize he's not good for you. Dr. Meyers believes that people often repeat toxic relationships because of childhood mistreatment, abandonment, rejection, neglect or abuse. In adulthood, there is an unconscious attempt to recreate, then solve and heal the original trauma experienced. Several factors lead to this repetition of choosing bad partners: fear, denial, an impulsive coping style, and distorted beliefs.

1. Fear keeps you from good partners and compels you to repeat what you're already familiar with. Past trauma reminds you it isn't safe to love or trust another or to be vulnerable.

2. Denial of past anger, sadness, emotional needs or painful feelings is ongoing. You must be accountable for your role in the dysfunction of the relationship and stop blaming your partner. Lack of accountability obliges you to repeat the patterns.

3. An impulsive coping style involves behaving without thinking of the destructive consequences. This includes jumping into a relationship too quickly from boredom, sadness or loneliness; and often includes addiction to high drama.

4. Distorted Beliefs cause you to be overly attracted to the fantasy of romance and not to a realistic relationship with a responsible, down-to-earth person.

Dr. Meyers writes that the only way to have lifelong love is to stop blaming and focusing on your partner; instead, focus on yourself and your own behaviors and choices. Stop dating someone as soon as you see early signs of potential problems. He references Judith Beck's book, *Cognitive Therapy*, which states most people's core beliefs about themselves are rooted in a negative perception of worthlessness or helplessness. Relationship Repeaters are people who tend towards not feeling good enough and have one or both core beliefs as a result of childhood experiences. How you feel about yourself in general does influence how you feel about your life overall and seriously influences whomever you choose to date.

A loving partner is one who will focus on your emotional needs, care about your feelings, and respect that his choices affect you in a negative or positive way. You must also have faith and believe that you are worthy to give and receive love, and that you *will* find a lasting love. A life or relationship coach can help put all your life spheres in order so that you have a healthy self-love and confidence. Only then will you refuse to accept any man's negative or neglectful treatment of you.

Dr. Meyers offers the following suggestions to help stop the repeating pattern:

1. Slow down the dating process so that you can make sound judgments.

2. Feel personally balanced to alleviate anxiety and mood changes.

3. Keep a journal to monitor your feelings and have a sponsor who will tell you honestly that you're going after the wrong guy and help you to make better decisions.

4. Have realistic expectations and don't obsess about the romance factor. Each person, on their own, should have a full, positive life and stay healthily functional and productive.

5. Know how to self-soothe and possess strong coping skills so that you don't become overly dependent on any man. Maintain your ongoing healthy and nourishing activities that will keep you balanced.

I heartily suggest you read his book in its entirety if you find this section resonates with you.

Chapter 3

The Warning Signs When Dating

Choose your life's mate carefully. From this one decision will come 90 percent of all your happiness or misery. – H. Jackson Brown, Jr.

EMOTIONAL MANIPULATORS ARE considered toxic people because of the pain and destruction they create. These self-centered people are habitually attracted to the codependent or the loving and giving partner. This leads to a strong chemical, magnetic attraction that resists change and leads to repetitive breakups, broken promises and abusive relationships.

Toxic people are resistant to therapy and often refuse to get help because they believe nothing is wrong with them. If they do try therapy, they are often forced into it and usually don't stick with it very long. In most cases, conventional therapy doesn't help change these personality types.

Disliking being alone, the emotional manipulator seeks the codependent to take care of them. They slowly take a controlling role in the relationship, as the codependent relinquishes personal power, keeping the manipulator happy and feeding his sense of power, neediness and control. Initially, when the manipulator feels desired and indispensable and is taken care of by their devoted partner, the "dance" of the new relationship moves well and is full of love and passion.

But the manipulator's constant control, demands, put-downs and abuse leads to a severe imbalance and often a backlash from the codependent. This, in turn, leads to a deeper need to control, pushing the manipulator into a tantrum of raging anger. If the manipulator meets a similar personality type, there is little attraction and the person would be seen as conceited, arrogant, or not trustworthy. Manipulators are repelled by their own personality type and find there is simply no chemistry.

When he meets a female of the opposite personality type, the manipulator feels huge infatuation, chemistry, sexual attraction and electrifying love that is intense and addictive. They feel as if they understand each other's past pain and create a dependence on one another. This romantic phase where they can't be without each other keeps them returning to the relationship after many breakups.

When a breakup occurs, the love addiction causes physical and psychological withdrawal and severe emotional pain. Loneliness, fear, and anxiety about the future; craving for their love object, constant urges to see, speak to or text their partner; all overtake their will to stay away. Consciously, they know their partner is bad for them, but the addiction becomes a constant battle to try and stay away. Eventually, they break their own promise to move on and too often choose to return to their lover.

The role each partner plays – giver and taker, respectively – is one of magnetic attraction. These roles, whether codependent or emotional manipulator, are fixed, resist change, and can be lifelong.

The Warning Signs When Dating

Still, each partner can become healthier and less controlling with intensive therapy and an understanding of their type, bringing their roles to a more stable balance.

Darwin's theory of evolution stated that opposites attract to reproduce. They make a strong match, with each making up for the other's weaknesses. But when the codependent questions their role, or displays a backlash against the control and anger of the emotional manipulator, these relations fall apart. Often the controlling person is actually weaker than the codependent whether professionally, financially, or in self-esteem. If the codependent waits too long to take back her power, the controller will destroy more than just the relationship.

Stable relationships require healthy values and balance in each partner. Both need a significant level of self-worth, self-respect, self-esteem and strong personal boundaries that protect them from unhealthy love.

Before you start dating, work with your coach or counselor on understanding personal destructive relationship patterns fueled by your past family dynamics or traumas. This will help to enhance your awareness of the type of person you attract. Know what a good relationship looks like, and know the warning signs of the toxic, emotional manipulator. Be sure you maintain a strong sense of self; discuss with your coach your requirements, wants and needs in a partner and don't deviate from the list.

Sometimes people try to talk themselves into a relationship because they feel lonely, and afraid that no one better will come along. Here are some of the signs that you're settling for less than you deserve:

- You see a person's potential but he has to be fixed, rescued, or seems overly needy for you.

- You see a lot in common but you are neglecting obvious concerns or differences.

- Your date is fun and sexy, owns a big home and fancy car or has some other quality that you're focusing on. But your intuition tells you something is wrong. He is overly outgoing, controlling, attention seeking, flirtatious with the opposite sex, selfish or arrogant.

- Your date is emotionally unavailable – meaning engaged, married, separated or in the process of divorce – or recently out of a relationship and not looking for anything serious.

- You don't want to be alone, so you overdo and emotionally chase the man to try to make this relationship work. You ignore your instinct that things are wrong; because he rarely contacts you, or when he does, it's for sexual reasons only.

- You keep forgiving his poor or neglectful behavior and provide him numerous chances to prove that he cares for you.

Here are additional warning signs to watch for while dating, as described by the "The Red Flags Checklist" from *Relationship Coaching Institute:*

- He has signs of an addiction: gambling, sex, food, alcohol, drugs, spending, or he's a workaholic. He describes these behaviors as normal, or "not a problem," but they seem excessive to you. Even worse, he brags about his "high sex drive" (run, fast!) or "works harder than most" to provide.

The Warning Signs When Dating

- You witness impulsivity, secrecy, lack of control with saving or spending, constant irresponsibility, immaturity or child-like behaviors including the need to break social rules.

- He's easily frustrated, and then blames you or another; or you witness rage directed toward another.

- He seems to control or talk down to others, inflating his ability to control wait staff, coworkers, employees, or clients.

- He acts emotionally cold, distant, and aloof, has trouble looking at you when you talk or is busy looking around the room for others to spot while with you.

- He still talks about an ex-lover with sadness and yearning for their relationship.

- You see signs of a lack of integrity in financial matters or when he deals with others.

- He is negative, judgmental, compares himself to others as being "better" or tries to one-up you. He lacks concern over things that matter to you.

- He takes no responsibility for his actions. He will not apologize, show remorse or any sense of guilt for his wrongdoings. He won't self-examine or admit fault, or consider your suggestions or feedback.

- He breaks promises, is often late, changes his mind, or twists your words trying to make you believe something else from what you know is factual and true.

- His self-description is not the truth and he tells lies about who he is or his status in his career.

- He constantly creates drama with you or others because his behavior is inconsistent and unreliable.

- He is self-centered and talks about himself a lot, talks over you when you try to share your opinion, or gets loud or yells at you "to be heard."

- When angry, he shuts down and refuses to communicate for days, will not take your calls, emails or respond to your texts, making you feel punished and ignored.

- You find yourself falling for what you see as his potential, or try to change him into what you want instead of seeing who he really is. You may be able to invoke a temporary change, but it won't last long.

It is easy to become a victim or prey to this type of individual if you aren't careful choosing what you want in a partner. Choice begins by clearly defining your desires, wants, needs, and requirements in a future partner. Once defined, silently compare every date to that well-memorized list. If they fall short, move on.

When you can live by your created list of desired qualities, you'll see a lot of one-and-done dates. You must date a lot of people to discover exactly what you want, and refuse to settle for less. Once you see a warning sign or two, or witness a lack of integrity in his character, you won't waste your time on a second date.

For example, I was on a date with someone who described his Catholic family life as loving and supportive, with a strong sense of religion. But later, he made two racial comments that totally turned me off. I am a loving, spiritual person who looks for the good in everyone and who does not discriminate. This man was missing the spiritual requirement I know I needed in my life, and that led me to ending the friendship after the second date.

In their book, *Not Your Mother's Rules – the new Secrets for Dating,* Ellen Fein and Sherrie Schneider advise being more concerned about "weeding out the buyers bewares" and to "put faith in attracting Mr. Right." If a man doesn't call, text or email you on a regular basis, he's not that interested. Three weeks of no contact is the limit, at which time you should discard the idea of dating him. You need to recognize that if there's no future with a particular man, stop dating him. The authors insist that you shouldn't accept a date after Wednesday, don't be the first to email on an online dating site, ignore "Winks" and "Want to meet you" approaches, and don't make the first phone call. Don't respond to late-night texts or phone calls, and wait several hours before you respond in the courting phase. Keep your response email and the first phone call short. Remain protective of your privacy and try to meet him briefly in person to see if you want to continue dating him. If a man is fiercely attracted to you, I agree that he should pursue and choose you, even online.

They also advise not to text or write to anyone online over the weekend (Friday 6:00 p.m. – Sunday 6:00 p.m.); you need to be – or appear – busy. Keep dating others until the man you want asks you to be exclusive. Make him work to see you; ask to meet in a location convenient for you and don't travel far to meet him. Dates should be light and breezy; don't hook-up too quickly or push for a relationship. A man who wants a relationship will clearly tell you he's ready for an exclusive commitment or marriage. Until you're in a steady relationship, continue meeting men at least once or twice a week. Switch up locations, events, and times; but try to go to places where men gather. If he asks to hang out, get a specific date and time; if he doesn't follow through he is an unreliable time waster and you need to move on!

Chapter 4

Types of Toxic People

Stop looking for a scapegoat in your life but be willing to face the truth within yourself and right your own wrongs. – Eileen Caddy

---

A) The Emotional Manipulators: Narcissistic, Borderline, and Bipolar Personality Disorders

*A man who is sure of himself is **not** angry at every slight done him, nor does he carry grudges. A man who fears for his own worth, however, **is** furious under such conditions.* – Jane Roberts

Personality disorders include those diagnosed as borderline, bipolar, narcissistic, antisocial, sociopath, psychopath, obsessive-compulsive, avoidant, and schizotypal clients. Patients with these traits are very difficult to treat, create repetitive crises within all their relationships, and require more time in therapy than any other type of client. They rarely choose to go to therapy, but show up when they are forced to, so their motivation to change remains very low. They stay in counseling until their current crisis is over, and rarely see anything wrong with themselves; instead, they blame others. Several of these categories of personality disorders are explained below. It is important that you realize that this type of person creates many challenges with their hidden agendas, generating severely toxic relationships.

1. *The Narcissist*

All emotional manipulators and toxic partners have narcissistic traits. As described by the DSM-IV-TR Diagnostic and Statistical Manual of Mental Disorders, a partner with this personality disorder shows the following traits that start in early adulthood:

1. There is a grandiose sense of self-importance, arrogance and haughty attitudes as they look for excessive admiration from others.

2. They exaggerate their talents and achievements and are preoccupied with fantasies or behaviors of unlimited power, beauty, success, or an ideal love.

3. They expect to be recognized as superior without the matching achievements.

4. They have a sense of entitlement and unreasonable expectations from others. They want to associate only with other, "special" or "high-status" people.

5. They take advantage of others to achieve their own gain.

6. They lack empathy toward another's pain, and refuse to recognize or identify with the feelings and needs of others.

7. They are jealous of others and think others envy them.

If your partner shows even half of these traits, you have a narcissist on your hands. They are generally selfish, self-centered, vain, materialistic, self-absorbed, worry only about themselves, and lack empathy.

They are never able to love another person or themselves because they are conceited, selfish, proud and aloof. However, mild narcissism can be healthy because it allows a sense of personal esteem and lets you know that you should be valued and important to your partner.

When you possess healthy self-esteem, a high level of confidence or mild narcissism, you can become successful business people, artists, entertainers, and trainers. Many famous business people and actors are considered mild narcissists without being harmful to other people; they simply have a high sense of self and don't meet the DSM-IV-TR criteria for the personality disorder.

These healthy "light" narcissists do meet their partner's and their loved one's emotional needs. They are able to share and give to others, and can stop their self-focus when necessary. They are not hurtful toward others, and are able to take responsibility for their mistakes, apologize, and learn from hurtful behavior. They do monitor their self-centered traits, using them to achieve, rather than to hurt others.

The diagnosis for Narcissistic Personality Disorder (NPD) is given when:

1. Extreme selfishness is exhibited, together with an excessive and constant need to be admired, adored, praised and appreciated.

2. Relationships are one-sided; these individuals never apologize nor accept responsibility or blame, and think of themselves as the superior partner.

3. Generosity is shown only when they feel personal gain will be made.
4. There is limited empathy toward others and greater concern with self-love or personal advantage.
5. There is bragging, exaggerating and the belief that they are expert in most things, as well as being gifted, special and superior in their thoughts and ways.
6. Glory, status, perfection in their partner, fame, or prestige is consistently and addictively sought.
7. Others are degraded and their own accomplishments seen as superior.
8. There are unreasonable expectations from others including their partner, with special and favorable treatments expected.
9. NPD may occur with other addictions.

When it comes to criticism, and you are involved with someone with NPS, watch out! They become over-reactive about being judged and are inordinately sensitive to criticism. They will make excuses for their actions, deny the truth, blame you and refuse to apologize. These defensive actions are severe when they perceive you are mistreating them. If you're imperfect (looking, acting or sexually), they cannot tolerate it, acting smug, defiant and judgmental toward you or your actions, hurting you with their passive-aggressive anger.

They don't recognize the extreme degree of harm caused by their actions, nor can they stop or regulate what they do, denying and failing to take responsibility for their destructive behavior.

Their needs will always override those of their partner. You will almost always be blamed for their perceived pain; when in actuality, they caused it themselves or you are the damaged party.

At least 16% of mental health clients are diagnosed with NPD, and up to 75% are men, according to Ross Rosenberg, M.Ed. and author of *The Human Magnet Syndrome: The Lure of Dysfunctional Relationships*. This diagnosis is found equally in all professions, social, economic and ethnic classes. They hide their true self, which causes them constant anxiety, shame and desperation, but, initially, they present with charm, confidence and charisma. Many become politicians, top executives, and famous sport figures.

The covert narcissist hides their traits and can come across as normal and altruistic. They may work for a charity or act as a humanitarian, pretending to be selfless and acting for the good of all. They could be considered an expert, leader, or spokesperson who does gain from their heightened status. These types often secretly seek admiration and control over others.

According to Rosenberg, the worst type of narcissism is called malignant. People with malignant narcissism are paranoid, suspect deceit, doubt loyalty and are killers within our society, like Stalin, Saddam Hussein, and Hitler. They are aggressive, controlling, manipulative and self-obsessed. They create a new system of right and wrong, and justify being harmful to others while trying to convince society their way is the right way. They may also be physically, sexually and emotionally abusive.

Conversely, the kindest and most productive narcissists are the ones who produce society's best achievements, are gifted leaders, have a great many followers and can motivate and inspire others. They possess far-reaching vision and purpose and are often spiritually based. Feeling "above it all," their self-confidence and sense of grandiosity can sometimes lead to extreme risk-taking. Many religious leaders and politicians fall into this category.

2. *Borderline Personality Disorder (BPD)*

BPD is defined as a persistent pattern of unstable personal relationships, self-image, and severe impulsivity that begins in early adulthood. As stated in *DSM-IV-TR Diagnostic and Statistical Manual of Mental Disorders*, a person may have this disorder if half of these traits exist:

1. Instability in thinking, behaviors, moods, self-image, and personal relationships.

2. Desperate efforts made to avoid imagined or real abandonment.

3. Unstable, intense interpersonal relationships having extremes of devaluation and idealization of the partner.

4. Persistently unstable self-image.

5. Self-damaging impulsivity in the following areas:
   a. Sex
   b. Spending
   c. Binge eating
   d. Substance abuse
   e. Reckless driving

6. Self-mutilation, gestures or threats of suicide, and frequent sabotaging of relationships.

7. Intense mood swings, irritability and anxiety.

8. Inappropriate and intense rages and tantrums that are hard to control.

9. Paranoia and chronic feelings of emptiness.

This is one of the most unstable psychological personality disorders and affects up to 6% of Americans. As many as 75% hurt themselves and up to 10% commit suicide. Women seek therapy more often, but there are no differences in BPD between men and women. Some do achieve stabilization with time after age 40, and it is said that those in their 20s are at the highest risk of self-harm.

They seek control by being demanding and unforgiving, and by having reactive mood swings that are difficult to control. Ultimately, they try to punish their partner when they perceive being abandoned. They are strongly connected and dependent on their partner's love. By attacking and hurting the partner they love, they sabotage their relationship and create the actual abandonment that they fear most. They have a black-or-white approach to thinking and are very judgmental as they simultaneously feel deep love and rage-filled hatred. Marilyn Monroe was a prime example of someone with BPD.

The following demonstrates some of their pervasive thought patterns:

1. I must be loved all the time to feel worthy.

2. I have no control over my emotions.

3. No one cares for me as much as I care for them.

4. I fight back and become bad if someone wrongs me.

5. I expect and can only be happy when I find that perfect, all-giving person to love me and take care of me unconditionally.

6. You should be blamed and punished if you are bad.

7. I must be completely successful to feel worthwhile.

The Borderline transfers their own negative feelings and behaviors onto their partner, who then behaves according to the false accusations, leaving the partner with the feeling of "walking on egg shells." They criticize and blame their partner for the imagined offense; externalizing responsibility for their own bad behaviors. They believe if they act out, you caused it and, therefore, it's your fault they did what they did.

Nothing you can say or do can fix this. Everything you suggest triggers an angry and negative response. The book, *I Hate You, Don't Leave Me,* by Kreisman and Straus, addresses this dilemma. The BPD fears love and intimacy because it makes them feel vulnerable and so they constantly test the degree of love their partner has for them.

Their personality is split between needing and craving love, and the fierce need for control and independence. They fear abandonment and often become enmeshed with their partner. Then, when too close, they'll seek a way to sabotage the relationship. They struggle with their own identity as well as having the narcissistic tendencies that strip away empathy for others. They use seduction or manipulation to meet their needs. But once they get too involved, or enter a commitment such as marriage, they feel overwhelmed and often leave the relationship.

If they feel criticized or suspect you don't love, worship or aren't committed enough to them, this sparks a rage of abandonment and a personal meltdown. They are out to destroy everything in their path, and will find the most hurtful way to punish their partner; destroying the very love that is most important to them.

Their partner is left bewildered when a minor, benign event can create such extreme feelings of humiliation, rejection, and self-contempt that lead to overwhelming aggression. If this aggression is turned inward, the borderline person will turn to drugs, alcohol or other addictions, or enter into depression and self-harm becomes a risk. After the partner leaves their victim they often follow up with seduction, flattery, and talk of previous romantic adventures to try to win them back.

These unfortunate souls come from families where they had abusive and/or neglectful parents who chronically caused emotional trauma and/or physical pain. Often there might have been an alcoholic or drug-addicted parent. Children who live in constant fear cannot trust and have attachment problems. They react with constant fear and are continually anxious and afraid to disappoint the abusive parent. They either willfully act out and become difficult, or just the opposite, will do anything to keep the peace, becoming the parent and taking care of the house, other siblings, or the victimized parent (often their mother).

Shame and lack of trust are a way of life. Their mother's needs are always a priority before their own, and the love and security they crave never comes from either parent. Abuse, neglect, criticism, lack of safety and not feeling good enough become the norm. They often develop a façade of charm to present to the outside world or develop humor to gain the attention they desire, becoming the class clown, or the charismatic, sexually seductive teen idol, or both. Think of John Travolta's character in *Saturday Night Fever*, or Fonzi from *Happy Days*. Deep down, they are needy, and don't feel important or valued. They often repress their rage and become emotionally shut down and passive-aggressive in adult years.

Borderline people do not usually seek help and if they do, they enter therapy only to avoid consequences or as a final attempt to save their relationship. They quickly stop therapy when their partner forgives them or if the therapist confronts them with the reality of their actions. They feel that they did nothing wrong, which makes them a poor candidate for change. Their psychological damage is so severe and the intensity of their childhood trauma so profound that it prevents the insight and inspiration they need to change. If their partner forgives them, soon after the honeymoon phase they cycle back into dysfunction after a period of peace.

3. *Bipolar Personality Disorder*

Bipolar disorder usually begins during late adolescence or early adulthood and may be inherited from a parent with the same diagnosis. It could also be caused by a chemical imbalance in the brain. Factors that increase the risk of developing this disorder include drug abuse, periods of high stress, major life changes, as well as the biological component. Untreated, the disorder can ruin relationships, job performance and has been strongly linked to suicide. It is a long-term illness that must be managed with medication and therapy throughout one's lifetime.

Partners with bipolar disorder show extreme mood swings that can present in three different ways: manic, depressive or a mixed episode. The latter includes both manic and depressive symptoms. Bipolar disorder wreaks serious havoc on a love relationship because of mood and personality changes, and impulsive actions that damage the security and trust within the relationship.

In a manic phase, one could be extremely happy with a very high energy level, or act aggressive, irritable and agitated. This phase could also bring on impulsivity resulting in negative consequences that need to be dealt with after the manic phase subsides. Impulsivity rules over judgment, and acting out could include spending large sums of money, being sexually promiscuous or cheating on your partner, defiantly abusing alcohol or drugs, or acting out to the point of getting arrested.

To be diagnosed as manic, this episode must last at least seven days, and include three or more of the following behaviors:

1. Impulsive, risky conduct that could involve spending or sexual promiscuity.
2. Racing thoughts and actions.
3. An inflated feeling of importance, power or greatness.
4. Overactive with minimal need for sleep.
5. Talks too fast and too much.
6. Easily distracted attention, shifting rapidly among many topics.
7. Intense focus on goal-oriented activity.

The diagnosis for a major depressive mood episode usually includes a loss of pleasure in activities and people previously enjoyed. Four or more of the following symptoms must exist, almost daily, over a two-week time period:

1. Loss of energy and extreme fatigue.
2. Chronically excessive sleep.
3. Indecisive and inability to focus or concentrate.
4. Inappropriate guilt or feelings of worthlessness.
5. Feeling sluggish or restless.

6. Significant weight loss and lack of appetite, or weight gain with significant appetite increase, showing change in body weight of 5% within one month.

7. Recurrent thoughts of death; planned or attempted suicide.

While in the depressive state, your partner could withdraw from you and the children, and lose pleasure in almost everything. Simple stressors or common work and financial stress can send your partner over the edge into dramatic anger and temper tantrums. He may also self-medicate with drugs, alcohol or by sexually acting out.

These relationships are extremely difficult, especially if treatment is refused. Medication that stabilizes mood, such as Lithium along with antidepressants, can help control symptoms (WebMD.com). Therapy is essential to learn how to control one's stress and acting-out behaviors. It is helpful when you accompany your partner to counseling to learn supportive techniques. Getting enough sleep, exercising, eating healthy, limiting caffeine and alcohol are all recommended. However, up to 90% of these marriages fail, so knowing early on if your partner is bipolar gives you options to stay or leave this high-risk relationship. I would suggest you save yourself future emotional heartbreak, and move on.

B) The Charming Con Artist: Antisocial Personality Disorder, Sociopaths and Psychopaths

Il Mondo! My heart belongs to you so take it, and promise me you'll never break it… (Song) "Il Mondo" – Patrizio; The Italian, CD (2005).

As Martha Stout, Ph.D., writes in her book, *The Sociopath Next Door: The Ruthless Versus the Rest of Us*, 4%, or one in 25 humans, is sociopathic or have an antisocial personality disorder (ASPD) yet live their lives with no conscious guilt, empathy, shame or remorsefulness. Dr. Phil McGraw's book, *Life Code – The New Rules for Winning in the Real World* is suggested reading as well. He identifies "the BAITERs (backstabbers, abusers, imposters, takers, exploiters and/or reckless people) through the "evil eight" identifiers. What most people think of when they hear the term "sociopath" is a violent criminal; however, these people who have no ability to love are our coworkers, neighbors, friends or our own partner.

The DSM-IV-TR defines antisocial personality disorder as an ongoing pattern or disregard for, and violation of the rights of others, if three of more of the following conditions exist:

- Deceitfulness, repetitive lying, or conning others for their personal pleasure or profit.
- Impulsivity or failure to plan ahead.
- Aggressiveness and irritability.
- Constant irresponsibility, repeated failures to hold consistent work or honor financial obligations.
- Failure to conform to social norms or lawful behaviors by repeating acts that could be or are grounds for arrest.
- Total lack of remorse and being indifferent to one they have mistreated, hurt or stolen from.
- This person is at least 18 years old and may have shown signs of conduct disorder before the age of 15.

Signs show intensity at between ages 20 and 30, and men are more commonly diagnosed. These men repeatedly violate social laws and the rights of others and don't learn from the consequences of their mistakes or punishments. They have an inflated sense of superiority that is narcissistic, ego-centered and arrogant and carry themselves with a sense of entitlement, and are especially demanding of their partner.

Their impulsivity leads to severe irresponsibility and a lack of self-control. They often make quick decisions on a whim with no concern or consideration for the harm it may cause others. Sudden disappearances or running away like a child are common behaviors, which set up a pattern of lost jobs and addictions. Many are addicted to sex, porn, gambling, drugs and alcohol and some are workaholics.

The ASPD man is often aggressive with a disregard for the safety of self or others and is easily enraged, causing psychological, physical or verbal abuse to their partners. They often refuse to control their sex drive and are highly promiscuous. They brag about a high sex drive, failing to see their practices as addictive. They are sexually exploitative, demanding and abusive to their partners.

Relationships with this type of man are heartbreaking because they are incapable of long periods of attachment and lack empathy. They exhibit a shallow affect with flat, insincere emotions. This person will show no remorse, or affection, once they have callously hurt you.

ASPD males are con artists who cheat others by means of fraud and deception. They are brilliant in hiding their sociopathic behavior. Being compulsive liars, they lie easily and well and without concern for you. These types will look you straight in the eye and convince you they're telling the truth. You need solid evidence before confronting them; still, they'll lie about their infraction! At that point, you know you're dealing with a sociopath. Start making swift moves to get out of the relationship. They may show artificial care for the feelings of others but only if they'll get something in return.

How did you fall for a sociopath? It's very easy to do, so don't beat yourself up for feeling attracted. They have charismatic, if superficial, charm and are great conversationalists. Charm is a necessity to manipulate, win over and control their prey. Ted Bundy is a great example of a man who was good looking, smooth, and quite articulate. He said what people wanted to hear, using charm to capture his victims.

These parasitic people manipulate their prey for personal gain, brilliantly choreographing a romantic, passionate relationship as they beguile you into falling in love with them. They are sexually dishonest and prone to many sexual or emotional affairs. Pretending to fall in love with you, they will make a commitment, often wanting to marry quickly for financial gain. They will want to move in to your home within a short period of time, showering you with gifts or a beautiful engagement ring, giving you enough gifts to convince you, your family and the world what "a great catch" he is.

Soon after marriage, they suddenly disappear, move onto another victim, or seek secret, sexual affairs to alleviate their boredom. These slick, pathological liars twist stories and blame others to evade responsibility and to get out of a tough situation. They will convince your family and friends that *you* are the dysfunctional one, the liar, the cheat or the one to blame. It's amazing to see families turn against the person they've known and loved for years, and fall prey to the convincing lies of your sociopathic partner. It's also heart-wrenching, because this is when they most need their family. Victims are left even more crushed, while the partner's self-esteem has been enhanced by having duped the spouse's entire family as well. The goal is to isolate you from any and all of your support systems, and their power trip means conning anyone they can to make themselves look better.

Because their need for stimulation is higher than necessary for most people, they're willing to take immense financial, social, physical or legal risks. Once caught, they "lack affect," showing shallow-to-no emotions for their victim. You, their lover, are often overwhelmed with the shocking discovery of their secret life, asking yourself, "Who is this person I fell in love with, and how could I not see it?"

Stop blaming yourself; remember that one in twenty-five sociopathic people con their dedicated partners all the time. I see so many brokenhearted, psychologically shattered victims in my counseling office, all coming off the stunning reality of life following the discovery of deception. Damage from sociopathic disorders lasts a very long time, robbing their victims of self-esteem, business or social reputations, peace of mind, confidence, financial security and the ability to trust. The perpetrator just doesn't care.

When surface charm disappears after ASPD men marry their victims, the marriages become loveless, short-term and one-sided. They will do what they want, when they want and the spouse must deal with it or, if confronted, they simply leave without remorse.

Many of my therapy clients keep trying to extract an apology from their lover. Stop asking – it won't come. The most important thing you can do for yourself is to learn these facts and realize the psychological deviance is not about you. It wasn't you who caused them to do what they did, so don't absorb the blame or let guilt fester in you.

Very few people are aware of this personality disorder and it is so prevalent! Remember that 75% of humans do think consciously about not wanting to hurt another person. Most of us feel remorse after hurting someone and are quick to apologize. Few of us are without guilt but we still can show regret and empathy even to a stranger.

Robert Hare, a University of British Columbia psychology professor, who developed the *Sociopathic and Psychopathy Checklist*, now the standard diagnostic tool for researchers and clinicians, states: "Everyone, including the experts, can be taken in, manipulated, conned and left bewildered by them. A good sociopath or psychopath can play a concerto on anyone's heartstrings. Your best defense is to understand the nature of these human predators."

Dr. Hare's Checklist of Sociopathic Traits

1. Superficial charm
2. Grandiose self-worth
3. Need for stimulation or proneness to boredom
4. Pathological lying
5. Cunning and manipulative
6. Lack of remorse or guilt
7. Shallow affect of emotions
8. Callousness and lack of empathy
9. Parasitic lifestyle
10. Poor behavioral controls
11. Promiscuous sexual behavior
12. Early behavior problems

13. Lack of realistic long-term goals

14. Impulsivity

15. Failure to accept responsibility for their own actions

16. Many short-term marital relationships

17. Juvenile delinquency

18. Revocation of condition release

19. Criminal versatility

Share this list with your friends. Memorize it so that if, or when, you see the ASPD person charming their way into your life, get out fast! They're very difficult to spot but you can, and must, save yourself by entering therapy to help recreate your life, and restore your own self-worth and sanity.

It is well documented that there is no effective treatment for the sociopath, and that they enter therapy only when court ordered, or if they see some gain for themselves. Since they don't think anything is wrong with them, they neither see nor feel their victim's pain, and they don't care about whom they hurt. They're quite happy to continue with their self-absorbed lives after they have devastated you.

The sociopath sees seduction as a game and likes to wreck people's lives for profit or for the sheer fun of it. These are the people who marry for money, undermine coworkers, tell horrendous lies to your face, and live a dark, secret life unknown to you. Prone to boredom, and with no self-monitoring, they do whatever they please to entertain themselves while assuring you that your relationship is fine.

They put on a perfect face for strangers, so when your life falls apart (and it will when you uncover the lies and manipulative actions played against you), you will invariably look like the crazy, nasty woman who hurt him so badly. They expertly hide their psychological makeup, knowing full well that it's radically different from that of most people. They run away, hide and never come back once you are on to them.

Some sociopaths are violent; some are not. Many desire power and money, are highly intelligent, and have the ability to become quite successful in their careers. Deep down, they may lack enough self-esteem to achieve the level of power they crave, so they become parasitic and often will marry only if they feel they can get something from their partner.

Lesser intelligent sociopaths can become frustrated, aggravated, and enraged at not reaching the career pinnacle they yearn for. Instead, they control others seen as less worthy or more vulnerable than themselves. Sociopaths prefer jobs that can control the helpless or those who will look up to them in their position of authority. This could be the boss who acts like a bully or manipulates others to make them appear incompetent, especially those perceived as more successful and accomplished.

Lacking a conscience, these men are happy to sit at home and watch TV while you do all the work. They will lie to you, and feel perfectly happy to stay lazy and unproductive while pretending to be working hard. They won't feel responsible or embarrassed by their actions, and play their own power game by secretly doing what they want without getting caught.

These men choose a spouse who is kind, supportive and will work hard for the benefit of the relationship. If you're a woman caught in this setting, seek counseling immediately to develop a plan to get out.

C) The Addicted and Types of Addiction

Realize that you cannot help a soul unless that soul really wants help and is ready to be helped. – Eileen Caddy

Mosby's Medical Dictionary (2009) defines addiction as a "compulsive, uncontrollable dependence on a chemical substance, habit or practice to such a degree that obtaining or ceasing use may cause severe emotional, mental, or physiologic reactions."

Many addicts suffer from a sense of grandiosity, narcissism, feelings of entitlement and inflated ego pride. These traits interfere with both professional and personal relationships that result in conflict, turmoil and pain, which leads them to reuse again.

As a licensed and certified alcohol and drug counselor (LCADC) who taught this credential for the State of New Jersey at Stockton College of New Jersey, I cannot say enough about how destructive an addiction is to the individual, you the partner, your relationship, and to the children. There is no way to love someone enough to get them to stop using. The addictive substance or behavior will always come first.

There are many types of addictions, and it isn't always clearly evident, while dating, that the person you're falling for has an addiction. This is always kept as a deep, hidden secret, and will remain that way until you discover it, usually long after falling in love. After discovery, prepare for lies and denial that will go on for months or years.

Some addictions are more prone to secrecy. They are: sexual/porn, food, pills and spending addictions. Addictions to alcohol, marijuana, harder drugs like crack or heroin, and gambling addictions usually show themselves early. You can spot someone with an alcohol issue if they consume more than two or three drinks (of heavy liquor) on your first date lasting one to three hours.

Gambling addiction shows itself early as the addict enjoys showing off how good he is and will want to take you to the casinos. Crack, heroin and other hard drugs show extreme changes in behavior, which is hard to hide.

Someone excessively charming, eager to engage in sex and shows extreme romance early on could be demonstrating signs of sexual addiction. The best way to protect yourself is by making the person you really like wait to be with you sexually – at least ninety days. This is called the Ninety-Day Rule; within three months, any warning signs of addiction should have emerged. This gives you enough time to watch and ensure the person you're falling for is stable and drama-free before getting too emotionally involved. Remember that we're talking about addictions; signs of the sociopath tend to emerge much later. Their trick is a slow game of roping you in for financial gain, which takes time especially if marriage is part of their plan.

A person with any addiction should be on your "red-flag warning list", and the relationship must be stopped as soon as the addiction is discovered. Don't fall in love with the addict's potential or empty promises of "getting clean." You will never love someone enough to have them break free from their addiction and you'll endure a destructive relationship. The best chance of stopping an addiction usually happens only after you leave your partner. A person should be clean and addiction-free for at least two years before you get serious or clean one year before getting back together.

Save your heart and save yourself and get out as soon as an addiction is discovered!

Types of Addiction

1. *The Sex Addict*

I'm going to spend more time on this addiction because it is one of the fastest growing, yet rarely talked about, addictions. It was once seen as casual male curiosity for men to read *Penthouse* or *Playboy* magazines. Today, with the Internet, pornography is readily available, often leading to a full-scale obsession, or addiction, ruining many lives and relationships.

One of the leading authors on Sexual Addiction, Patrick Carnes, Ph.D., author of *Out of the Shadows, Understanding Sexual Addiction,* defines sexual addiction as "a pathological relationship to a mood-altering experience." The secret, dark life of the sex addict becomes more important than everything previously valued, including their partner, family and work.

Sex addiction is a cycle where a person (usually male) is thinking about the next time he can get to his pornography, set up a conquest, or plans the next sexual encounter immediately after having one. These addicts engage in risky behaviors, often having sex with strangers, prostitutes, exposing themselves, or engaging in voyeurism. They take significant risks to satisfy their craving, often losing their loving partner, high-paying job, reputation in the community, children, even their lives. It's one of the hardest addictions to break. Ask your date at the beginning of dating if he watches pornography, and how often. If you're presented with the excuse, "All men watch porn and it's not an issue," believe me, it is. Sex addicts are in heavy denial and usually lose everyone once their secret life is discovered. These men fail to see the disrespect and form of emotional and sexual abuse that pornography is to their woman.

An addiction exists when the partner puts his sexual needs above the importance of all other relationships. The addict can also make his spouse a sexual obsession and become demanding for daily sex or to have several encounters a day, be critical of his partner's performance, or make her feel victimized in some way. As a romance junkie, the addict could turn to email, instant messaging, or to chat rooms to resolve past or current issues involving intimacy, abandonment, self-esteem or loneliness. Investing time, money and obsessive attention into these false relationships leads to the erosion of real-life love relationships.

The sex addict risks everything, including self-respect, to obtain the attention craved or to engage in the sexual obsession. As compulsion leads to an unmanageable life, all meaningful relationships are compromised. Sex becomes the most crucial indicator of love from his coaddictive partner and there's failure to see all her other positive attributes.

As the addict's partner strives to keep her man happy, she feels cut out, neglected and confused while the addict is thoughtful and generous toward others, but shows little or no personal warmth or kindness to her. This makes her try harder, or become more sexually attentive to please him, which leads to resentment; he'll engage in the sex but show minimal emotional connection to her while in the act. Nothing is ever enough. You could enjoy a great sexual session only to have him demand more sex right afterward. He'll brag that he could have sex three or four times a day. Be assured that this is not a compliment; it's a sexual addiction.

Stress and anxiety can trigger the compulsion and it tends to get worse in later years. Addicts live in constant fear and anxiety that their secret life will be discovered along with their shame and pain. To keep their secret world safe, they learn to project a brilliant social exterior and often appear "full of themselves" or grandiose. The stress of being revealed creates a powerless feeling that alienates them from loved ones while lies increase and grow around what they say and do. Sex addicts live a life that lacks integrity and become expert liars to cover up their addiction, then show little to no remorse once caught, explaining it away as "normal male desires."

Addicts believe that they would be abandoned by everyone if the truth were known. Despite the fear of vulnerability or dependence on another, the pretense of being in charge is maintained through lies and charming self-control. You'll need solid evidence to prove deceptions, and even then, lies and excuses will amazingly continue. They'll never admit the truth about their affairs and lie to the end to protect their secrets. Trust that what you may find is the tip of the iceberg. Keep looking for tangible evidence prior to confrontation. Once confronted, expect an addict to blame you, or smugly state, "All men watch porn and I'm proud that I have a high sex drive." Get out quickly and protect yourself with evidence as he will try to turn your support system against you. Don't expect an apology, because most of these men are sociopaths.

Many become sexually addicted after growing up to believe that they are unworthy and a bad person. This leads to chronic feelings of inadequacy and desperation, which perpetuates a sense of failure and low self-esteem. Without parental affirmation of love and self-worth, a child's sexual development can become severely derailed because of inferior parental care.

The child confuses sex with nurturing and comfort and associates love and security with sexuality. Many children masturbate as a self-soothing coping mechanism to relieve constant anxiety of a dysfunctional household. Often times, sex addicts were sexually abused as children or entered into an adult-oriented sex life under the age of eleven. Addicts often discover their behavior is similar to that of their parents or other relatives as compulsive sexual acting out passes down through generations. The core belief of the sex addict emerges early and quite clearly since it's believed that "sex is my most important need." Sexual contact is also seen as a victory or a score, and indeed, it is a powerful high for them. Therefore, an adult love relationship often starts out being romantic, passionate and sexual, but is soon replaced with secret, outside sexual stimulation once the relationship "settles down." This hidden compulsion and obsessive, sexually addictive activity replaces the primary love relationship.

A constant, underlying threat of parental abandonment is always present in the childhood life of a sex addict. Feeling unloved, unwanted and unworthy leads to an endless concern for survival. Ironically, addicts reject unconditional love and, therefore, are unable to trust anyone they love. If they do want a relationship, it's more because they want something from that person. The more prevalent the childhood feelings of abandonment, abuse, punishment and humiliation might be, the stronger the sexual addictive urges. The relentless certainty of rejection compels them to reject their partner first, regardless of their own strong feelings. This behavior defines a commitment-phobic person.

As soon as the relationship gets serious, or results in marriage, they feel suffocated and act to purposely sabotage the relationship. Later, feelings of abandonment set in, and they will often try to reconnect with their partner, giving false hope that they've changed. They will hold on to their partner for a sense of security while seducing others, looking for their next sexual or financial victory.

Sexual addiction has become rampant since the development of the Internet. Cheating has been made easier with websites like Ashley Madison (for married people who want to cheat), Adult

Friend Finder (people looking for a quick sexual score), and other sites that make fast money luring people to effortless sexual hookups. These sites bombard the viewer with images within seconds of opening their site, and then they loop to other porn sites, accelerating the addiction process.

The porn user becomes fixated on the visuals, and as neural pathways become overloaded, arousal templates in the brain are altered. As the sexually explicit images become addictive; the addict is absorbed with Internet porn and chat rooms, losing touch with reality. He becomes emotionally distant, moody, critical of his partner and children, and essentially a miserable person to be around.

Cybersex is considered to be similar to crack cocaine for the sex addict. Beginning with pornographic images, the addict's compulsion graduates to movies, live mutual sex on Skype cams, chat rooms, and eventually with real-life prostitutes, both online and offline. Anonymity helps fuel the fire, allowing an addict to beef up his ego as he reinvents himself into anyone he wishes to be. Because prostitutes are paid, they are in the business of lying about how great and special the addict is, prompting the self-loathing addict to return for more.

He lives in denial, trying to convince himself it really isn't cheating since it's all virtual and online. His impaired, delusional thinking convinces him that it's harmless and without consequences. Cybersex addicts cannot stop their behaviors for long and tend to spiral, spending hours on the computer claiming to be working while indulging in pornography after their partner falls asleep. They become obsessed with the images, and disconnect from elements of real life.

As arousal occurs in the brain, serotonin levels decline and dopamine levels rise, initiating a "high" feeling. Sexual behavior, thoughts and feelings are distorted. There are three neural pathways in sex, one that triggers the chemistry of romance and includes arousal, intensity and obsession. Another initiates feelings of attachment that lead to bonding.

John Money, a John Hopkins University researcher, found in 1980 that the sexual neural pathways could be the "prototype of all addictions." He wrote about "a love map" that forms between the ages of five and eight years, establishing a template of what we find sexually arousing. We then act on that template. Physical or sexual abuse or early sexual experiences severely distorts this love map, leading to self-destructive forms of sexual arousal.

Even Facebook, or its affiliated online games, has become one of the most common forms of cheating for clients I see in my practice. Facebook encourages communication among old friends from the past, either publicly or privately by instant chat, or by sending messages behind "the wall." My women clients tend to start affairs through Facebook, while my male clients are more inclined to go to interactive porn sites (often using live Skype chat) or connect with ladies through sex ads on Craig's list. There is now software that hides cell-phone communication with a secret lover. It seems harder than ever to sustain a respectful relationship against a background of more than enough software and Internet enticements to aid cheating.

Sexual addiction (SA) groups do exist, and are growing as this addiction becomes more widespread. Addicts use the twelve step philosophy similar to AA. There is valuable information for getting help on the sexual-addiction website, www.saa-recovery.org. This organization, along with weekly, six-month, or more, of weekly therapy sessions, has helped many of my sexually addicted male clients find quality love relationships while leaving the dark addiction behind. They normally come to counseling once they have lost their wives, children, and/or jobs.

Many addicts won't seek help as they convince themselves they can control their behavior. Level-one addicts begin their addiction by occasionally binging on pornography and then can sometimes stop for weeks or months. They rationalize the behavior with the belief that this is "normal" and it won't impact their lives. Yet a secret life of lies and deceit, including shame and anxiety, will lead to the compulsion to use. Eventually, obsessive thoughts and sexual behavior leads to higher risk, social consequences and a violation of society's norms and marital vows. Indulgence in pornography or an affair at work results in job firing, loss of respect, and often dissolution of the family.

This addiction is tragic for the female or male partner. The healthy spouse is shocked by the lies, duplicity and the extent to which the "secret life" had been maintained for years throughout the relationship. An excellent book that addresses and helps traumatized partners is one by Stefanie Carnes, Ph.D., entitled *Mending a Shattered Heart, A Guide for Partners of Sex Addicts*.

The transformational leader Osho, author of *Intimacy – Trusting Oneself and the Other*, asks the question, "Why do people like to see pictures of naked women? Are women themselves not enough? They are, they are more than enough! So what is the need? A picture is a dream, it is not real, it is never angry, it is not a real-life woman who cannot be perfect. A picture is just mental. Those who suppress sex in the body become mentally sexual. Then their mind moves in sexuality, and then it is a disease. The sex will follow you; it is your shadow. Wherever you go, your shadow will be with you. Neither fight nor flight will help. Where will you go? Wherever you go, you will carry yourself with you, and your shadow will be there."

Osho continues, "If you feel hungry it is okay, eat; but if you think about food continuously, then it is an obsession and a disease. When you attempt to suppress it, the more anger possesses the core of your being. When you constantly suppress, you will be constantly angry and it will become a poison that flows like blood through your veins, and it will spread into all your relationships." Another passage says, "Even if you are in love with someone, the anger will be there and the love will become violent."

He believed that those who are addicted always feel shadowed, anxious and afraid no matter how fast or how far they run. This excellent book provides sharp insight into the unavoidably traumatic ending of love that occurs when you're involved with a person trapped within a toxic sexual addiction. It also provides a distinct understanding of the true nature of intimacy and love.

A woman client married twenty-four years discovered the tragedy of her husband's pornography addiction. He swore it involved only movies watched on his cell phone. She instinctively knew there was more and after she persisted, he finally admitted to several sexual encounters, years of watching porn, and masturbating in his employer's truck. In this situation the husband apologized and begged to be given another chance. The wife felt too deceived and she filed for divorce. He did come to my counseling center, and I encouraged him to buy the books I recommended here, and to join the SA Group in our area. He has done so and is still with the group, acknowledging fully his addiction and remorse. He has allowed himself the chance of changing his life but will have to stay with the counseling now that he is facing divorce.

Another woman came to see me regarding her husband's constant affairs, his pushing sexual experimentation upon her and his constant need for sex (they are in their late 50s). She discovered another affair, with "a young, blonde bimbo" he was financially supporting. At the result of her telling him she wanted a divorce, he went out to the back of their home and shot himself. He realized he couldn't stop the addiction that had ruined his marriage, his children's respect, and his life. He chose to die instead of ever apologizing to her for the pain he had caused throughout their entire marriage. This man was also borderline, narcissistic, sociopathic and lacked remorse, which ultimately led to his demise.

A third client I have lost his marriage and was seeking sexual partners through Craig's list. He didn't think he had an addiction, though he masturbated four times a day, and watched pornography constantly. He lied to his wife for years, and always had "a girl or two on the side." After reading the Sexual Addictions Checklist I provided, he denied at first that he had a problem. Once his wife left him and filed for divorce, he faced the reality of his situation. He is in the SA Group, but his wife chose to move on. Currently, he's attempting to stay "sober" for 90 days: no porn, masturbation, sexual chat rooms, alcohol or pot (which lessens his defenses). At ten days in, his struggles are considerable. He has a new girlfriend, and calls having sex with her "legitimate, healthy sex." I call it denial, delusional, and looking for excuses. He had sex with her on the second date. After two months he broke up with her, seeing her toxic dysfunction that initially had attracted him. Six months later, with weekly therapy, he is in a healthy relationship, abstains from pot and alcohol, and has no desire for internet porn. He has put a porn-buster software program on his computer to ensure abstinence. He's extremely happy and waited 90 days to become sexual with his new lady. Eight months later, they are still happily together and he is porn-free.

A fourth client, a woman engaged to a man she has a young child with, was awakened at 4:00 a.m. by the FBI who had come to arrest her fiancé. He had been caught engaging for years in pre-teen pornography sites. This addiction destroys the women caught up in this mess.

As soon as you discover this addiction, you should strongly consider leaving your partner if they refuse to get help. This is one of the hardest addictions to overcome. Left to their own efforts, sex addicts will relapse since addiction is "a disorder that is characterized by relapse." The years of lies and deceit clearly demonstrates your partner's character flaws and lack of integrity. The need stays as deeply ingrained as lying had as a survival skill in early developmental years. Sex addicts need the SA groups and years of therapy to help break the sexual compulsion. With help, they can learn how to live an honest life and regain the ability to have a healthy, sincere, sexually intimate relationship with a real woman.

2. *The Alcoholic/Drug Addict*

Many outstanding books have been written addressing alcohol and drug addiction. Most people wouldn't marry knowing their future spouse is an addict or alcoholic. But there are warning signs to be aware of while dating. Here are some indicators that your partner may be alcoholic:

1. On the first date and within a short time period, more than three "heavy" drinks are ordered (e.g., martini, scotch, or straight vodka).

2. Your partner needs alcohol almost daily to relax, calm down, reduce stress or fall asleep.

3. Your partner is unable, despite best efforts to submit to your request, to control the amount of alcohol consumed or time spent drinking.

4. Your partner needs to continually drink more to feel the same effects, or is experiencing memory blackouts.

5. Friends and family members have expressed concern.

6. Your partner is currently in trouble with the law because of drinking, or has been charged with a recent DUI (driving under the influence of alcohol or drugs).

7. Your partner drinks early in the morning, when alone, or hides alcohol usage from you and others.

The best method to receive treatment is with a combination of individual therapy (with a LCADC or CAP), group therapy, attending Alcoholics Anonymous meetings, and possibly some of the medications used to treat underlying issues such as depression or anxiety. Many people overuse alcohol to self-medicate stress or due to a mental health problem such as bipolar personality disorder. Individual therapy should examine all your life spheres to examine why you're drinking too much. This would include examining the state of all your relationships, work environment, family history, financial concerns and overall physical wellness.

A drug addiction can start innocently enough by using prescribed medications for pain, after a surgery, or when dealing with a death or emotional crises. Over time, one becomes dependent on the drug to relieve stress or forget a problem that has been difficult to deal with. Losing your job or home, undergoing financial or relationship crisis, or being diagnosed with an illness are other reasons why people use drugs to numb their pain. Many prescription pills are highly addictive, and can quickly lead to a full-blown physical and psychological addiction, adding problems to the original issue. Detoxification (detox) is often required to help wean you off the drug safely and to manage the uncomfortable symptoms of withdrawal.

Signs of a drug addiction include:

1. Using the drug daily or several times a day.
2. Using larger amount than what was prescribed.
3. Inability to stop taking the drug and the belief that you need it to handle everyday problems.
4. Focusing time, attention and energy in procuring the drug, and buying it even when you can't afford it.

Some signs your loved one may have a drug addiction include:

1. Mood swings, anger, irritability, bad attitude and becoming verbally or emotionally abusive.
2. Loss of sleep, low desire for sex, and eating excessively.
3. Lying and sneaky behavior, i.e., a secret life.
4. Financial or legal problems, trouble with a business partner or at work, with friends or family.
5. Neglects appearance, lacks hope for the future.
6. Isolation from others, doesn't want to go out or see friends or family, desire to party with non-judgmental strangers.

If you see a problem with alcohol or drug use early on in a potential partner, get out of the relationship before becoming too invested. These people are usually "the life of the party," flirtatious, sexual and socially outgoing after a few drinks, but may be moody, distant, depressed, tired and angry the day after without their alcohol or drugs. Early on while dating, they will hide the amount consumed, so it's best to carry on dating for at least ninety days to see if there are addiction issues. Usually, something will emerge within that three-month period.

Is it safe to date or become involved with someone who is a former addict or alcoholic? You may have heard the term "dry drunk" to describe an alcoholic or drug user who no longer actively uses their drug but may sustain some of the faulty thinking and behavior patterns, or display the strongly negative emotions of one who is chemically addicted. Proceed slowly. Many people do take their recovery seriously and engage in individual counseling to understand and change childhood patterns that may have led to addiction. Take the time to look carefully at all aspects of the person to ensure you feel they are emotionally and physically healthy. You have a choice, so it's always best to go for the healthy, non-addictive partner to protect yourself.

Other Addictions: Gambling, spending, over-eating, hoarding, online games, email, and video games

I will discuss each of these addictions briefly to make you aware of the signs that the person you're dating may have a problem. Addicts are very skilled at hiding their behavior, so stay alert, and guard your heart!

3. *Gambling addiction:* gambling, slots, sports betting, bingo, lotto, online gambling. All these addictions have to do with the thrill of winning or the possibility of winning. The gambler will often take you to a casino to show you his skills. Involvement in any of these betting activities, whether daily or several times a week could be an indication of an addiction problem. These addicts brag about their winnings, and lie about the amount they lose.

4. ***Internet, email and Facebook use, online games, texting, and smart phone addictions:*** These are becoming more common due to society's usage and dependence on computers and phones. If your online activity becomes excessive, or you feel stressed, anxious, or irritable when not online, or if you constantly check your email and ignore your partner and children, you may be addicted. Many couples break up over this type of an addiction because the healthy partner feels ignored, unimportant and lonely.

5. ***Food Addictions and Eating Disorders including Binge Eating, Purging and Anorexic behavior:*** The majority of those with food addictions are women, but men can be affected as well. These people become addicted to carbs, sugar, fats or sweets. Consuming large quantities of these foods actually changes brain chemistry and creates withdrawal symptoms if the person stops excessive consumption.

    With binging, a lot of food is eaten in a short amount of time, and the person may or may not choose to purge (vomit) the food afterward or exercise compulsively to lose the excess calories. This behavior escalates when the person is anxious, depressed or stressed out. This often begins when a child feels emotionally abused or unloved, and uses food to self-soothe. Powerless to stop the eating pattern, depression can follow over the amount of food eaten, making this a vicious cycle. Many women who were sexually molested or abused overeat so that men will not be attracted to their bodies. They feel "safer" being overweight as they believe men will not sexually desire them.

    Anorexia is the use of control over food, usually in response to feeling a lack of control in other areas of one's life. There is an intense need to control calories, weight and food consumption. Anorexics believe that being skinny is attractive, but they take it to so severe an extreme that it often leads to death. This intense monitoring of food and weight usually starts in childhood or in teenage years. They may have had a very controlling, abusive parent or may have taken ballet, gymnastics or wrestling where weight monitoring is crucial. High-fashion models are vulnerable to anorexia because they're encouraged to believe that super skinny is sexy and the ideal to achieve. Remember, instead, that healthy is sexy!

6. *Spending and Hoarding:*

Is hoarding an addiction or a compulsion? According to the DSM-IV-TR, compulsions are "repetitive behaviors or mental acts that a person feels driven to perform in response to an obsession; and which acts are aimed at preventing or reducing distress or preventing some dreaded event or situation."

What starts as a compulsive behavior tends to become an addiction, such as those with impulsive spending habits. Overspending and a powerful need for material goods reflect a need for instant gratification possibly due to extreme stress, anxiety or depression. This can lead to a hoarding of material goods, animals, or a specific collection of items to the point where their homes are disgustingly cluttered. Those with spending addictions often hide their purchases and create large debts before their secret spending is uncovered, often ruining marriages and the possibility of a secure future.

Rescuing and bailing out someone like this from debt is a momentary fix. Like the addict, *you* cannot love someone enough, or fix this person for the long term. Clinical help often along with an anti-anxiety or mood medication is necessary as there is almost always a relapse with the compulsive behaviors.

In the current DSM-IV-TR, compulsive hoarding is considered as part of the behavioral criteria for a diagnosis of obsessive-compulsive disorder (OCD). However, the latest research suggests that hoarding is not a compulsion related to OCD. It is considered as an independent diagnosis in the fifth edition of the DSM (Mataix-Cols et al., 2010).

Hoarders simply cannot part with their "stuff." Animals become like family and material goods that aren't needed are purchased to bring the buyer a sense of love and security for a few moments. Throwing out these items is like parting with their right arm; they need their "stuff" and the idea of getting rid of any of it makes them physically and mentally ill.

What is behind this compulsivity and need for instant gratification? As reported on the website, http://mag.newsweek.com/2011/10/30/the-new-science-behind-your-spending-addiction.html, measurable differences between the brains of people who are able to save and those who spend lavishly have been discovered by brain scientists. They refer to the gray matter of the brain as the "money brain" or the part that monitors consequences, the sense of regard for self and others, motivation, memory and the ability to make crucial decisions. This research has lead behavioral scientists to identify personality types as well as traits of spenders and savers. The spender's brain is more impulsive, not wired to find pleasure in future rewards and cannot anticipate the consequences of spending impulsively. Be sure to choose a saver for a partner.

In a well-known 1960 experiment conducted by psychologist Walter Mischel at Stanford University, four-year-olds were presented with a marshmallow left in front of them while the experimenter exited the room. The children were told that two marshmallows would be the reward if they would wait until the scientist returned before eating the first one, thus measuring the ability to delay gratification. More than ten years later, the children able and willing to wait scored higher in their SAT tests supporting the idea that impulse control and other forms of emotional intelligence are linked to academic performance, and those who could delay gratification were less likely to be addicted to drugs, compulsive behaviors and less likely to be obese.

In people able to delay gratification, the brain's rational and thoughtful prefrontal cortex shows more activity than does the right frontal gyrus that inhibits impulsivity and the need to "have it now." These tend to be happier, more successful people who have a good support system.

Poor delayers who need instant gratification showed lower activity in these brain areas and higher activity in areas of the limbic system. Being able to save and sustain a goal is affiliated with having a good short-term memory and the ability to project and plan into the future. The higher levels of oxytocin in the healthy brain reduce anxiety and help us make better decisions.

Research into the younger generation shows a large percentage having problems with delaying gratification partially because they tend to be less patient, more impulsive, and believe they have plenty of time to save. Studies also show that children spoiled and given what they wanted instantly show more impulsivity and more irrational spending as young adults.

Helpful treatments for these disorders include: working with a Clutter Coach along with Cognitive Behavioral Therapy (CBT) to focus on replacing unhealthy, negative and irrational thoughts, beliefs and behaviors with healthier, more positive ones; teaching better decision making and healthier coping skills. (Sanxena and Maidment, 2004). In addition, this research shows that antidepressants and anxiolytics are effective in treating co-morbid disorders such as anxiety and depression, both often found in those with addiction and compulsive hoarding.

While dating, watch your partner's level of impulsivity and reckless spending. Ask if he has debt, and see if he has clear goals for the future. Monitor behavior to see if he is anxious, or has a calm, confident demeanor and a sense of personal security. In general, ask yourself if he has his life together and a solid plan for his future.

If he is obsessive, he may be an over-cleaner, a super-perfectionist, checker (lights, stove and locks), over-active hand washer, and show other signs of being afraid of germs. Very often there is ritual tied to obsessions and counting, like counting thirteen times to check the stove, then seven times to check the locks upon leaving the house. This extra time causes a lot of stress on himself and his partner but can be eased with medication.

7. *Other addictions worth mentioning:*

   1. TV addiction

   2. Exercise addiction

   3. Smoking (decreasing due to social stigma, restaurant and workplace rules, and the electronic cigarette)

Knowing the signs of addiction and compulsive behavior is important when starting to date and getting to know someone. However, these behaviors are often well hidden and emerge after you're emotionally invested. Many addictions can be helped, but only if the addicted party clearly wants the help and is invested in treatment for a long period of time. Many with addictions will stop for a while, verbally promising not to use in order to keep their partner and the relationship. They may believe in their promise to control and stop their addiction, but it's very difficult to do so without help.

If you discover an addiction, see if your partner agrees to get counseling. Another chance with you is the most loving, kind and supportive gift you can offer, but with the stated boundary that if there is a relapse, you're done with the relationship. You will need individual and couples therapy to heal from his lies and deceit and to help rebuild your trust. I do believe that people can change, but *only* if they *really want to*. If your partner relapses, or you catch them in more deception, you need to love yourself more, and move on to a healthier love relationship.

D) The ACOA Personality Type

You must begin to trust yourself. If you do not then you will forever be looking to others to prove your own merit to you, and you will never be satisfied. You will always be asking others what to do, and at the same time, resenting those from whom you seek such aid. – Jane Roberts

I see this toxic personality type in my therapy office all the time. Clients with ongoing ACOA issues enter therapy with their devastated partner who feels powerless because she doesn't understand the hurtful behaviors or know how to help.

ACOA stands for Adult Children of Alcoholics (or any adults who suffered trauma as children). They learned at a very young age how to deny their pain by shutting down their emotions. These children grew up in homes where there was one or more of the following issues:

- Abandonment from one parent leaving the family (physically, emotionally or due to addiction), or enmeshment by the opposite sex parent. No-fault abandonment might also have occurred, as in a parent dying early due to illness or accident; or a parent who must travel due to his career.

- Emotional or verbal abuse from an authoritarian or abusive parent.

- Physical or sexual abuse, rape or molestation.

- Extreme family poverty, financial worries, lack of food, warmth or shelter.

- Emotional neglect or lack of love, safety or security.

- Parental addiction to alcohol, drugs, sexual promiscuity, gambling, food, spending, etc.

- Competition amongst siblings resulting in feelings of worthlessness.

- Being teased or bullied from cohorts or family.

- Growing up in extreme clutter with a depressed or anxious parent, or with the opposite type, an OCD-cleaning or perfectionistic, demanding parent.

- Living within a parental domestic violence situation or knowing a parent cheated and lied.

- Any other family trauma; e.g., frequent relocation, a house loss due to fire or storm, a physically sick or addicted sibling or parent.

These situations that may have occurred during childhood can cause you to choose unhealthy, toxic partners. You can become codependent or love addicted, which often leads to breakups and grief.

Of course, even having come from a loving and positive parental household that left you with good childhood memories, you could still end up in a bad relationship. Your own history could encourage you to continue trying to help a toxic person or a bad relationship as you may hold onto an idealized vision of what a marriage could be. You may fall in love with a man's potential and ignore deceit or hurtful situations. Seeing the good in another is a positive trait, but don't fall into the trap of thinking you can "fix" another person.

The ACOA can initially be loving, charming, romantic, sexy, affectionate, giving, fun, outgoing, socially confident, and successful in their careers; all traits that would surely lead to a great partner! But dysfunctional traits may emerge that question the character of your fabulous new partner.

The ACOA personality may show a few or all of the following traits, across a severity range of 1-to-10, that can lead to personal and relationship dysfunction.

1. Low self-esteem but with a high lust and sex drive; overcompensates by seducing others, using sex to validate worth; low-value morals; feels shame and becomes impotent and cold; excessive need for partner's attention.

2. Can be irresponsible, detached, messy, impulsive, a spender, an underachiever, often plays the victim role, can be uncaring, and blames others when things go wrong.

3. Fear of abandonment, insecure, hates rejection or being alone, emotionally chases his partner looking for attention or validation, worries constantly.

4. Fear of those in authority; strong sense of inadequacy; takes things very personally; slow, or refuses, to apologize or forgive.

5. Shuts down emotionally; has distorted feelings, resulting in many short-term relationships.
6. Need for control and to be the center of attention; manipulates, lies, makes excuses, embellishes truths.
7. People pleasing or care giving only to be liked.
8. Resentful, angry and bitter.
9. Fear of change, loss, and rejection.
10. Need for approval, intolerant of criticism.
11. Anxious, jealous, inappropriate expressions of anger, prone to depression and self-pity.
12. Lacks trust and fears failure.
13. Rescues, ignores personal needs, feels responsible, can be codependent.
14. Shows false pride and arrogance; overly serious and perfectionistic to hide insecurities; can be compulsive about work (workaholic), or an over-achiever to prove personal worth to the world.

If, during childhood years, the ACOA tried to voice wants, needs or opinion and suffered rejection, abandonment, physical or emotional abuse, they learned and developed behaviors that helped them survive and cope. The tragedy lies in the fact that these very behaviors and imprinted habits now sabotage and destroy the adult love relationships they crave.

The ACOA mask their feelings by overworking, overeating, over spending, controlling others, using humor or charm to manipulate, abusing alcohol or drugs, using sex to soothe anxiety, or sustaining other addictions. They have trouble communicating their fears, anger, pain or needs, only to explode in an angry outburst if they feel an injustice has been done to them.

They have a dark side, often called "the shadow" or their "secret life" that haunts and follows them throughout adulthood. Engaging secretively gives them a sense of power and control that only they know about, which is a passive-aggressive way to fight with the ones they love.

They feel constant anxiety, self-loathing, fear control or commitment, live in despair, hide their shameful feelings of inadequacy, and want to punish those who hurt them in even the slightest way. They cannot admit to their wrongdoings, show no remorse, and often blame their partners. They use childlike survival skills against their partners and don't see them as abnormal, thus being called "the adult child."

Sylvia Kay Fisher and Ronnie H. Fisher put together the ACOA checklist that can be found in a Google search. It is used to assess many of the issues associated with the ACOA, and brings awareness to issues of low self-esteem, perfectionism, need for approval, impulsivity, conflicted personal relationships, and sublimation of personal needs. I use this assessment tool with my clients to dig deeper into their past memories and to explore their adult actions from a basis of childhood pain.

There are 6 sections in the ACOA checklist assessment tool, but I will mention some of the most common signs of the ACOA personality type here.

    A. Low Self Esteem

        1. I often feel that I am unworthy.

        2. I don't expect people to understand me.

3. There are very few people that really care about me.
4. Sometimes I feel I don't deserve to be loved.
5. I don't deserve to be happy.
6. I feel I am a weak person.
7. I worry people will think I'm incompetent.
8. Success is easier for other people.
9. I fail at most things I try.
10. I have trouble believing people when they tell me they like me.

B. Perfectionism
1. I take my responsibilities very seriously.
2. I hate when I don't have things under control.
3. I have trouble completing all the tasks I take on.
4. I don't laugh very often.
5. I become upset when my plans change unexpectedly.
6. I am considered responsible to a fault.
7. People say I take things too seriously.
8. I tend to be a perfectionist and want things just right, or my way.
9. It bothers me to see people relax so easily.
10. I can overreact to the smallest change in my routine.

C. Conflicted Personal Relationships
    1. I have a lot of fights and conflicts with my family.
    2. I get "sucked in" to fights even when I try to avoid them with family members.
    3. I have trouble staying in relationships for a long period of time.
    4. I have trouble communicating with those I care about.
    5. I'm not sure what a normal love relationship would look like.
    6. It is hard for me to connect with other people.
    7. I don't know what a normal family looks like.
    8. I often feel different from those around me.
    9. I sometimes wonder what is would be like to be happy.
    10. I am very loyal to friends and family when they don't deserve it.

D. Need for Approval
    1. I am afraid of what others think of me.
    2. People think I can smooth over conflicts before they escalate.
    3. Other people's opinions of me are very important to me.
    4. I avoid conflicts at all costs.

5. I find myself lying to others for no reason.
6. I give up on things I want to avoid a fight.
7. I worry others don't like me.
8. I would rather lie than tell someone the truth and make them angry.
9. I have backed down from something I believe in so someone won't be mad at me.
10. It is important that all or most people in my life like me.

E. Impulsivity
1. People think I am irresponsible and apt to get into trouble.
2. I often behave impulsively resulting in problems for myself and others.
3. I am in my element when things are disorganized.
4. I usually don't pay attention to details when working on tasks.
5. I often do things without thinking about the consequences for myself or others.

F. Sublimation of Personal Needs
1. I take care of other people's needs before my own.
2. Members of my family make demands on me and expect me to meet them.

3. I feel guilty if I do something nice for myself.

4. I usually ignore my own preferences in favor of those of people around me.

5. I try to satisfy requests made by family members even when it is difficult for me to do so.

There is a scoring system to this checklist, but to avoid self-analysis, or labeling your partner, I recommend that if you see yourself or your partner unmistakably described in any two areas, do seek out a therapist who specifically understands the ACOA personality type.

There is help for the ACOA and a promising prognosis for change. I see the change process as a large rainbow. The client starts on one side, where there is a huge learning curve. They may, and often do, relapse as they start their climb, but if they don't stay throughout the program of spiritual education, behavior modification and the twelve-step plan, they risk relapsing and sliding all the way back, never to reach the other side of the rainbow. With intensive therapy, reading, and understanding their past, many clients reach the other side to find the "pot of gold." They can enjoy a life lived with integrity, honor and honesty, enabling the removal of high levels of anxiety.

Many of my ACOA client's start the program, read the two suggested books, begin studying spiritual concepts and start attending religious services. They feel gratified to finally understand what drives their actions. If they do achieve a spiritual base, which is essential to growth and recovery, and stay with the study and self-help programs, they *will* get to the other side and welcome the feeling of peace and relief.

They have the tools to handle bad moments and their actions will no longer be so impulsive or extreme that they lose their loving partner. But without spending the time in therapy, doing the readings and spiritual practice daily, the heavily ingrained childhood patterns can reemerge and destroy a love relationship.

Old patterns the ACOA use for self-comfort can be broken. Some of these dysfunctional choices for relief of symptoms include:

1. An addictive use of masturbation, fantasies and sex to escape reality.

2. People-pleasing to raise self-esteem.

3. Using alcohol or drugs, spending, eating, gambling or other addictions to escape pain.

4. Isolation from others.

5. Using lies and seduction to feel the rush of manipulation and control of another.

I have several clients who have done wonderfully well in their healing, after coming to me on the brink of despair, or having lost their partner, family, children, job, and income. Some had long-lasting secrets they had never told anyone, like my client who had been sexually molested by a family member and held the secret deep inside by over-eating, spending, and developing a sexual addiction.

If the ACOA is invested in a total cleansing of past issues, healing can be realized with daily monitoring of thoughts and behavior, study and reading, as well as open and candid communication about their issues with their partner. There *is* a pot of gold at the end of that rainbow.

Specifically, the ACOA needs a therapist and sponsor within a twelve-step program to help them recover. Choose a mentor who has recovered and whose life you respect. Their qualities are what you hope to acquire for yourself:

1. Honesty in sharing your personal stories and in the way you live your life; total rejection of more lies and excuses.

2. True belief in a higher power; prayer or meditation twice each day. Read inspiring and spiritual books from Joel Osteen, Gary Kudov, Deepak Chopra, and others recommended in the back of this book.

3. Dedication to living your life with integrity, which I define as "doing the right things when no one is looking, because ultimately, God is watching, and you're going to get caught." So do nothing to embarrass or harm yourself or others.

4. Be willing to listen to your therapist and mentors; and practice daily what they teach. If easier, divide your day into one-third segments. Do the right thing from rising to lunch, from lunch to dinner, and from dinner to bedtime. Celebrate a good day and pray for accomplishments to be fulfilled tomorrow. Keep track of your good days to inspire you to have more of them.

5. When you feel doubtful of whether to make a specific choice, take a certain action or say a certain thing, ask yourself the four essential questions:
    a. If I do this, can it harm me in any way?
    b. Will it harm my partner, the one I love?
    c. Will it harm my children or extended family?

d. Will it hurt my reputation on the job or within my community?

Here's another saying to help you: *"If in doubt, go without."* In other words, don't take the action, say the words, or make the choice if it could lead to a poor outcome or an act of deceit. Don't make a choice if you feel uncertain; wait and meditate or pray on it.

Joel Osteen's book, *Your Best Life Now*, is a great read about living a life full of integrity. Living this way shows your absolute confidence because you truly like the person you are.

Someone I know always asked himself, "Would Joel do it?" (If Joel Osteen wouldn't do it, then he wouldn't either.) This person was doing very well on his journey of healing from ACOA tendencies, but fell short when his commitment-phobic anxiety overwhelmed him at the time of his marriage. Ultimately, he relapsed back to his secret life of pornography addiction, lies and deceit, losing the marriage and the woman he adored.

With personality disorders and addictive behaviors, there is frequent relapse in healing. You are fighting years of negative imprinting and survival skills that worked throughout childhood, but have destroyed your happiness in adult relationships.

There is help, but the ACOA must be committed to the process for the sake of their emotional growth, healing and peace of mind. Don't agree to attend counseling because your partner demands it to save your marriage and family. Do it because you know you need it, and desire to be a better person for the benefit of yourself.

In therapy, you can learn to express your feelings in a healthy way, set limits, be accountable, find ways to reduce anxiety, learn to be honest, take care of yourself and exercise integrity. When you learn to relinquish control over others, and focus on your own health, growth, goals and healing, you will have more confidence, less fear and fewer reasons to act out.

Goal setting with your coach, learning to be true to your word, accepting responsibilities and being supportive rather than deceptive in relationships will help raise self-esteem. Learn how to get out of "the dark side," by finding faith and living in the light. Spiritual reading is helpful, as is finding a church, temple or synagogue for weekly prayer.

Steps 8 and 9 of the 12-step program ask the ACOA to make a list of all those they have harmed and make amends to them all. They need to face their faults, accept responsibility, stop placing blame on others and be honorable enough to apologize in person or by a sincere letter asking for forgiveness from those they hurt.

One client said in his first session, "God forgives me, so I don't have to apologize to my wife for my sexual addiction." He missed the mark completely and needs to go to step one and stay in therapy to see the light.

If you are with an ACOA, it is important that you enter therapy with a counselor that knows this personality type. You will come to understand your partner's behavior and not take his acting out so personally.

If your partner refuses help through therapy and a twelve-step program, or relapses and continues with destructive behaviors that hurt you and destroy your trust, you must love yourself more and get out of the constant and cheap drama that characterizes life with the ACOA.

I also suggest the superb book by Janet Woitiz, *The ACOA Sourcebook* for all my clients to read, as well as *The 12-Steps for Adult Children* published by RPI Publishing, written by adult children in their recovery.

E) The Chronic Cheater – Emotional and Sexual Affairs

So sad that you're leaving, takes time to believe it – but after it's all said and done, you're going to be the lonely one… – Cher, Believe (1998)

Nothing is more devastating than finding out your loving partner has been cheating on you. At one time, this was a male-dominated behavior, but today's statistics show that women cheat equally as much as men, but for different reasons.

Affairs are often the result of a broken marriage, and it is the person's fault that goes outside of the relationship, not the person they chose to be with. The unhappy spouse should have gone to their partner and told them of their concerns, wants and needs. It often helps to go to couples' counseling or to have a relationship coach to help you speak freely to your partner.

The article by Molly Edmonds, "Do Men and Women Cheat for Different Reasons?" (http://people.howstuffworks.com/men-women-cheating1.htm) reports that marriage counselor M. Gary Neuman claims one in 2.7 men will cheat at some point [source: CNN]. It also appears that men cheat more than women, but women have been cheating more frequently in recent years.

Describing the reasons men and women cheat, she reports that men seek quantity and women seek quality. Men cheat to have more sex, and women have affairs because they want an emotional connection that is missing in their relationship. According to Neuman, "92% of cheating men say it's not about the sex, it's about feeling under appreciated," so men report they seek intimacy and attention because they feel neglected by their steady partner.

Other sources say that for men, the biggest factor was sexual excitability, but for women it was not being happy in their relationship and feeling that their partner didn't have the same sexual values as they did.

Neither cared about the consequences of their actions. It has long been assumed that women's cheating rates have caught up with men's because they're in the workplace and travel more in business. Distance from home and spouse opens up opportunities to cheat while escaping the routine of household and family responsibilities.

Cyber affairs also account for the increased ease of cheating, making it simple to hook up with old flames. Women's affairs primarily play into the romance and passionate urges neglected by their husbands over time.

Affairs make women feel loved, valued, sexy and exciting. It takes them away from the drudgery of household chores, the role of "mommy" and makes them feel like a desired, sexy woman again. If a husband has stopped romancing his wife, or neglects his hygiene, weight and image, this behavior tells his wife she is no longer important to him. Lack of communication, or talking to her without love or empathy, is another trigger for women. They seek men who can openly communicate and who are actively engaged emotionally. This is the "work" men must do to keep their women happy.

Men primarily look for fast and easy hookups that won't complicate their lives, or so they think. Yes, some websites play into the notion of fast hookups, or some men engage in sexual chat rooms believing they "aren't cheating." But whenever you emotionally or sexually share your time and energy with another person, and need to lie about doing so, this constitutes an affair, whether sexual, emotional or techno-cheating through the computer.

The issues are the same whether one is straight or gay, male or female. At the beginning of a relationship, there is passion, romance, excitement and interest in your partner. When the initial excitement wears off, you must actively and creatively keep the sexual interest and romance alive. A good, loving relationship requires ongoing attention and dedication.

Everyday life, stress and work routines kill libido. That is why a date night at least once a week (twice is preferred) keeps you focused on each other. This is not necessarily a dinner date, and should not be a movie date because the idea is to connect through flirting, communication, romance and passion. I usually recommend a venue with music where a couple can have cocktails and a snack, a comedy club, a day in the country, or an overnight stay a few hours away.

Ladies, do keep wearing the sexy things you wore when you dated, and don't turn into a nagging, dowdy housewife. Men, take care of your image, don't be a coach potato, or make football or golf more important than your lady. Although these statements sound stereotypical, they're also, unfortunately, true-life scenarios for many of my clients.

People are exhausted from long work hours, family responsibilities and financial stress. Many see their partners as their last concern, putting the kids and everything else before them. This is a huge mistake; you both must carve out the time to focus emotionally and sexually on each other. Because men are so sexually focused (their sexual center in their brain is seven times the size of women's), a woman must make sure her man is getting enough sexual activity (two to three times a week), initiate sex and intimacy often, be sexually creative and help spice up the bedroom. Read erotica to help learn techniques that could please your man.

Men have been visual creatures from the time of cavemen days; it relates back to ancient reptilian brain activity. They fall in love visually first and crave the sight of lingerie, high heels, fitted skirts, tops and dresses, and a lady who takes care of herself (hair, skin, nails and light makeup). Work hard to keep your look similar to the day he fell in love with you. Aging is natural, but always dress appealingly. Be able to communicate your sexual needs as men want to hear what you need, want and like sexually. They really do want to love and please you, and the way a man shows his connection and love for you is through making love.

Men, don't ask for sex on a daily basis, making it feel like another chore a woman must perform each day. Don't demand sex or act miserable because you're not having it when you want it. Your woman makes love with the brain first, meaning that you must connect emotionally for her to feel safe and connected enough to want to open herself to you. This issue of "feeling safe" is hard wired into her "old reptilian" brain and again goes back to cavewomen days, where a woman made love to a man she felt would take care of her and her children. If your woman isn't feeling sexual, get her out of the house, away from the kids and housework, and make her feel special.

Romance is the key to her heart and the secret to men getting more sex, so why do they stop doing this? Don't complain about sex; make her feel like a million dollars and you'll get all the sex you want. Cards and flowers for no reason, romantic email letters, sexy texts throughout the day, special gifts (jewelry is best) on her birthday, Valentine's Day, your anniversary, and remembering the day you met makes your woman feel valued and important. Never stop kissing and hugging her, holding her hand or flirting with her. Let the kids see you be romantic and loving – it sets a great example.

Both partners need to stay fit and toned, watch their weight, groom themselves, watch TV less, romance their partner in an ongoing fashion, be creative sexually (getting sex out of the bedroom for fun and variety), and find fun and romantic activities they can do together.

Most couples that come to me as the result of an affair can work through their issues in time with open communication, love, and honesty to recreate a more loving, sexually exciting and passionate relationship.

The guilty partner must be patient and completely open, honest and gentle with their partner as they heal from lies and broken trust. All computers, email, Facebook and cell phones should have no passwords or codes unknown to either partner. Don't spend a lot of time on your cell phone or computer; instead, invest that time with your partner and discuss feelings in an open and empathetic way.

If you have an affair, and your partner feels sad, mad, jealous or anxious over "the other man" or other deceptions, this is normal and to be expected. You cannot expect him to "just get over it" and pretend the cheating didn't happen. If he vents to you, or rehashes the details he discovered about the affair, tell him how sorry you feel to have caused him such pain. Tell him again that you love him and want to dedicate and devote yourself to the relationship and to rebuilding his trust. Empathy means putting yourself in his shoes. Would you be mad for a long period of time if your man cheated on you? Do whatever must be done to rebuild the trust, and be kind and patient.

If you've been cheated on I suggest you forgive once, and understand clearly why your partner strayed and where the marriage broke down. Apologize for your part in the failure of your relationship and restate your dedication to making things work. At the same time, point out the boundary line – this can never happen again, or you will be forced to end the marriage.

I have had many marital couples who present with an affair. I usually encourage them to forgive their partner, the most spiritual and difficult thing a person can do. I encourage them both to admit their faults, apologize to one another, and to speak about their needs to make their relationship better and stronger. I've known both men and women who have had the courage to do this.

Many marriages have moved on to much happier times, but sadly, the cheating partner often strays again. We examine the possibility of there being deeper mental health issues, like having a sexual addiction, or needy ACOA traits that cause constant attention seeking to feed ego and self-esteem, or engaging in a secret life to feel empowered. If this is the case, it's imperative that the healthy partner leave the relationship, get counseling and coaching to reinvent themselves and to rebuild their own lives

F) The Jealous and Controlling Paranoid

Jealousy is really a demand that someone love you in a certain way, it comes from a lack of self-esteem. – Dr. Wayne W. Dyer

Jealousy ruins a great relationship. Ask yourself if these behaviors are something you repeat from a past childhood imprint, or is your partner trying to make you jealous in order to control you in abusive ways?

Let's first examine why you become jealous. If you grew up with a cheating father, then it's in your childhood imprinting to be distrustful of most men you get close to. Also, examine the type of boyfriends you've had. Were they loyal, or did they flirt in front of you or cheat with another? This is a subject that you should address in counseling.

Your lack of trust may rise from painful experiences as a child and teen, but it's important that you address this. As a dating woman, be sure you allow the man to make the first move to show his interest in you. Raise your self-confidence to the point where you won't stay with any man if you see the described warning signs. Date only men you can totally be yourself with and those you don't have to impress in any special way. Work with your relationship coach to define your wants, needs and requirements in a healthy partner and refuse to deviate from that plan. Take your time when dating someone to ensure they are healthy and able to love and commit. With high self-esteem, if you date someone who goes out of his way to make you jealous, you'll recognize he has issues and stop dating him.

Signs He is Playing Jealousy Games

1. He doesn't call when he says he will, but expects you to pick up all his calls or respond to his texts. He's secretive with his phone, computer and his time. Either he's purposely trying to make you jealous or engaging in deceitful behavior.

2. He makes eyes at women when you're out together, especially when you're talking to him, making you feel unimportant.

3. He remarks on other women's beauty, or compares your breast size, height, weight, outfit, hair color or makeup to another woman's, suggesting "you try it too," an emotionally abusive way to put you down by implying that he prefers her.

4. He will compete with everything you do or say, needing to feel that he "won" or is better than you and your accomplishments. He often insists during conversations that you're wrong and he's right, or he minimizes your opinions, suggestions, or achievements.

5. He must have the last word, will talk over you, negate what you say, or just not listen. He'll be sarcastic, blaming and unforgiving, and will do anything to make you look bad or insignificant. His self-esteem is low and the only way he can feel powerful is to make you feel or look inferior.

6. He will try to convince you that he's jealous because he loves you so much. Men who have a healthy self-esteem don't play the jealousy game. They will give you the love and attention you deserve without hurting you in the process. Jealousy is selfish and used by toxic men who know they don't deserve you.

Everyone can feel jealous or suspicious every now and then, especially when you really care for someone. But feeling jealous on a daily basis is an issue. Insecure people tend to imagine worst-case scenarios or compare themselves unfavorably to their supposed rival. They experience overwhelming anxiety after misinterpreting an innocent event, making them believe that their partner might leave them for someone else.

Negative thoughts, low self-esteem, and insecurities can give rise to more self-loathing and doubt, leading to irrational conclusions about a partner. Exceedingly jealous people invariably drive their partner away by acting controlling, invasive, needy and demanding. They create the scenario they most feared – losing their partner.

Types of Toxic People

Learning how to communicate and work through moments of jealousy effectively is crucial to maintaining a loving, healthy and trusting relationship. Talk with your partner about why you feel insecure and request that he do something differently. Try to avoid blatant blame and any accusations that you can't prove. Thank your partner for listening to your concerns and appreciating your feelings. Use positive language to change your negative thoughts and to eliminate doubts.

Another way to deal with jealousy is to use humor, or leave the bar or table to use the ladies' room while he rambles on about why he got caught coming on to another woman. Or ignore the woman he's staring at and turn to look in another direction to catch the eyes of a handsome man. Two can play the game, or better yet, decide to stop playing games completely, and leave him.

If a man is obnoxiously hitting on another female in front of you or trying to make you jealous, nothing works better then calmly saying, "You like that girl, go get her," then get up and leave with a big, confident smile on your face. Walking out on a man in the middle of a restaurant will leave him feeling humiliated. Let her have the arrogant idiot. And don't pick up his phone calls ever again.

Don't ever let a man make you feel inadequate or not good enough. The man seeking attention from other women while out with you, does so because his own self-esteem is piteously low. There are toxic emotional and mental health issues lurking deep within him. You don't need his kind of love and attention because you love yourself more and will get out with your self-esteem intact! You go, girl!

Every toxic person uses control, whether overtly and obviously, or covertly and passively. Control is always about a lack of self-esteem, and wounded childhood issues. It could present as a

113

deep concern or caring for someone, and you'll hear words like, "I'm a gentleman who was taught to do for you." Yes, a gentleman who opens the door, helps you on with your coat and closes the car door is wonderful. It's nice for him to offer to order for you, but really, you know exactly the way you want your own restaurant dish to be made. There are polite gestures, and then there is control.

Toxic people try to control by use of emotional manipulation to get what they want. They felt utterly powerless as a child, possibly coming from a physical and emotionally abusive family, absent, neglectful or cold parents, or alcoholic or addictive parents. With no control as children, the need is obsessive in adulthood.

Seduction is a means of control, which is why many dysfunctional behavioral issues are grounded in overuse of passion, sex and romance.

Here are other warning signs to look for in people with control issues:

1. They make promises but never deliver, will "yes" you to death, but never follow through, and procrastinate only to infuriate you.

2. They try to make you feel guilty, ashamed, wrong, weak, or unworthy.

3. They will use intimidation to keep you from getting what you want. They will use verbal or physical abuse to put you down.

4. They will act out, whine, explode with anger, give you the silent treatment, use your kids/friends/family against you and do anything to convince your support system that you're crazy.

5. They will bully, dominate, use sexual demands, jealousy, perfectionism and insist things be done a certain way. If it's not his way, he will slowly destroy you and make sure you don't have things your way.

6. They often choose jobs that make them feel in a position of power, or one that society sees as powerful; for example, police officers, firemen, doctors, EMTs, nurses, attorneys, judges, and business executives. The need for the power of authority held by individuals in these positions doesn't necessarily reflect abusive control over their partner, but, very often, it does.

7. They try to isolate you from family and friends being jealous of your time spent with them. They want you to become dependent upon them so you will be easier to control.

Control freaks often look for a weaker individual who will be codependent upon them. Some are attracted to the power game of winning a strongly confident, successful partner they ultimately hope to dominate. That is their ultimate high.

Watch how they talk to service people, wait staff, bartenders, and people in a crowd. Do they act superior, bossy, rude, demanding, intimidating, or insist on having their way? See these signs early and don't be blinded by words like "I just want to take care of you to show you how much I love you." They may just want to control you and make you subservient to their wants, needs and desires. Be cautious and never let your personal life, power, and support system be taken away or controlled by another.

G) The Passive-Aggressive, Poor Communicators

No matter how hard I try; you keep pushing me aside – and I just can't break through; there's no talking to you... – Cher *Believe* (1998).

These people are described as cold, difficult, impossible, and never say exactly what they mean. They often are passionate and romantic one moment and then distant and critical another. Although they show good intentions and a spirit of innocence, they shun responsibility and are selfish and petty. You often feel manipulated, betrayed and hurt, never knowing when they'll be cold and distant.

Despite underlying anger and aggression, they will appear passive to most. When distressed, they will do things purposely to upset you but continue to act innocent.

Aggressive traits include doing something to control, upset, or derail another. Anger is a normal human feeling but the passive-aggressive doesn't manage their anger well. They tend to suppress it over a long period of time, adding up all the "injustices" in their mind, which results in excessive and inappropriate anger. Self-doubt and negative internal thoughts fuel their anger, with relief felt only from a destructive action targeted at you.

Some examples of this aggression:

- They procrastinate on a job they promised to complete.
- They are late for an event that is important to you.
- They deny, avoid or lie so you won't get upset.
- They never tell how they really feel.

Types of Toxic People

- They negate your legitimate complaints about their behavior and twist things to make themselves look like the damaged, or wronged, party.

- They start fights to create distance and a lack of intimacy.

- They will do things to purposely frustrate you.

- They are unable to finish tasks and resent your offering to help.

- They play the victim and won't claim responsibility.

- They ignore reality, tell deceiving stories and offer excuses.

- They are constantly late and exhibit selective memory.

- They can never forgive or forget, constantly throwing your past mistakes into a new argument.

- They will say something mean to put you down, raise themselves up, and gloss over it by insisting, "I'm only kidding."

- There are long periods of angry silence, or a specific subject will be changed on questioning.

- One minute you're adored, and can do no wrong, and then unexpectedly there will be a verbal dig to put you down.

- They will accumulate a mental list of all your unfair wrongdoings (usually being upset over something hurtful he did to you); when the list gets too long, they'll explode over something that seems mundane.

The passive-aggressive man doesn't understand why he behaves as he does. He is unable to communicate his wants and needs, keeps them buried inside for a long time, and then suddenly acts in strange, inconsiderate and destructive ways to hurt his partner. His air of innocence is at odds with his inappropriate ways to express anger, so what he says and does is confusing.

The passive part of this personality is initially seen as shy, modest or humble. The individual appears quite nice and agreeable. In time, the passive element will be shown in different ways.

- He shows little incentive to get what he wants.
- He often seeks approval and doesn't make a fuss.
- He desperately wants to be liked and is a "yes-man."
- He can't handle responsibilities and is a poor leader.
- He acts like a dependent child.
- He wants to be babied and nurtured by a strong partner.
- He avoids assertion and confrontation.
- He fears dependency so he tries to control you.
- He will withhold sex to punish you or make you feel undesirable.
- He feels inadequate and lacks self-respect.
- He feels constant resentment and fear, yet hides behind a "Mr. Good Guy" social persona, making you look crazy for getting upset with him.
- You are the object of his anger and he resists your requests and expectations.

Types of Toxic People

- He is needy and greedy; you can never give him enough love and attention.

- He's hard to get close to and acts sweet, then irritated.

- He shows little concern for your feelings or your time.

These two traits, passivity and aggression, occur simultaneously, making the passive-aggressive very difficult and complex. They do have some wonderful parts in their personality, but the bad side is infuriating and can lead you to your own self-doubt and blame.

What is the attraction? Initially, these men are charming, seductive, boyish and innocently needy. They're seen as kind, amenable, generous and slightly aloof – and you want to be the one who wins his heart. It can be difficult to spot a passive-aggressive, but knowing the traits will help.

Also, you must ask yourself if you're a victim type (sensitive and hesitant to communicate your feelings, often apologetic, fear loneliness, willingness to give yet often accepts less). The victim type likes the space that the passive-aggressive initially gives them. The passive-aggressive may have had parents that fought a lot, withheld love, did not express affection or emotions, made empty promises or may have been critical. Often a child from this household learns not to speak up and gives in to keep the peace.

It is often a no-win relationship, with you doing all the work to communicate and make sense of things as he emotionally withdraws or inappropriately explodes with anger.

Is there help for your passive-aggressive partner and can your relationship be saved? Yes, but the first step is for you to identify and understand his behavior; you are then less threatened by him.

Know that his fears are the basis of his aggression. You can choose to act and respond differently or choose to leave the relationship.

First, he must be willing to get help, and with time and therapy, his good personality traits can prevail. He must learn to express his needs and wants as they emerge as opposed to keeping them deeply hidden. Exploring ways to raise his sense of self and adapting a daily and weekly schedule so that deadlines are met as promised can give him a sense of fulfillment and self-control.

Second, you can change yourself but you cannot force change upon another. Look at your own behavior to see if you invite this type of person into your life. If you're demanding, never take no for an answer, are resentful, demeaning, or play a mothering role, you set yourself up for this type of man.

Sometimes the woman plays the role of a rescuer, helping the man when he's down. She falls in love with the man's potential and tries to fix him, becomes his support system and believes he needs her help in his career or personal life. These actions are well intended, and, at first, he likes the attention and feels appreciative.

But when you're the one constantly protecting his ego by making him look good to the world, cleaning up his mistakes, making excuses for his laziness, procrastination, tardiness, carelessness, or bad choices, your maternal instinct makes him feel like a child. Feelings of incompetence will emasculate him and further lead to feelings of low self-esteem and impotence that will turn to anger.

Once reliable, he becomes dependent as you enable him to be lazy if only to keep the peace. You must allow him enough space to make his own mistakes, which will force him to grow up. He may well see your reluctance to help him as rejection, making him feel you don't care enough or feel sorry for his circumstances, but it's what you must do to bring the relationship into better balance. Also, when forced into the role of "mother" due to his loss of masculine power and irresponsibility, your sexual attraction to him will be hugely diminished or stop altogether.

With your coach or therapist, you'll learn not to become too dependent or allow yourself to be mistreated. You'll acquire the skills to regain your self-esteem, understand that love never equals abuse, you won't settle for less and will gain the confidence you need to attract healthy love into your life.

H) The Angry and Critical, Mood Disorders

We are injured and hurt emotionally – not so much by other people or what they say or don't say – but by our own attitude and our own response. – Maxwell Maltz

When you are with a partner, their moods, good or bad, affect you. When you work to stay peaceful and spiritually based, and use positive self-talk for a healthy mind-set, it becomes difficult to live with a negative, moody, depressed or anxious partner. It is essential when you're dating that your sense of self matches your outlook on life. If you feel successful, content, and happy about your place in life, while your partner has a "pity-me" attitude, feels chronically depressed, overanxious and nervous, or shows inconsistent moods, your peace of mind will soon disappear.

One of the mood disorders in the DSM-IV-TR is bipolar disorder, which has its own section in this book. A second category is depression and dysthymic disorder. Dysthymia is considered a long-lasting mood of depression for most of the day, observable by others, lasting for at least two years. These symptoms cause significant distress and impairment in occupational, social or other important functional areas, and are not due to the direct physiological effects of a substance.

Two or more of the following symptoms usually exist:

1. Low energy or fatigue.
2. Insomnia or over sleeping.
3. Poor appetite or overeating.
4. Low self-esteem.
5. Feelings of hopelessness.
6. Poor concentration or difficulty making decisions.

With a major depressive episode lasting longer than two months, a constant state of depression and loss of interest in five or more of the following symptoms are present:

1. Depressed mood most of each day (irritable, teary, and sad).
2. Diminished interest or pleasure in almost all daily activities.
3. Significant weight loss or gain.
4. Persistent insomnia or hypersomnia.
5. Daily fatigue or loss of energy.
6. Feelings of worthlessness or excessive guilt.
7. Indecisive, diminished ability to think or concentrate.
8. Suicidal ideation with or without a specific plan, or a suicide attempt, or recurrent thoughts of death

Depression is a debilitating illness often misunderstood by others who want the person to "just get over their sadness." While time heals some cases of depression or bereavement associated with a specific loss or event, major depression tends to be chronic and is caused by chemical imbalances in the brain. Rarely will lifelong depression go away on its own and no amount of willpower or pressure from others will make it disappear.

Feeling like prisoners in their own skin, chronically depressed people cannot help how they feel and it's essential they seek both counseling help and medication management.

The spouse of a depressed partner feels abandoned, ignored, overwhelmed, lonely, and often has to pick up the slack. If anxiety accompanies the depression, the depressed party is often insecure, needy, suspicious, fearful and clingy. In addition, if he feels the least bit slighted or ignored, he can become enraged. These negative behaviors can cause a complete collapse of the relationship. The depressed person has no idea what to do nor has the energy to help himself.

Benefits from medication can be quite dramatic yet can have side effects so check with your doctor. However, even with medication, the signs of depression may not vanish completely. Body pain, sadness, apathy, exhaustion and anger may still exist. Sufferers may lack enthusiasm for you and for life, making them not much fun and a constant drain on your energy. They may have trouble retaining a job as memory, concentration, social and organizational skills all are compromised.

Patience, tolerance and support are needed to help your partner. With medication and therapy, there is great help for depression, as long as the help is wanted and there is dedication to ongoing treatment.

I) The Dramatic Histrionic

I guess you can tease me about being a drama queen, because that did heighten the drama. – Greg Louganis

Histrionic personality disorder (HPD) people crave attention, need other's approval, and are dramatic and theatrical in their inappropriate and loud expressions of emotion. They become uncomfortable when not the center of attention and consistently use their physical appearance to draw attention to themselves. They tend to sexually seduce others by acting provocative and flirtatious. This behavior starts at an early age. They tend to believe that their relationships are more intimate than they actually are. Histrionics are easily influenced by others or their circumstances.

This personality type is four times more prevalent in women than in men, affects 2–3% of the general population, and is seen in up to 15% of those with mental health issues. The same traits seen in men are usually diagnosed as narcissistic personality disorder. HPDs are very manipulative and self-indulgent. They will try to achieve their own needs by searching for high stimulation and excitement.

HPD people tend to exaggerate their difficulties, pains, or illnesses. They want people to feel sorry for them while failing to see their own personal situation realistically. They are easily frustrated, moody, easily bored and often unstable in the workplace. Their yearning for excitement leads them to take great risks, with results often ending in disaster, which can lead to depression. Because of their feelings of high self-importance, they're sensitive to criticism or disapproval and show a strong unwillingness to change. They are impulsive and hate to delay gratification, making rash decisions that end up hurting them, often financially and in relationships.

Their intense, unstable emotions and sense of self-esteem are dependent upon the approval of others because they possess a very low self-worth. They rarely think they need therapy, but if they enter treatment, they don't stay long. The goals of counseling would be to help uncover fears and the motivations that lead to faulty thoughts, choices and behavior, as well as to teach a better and more positive way to relate to others. Medication could help to treat the anxiety and depression that often coexist with this disorder.

Many people with HPD are able to function well socially and at work; however, those with severe cases experience significant problems in their relationships and daily lives. Projects are started and never finished. They can be impulsive and lack organization.

Prone to boredom, they often seek outside attention and engage in affairs. Once the steady partner in their life stops giving them attention and praise, they seek it elsewhere. Their self-absorption diminishes empathy and concern for their partner, making their relationships shallow at best. It becomes evident early on that you're with a histrionic personality type. The drama queen or king can be a demanding tyrant, like a spoiled child demanding immediate attention. Steer clear and move on.

J) The Avoidant Commitment Phobic:

Falling in love and having a relationship are two different things.
– Keanu Reeves

Men with commitment conflicts are extremely seductive. They are expert at playing into your fantasies. When you see a seductive Romeo, the type you instantly fall for, that's the time to take off your blinders and live in the real world or prepare to have your heart shattered.

These men get high on the power of winning a beautiful, smart, accomplished, confident woman. Then, as the relationship gets exclusive, they become anxious. One minute they're in the hot chase, and then, shortly after, they won't show up for a date, forget to call, become suddenly unavailable, or simply just vanish.

If you were with your partner for a long time, and he left you suddenly, you feel stunned because there appeared to be no reason, explanation, or major fight to explain his leaving. Everything seemed fabulous, sexy, loving, special and fun for both of you. His action of leaving can throw you into post-traumatic shock. Your man has run away from love, passion, friendship and the type of affection he said he desperately needed and wanted in his life. Everyone else is also stunned that the couple "so in love" has fallen apart. So, what happened?

Your man exhibited a typical avoidant response in feeling claustrophobic and too close to you, triggering the caveman reaction of "fight or flight." The man who fought so hard to win you panics the moment that he has you. Men with commitment phobia are everywhere; and their problem is a hard one to fix. Both men and women can experience fears that lead them to sabotage a perfectly good relationship.

The most profound problems happen once a commitment phobic makes a promise to be monogamous, exclusive, married, and responsible. They leave as soon as they feel too squeezed into the commitment they promised you.

Know that this is not about what you did wrong, because you did nothing wrong! You couldn't have been more loving, understanding, giving, sexy, patient or kind enough. You ask yourself if you were too needy, if you let the relationship move too fast, or question whether you failed to show him the love he needed. Or, you beat yourself up for "not seeing he was a fraud, or being stupid to trust too soon." You ask yourself, "How could I have missed this weakness in character before falling in love with him?" Please stop doing this. You must know this is *NOT* about you, your ability to love, or your level of intelligence. His weakness and callous lack of ability to connect is about him.

This happened because your partner has a severe mental and emotional health disorder and whatever you suggest to help the relationship or calm his fears, will only make things worse. Offering suggestions on how to make things work will be seen as a trick. Anything you recommend will never be good enough and all he wants is to stay out of the relationship he's so afraid of. He will refuse individual and couples counseling because he knows what he did was wrong, and the counselor will call him on it. He's afraid of you, afraid of the feeling of "forever" and will never be able to truly love anyone in a healthy, honest way with a basis of integrity.

You need immediate coaching or counseling support so that you understand this is not about you or what you did; it is about his inability to love any woman in a healthy, mature way that involves trust.

A commitment phobic husband becomes emotionally abusive, forgetting his wife has deeply human feelings and real love for him. His anxiety is so out of control that he no longer sees her clearly and has no empathy, kindness or concern for her. He alternates between feelings of disgust and love. He uses other women sexually to act out his anger and tells them he's single. He may have been unfaithful or acted out in a passive-aggressive way while married, but then will calm down and remain single once leaving the marriage. He leaves clues so you will find out about his affair or start outrageous fights so that you'll want to leave the marriage, thereby making you "the guilty party who broke up the relationship." He has no interest in talking about or fixing the problems he created, and if he does discuss why he left, he'll place the blame on you. He just wants out and will often leave when you aren't around to witness his move, being too cowardly to face you.

Many men have a fear of commitment. An example is the man who won't call after a wonderful first date or a fabulous sexual encounter, or the man who blatantly sabotages the relationship at the point you start to talk about marriage. If he becomes scared, but afraid to leave the love he wants, then he may become passive-aggressive and act out in way to sabotage the relationship so that you're the one to break things off.

The thought of being together forever is a concept of both fantasy and terror for him, to the extent that he may become abusive or start emotional or physical affairs in secret. He blames you for making him anxious when you actually did nothing outside your usual behavior. His fear of intimacy becomes so intensified that he will destroy and leave a great love and marriage.

The sad thing is that this man desperately wants and needs love. When you met he was vulnerable, open, kind, and made you feel safe with his attentive care and affection. He couldn't give you enough and wanted to please you in many thoughtful ways. He led you to believe he wanted "forever" with you, and might have written love letters, songs, or performed other grand gestures of true love. Your relationship was admired and women would say, "You're so lucky to have him, you're perfect together!" Then, out of nowhere, he suddenly leaves, shattering your world and leaving everyone wondering what could have happened.

He likely had an abusive or neglectful upbringing that involved abandonment. He craves the type of romantic love he had dreamed of since he was young, picturing the perfect woman and the ideal relationship. At the first sign of something that doesn't fit into his fantasized vision, he panics and wants to move on to look for it again. He neither trusts nor is he capable of being in a real love relationship.

These men are charming, attractive, arrogant, and confident. They exude power but are sensitive, attentive and open with their feelings. They tend to get seriously involved quickly, and because they show intense interest, you want to return it because they make you feel safe, secure and loved. The sex is incredibly erotic, sensual and giving. He would do anything to please you while you're lost in the desires you only imagined could have existed.

Soon after this level of intimacy, when he believes you have dropped your guard and may be falling in love, a new pattern emerges. He starts by creating a little distance from you. There are small contradictions in his behavior with the excuses given to hide small lies or actions. Stories are told, and you want to believe them as he assures you what he's saying is true, forcing you to ignore your intuition. You're now being manipulated by a toxic man who cannot truly love. You'll feel very confused as you begin to witness his emotional distancing and the signs of two different personality types emerging.

He wants to see his friends more, he stays later at work, he won't see you as often, nor will he respond to your phone calls and texts. He'll respond after several days and act as though nothing is wrong while brushing off his distance as merely being busy at work or with some other excuse that you'll accept.

He assures you that he loves, needs and wants you and nobody else. While skeptical, you accept his excuses and explanations to give him and your love a chance. If you hesitate to see him again, he charms you into another date that usually involves a sexual night in bed or going somewhere that's meant for just the two of you.

His assurances differ from his actions. No one will believe how powerfully he came on to you while hearing about how heartlessly he chose to leave you. The way he sabotages the relationship is especially hurtful. He will do the one thing he promised never to do to you, whether that's engaging in an emotional or physical affair, or returning to an addiction like porn, drugs, alcoholic binges, etc. This is a test phase; he wants to hurt you in the cruelest possible way to see if you'll still love him "unconditionally." When you leave because you refuse to tolerate his toxic, abusive behaviors, he throws guilt and blame at you, saying, "You never could love me enough." Let's be clear, these men can never be loved enough – they always crave more, often due to abandonment issues.

These men have all the excuses in the world as to why they had to break things off but none that make real sense. Or they will lie and distort the truth, making you look like the villain, and act so slick that they can convince your friends and family "how mean you were" or that " your actions were unforgiveable."

Your behavior was more likely a normal reaction to his actions that were intolerable and unacceptable in a committed relationship or marriage. Be confident when you feel you did nothing wrong. Society has taught women to respond to the handsome prince that brings Sleeping Beauty to life; the knight in shining armor who defends her honor; Romeo pleading his case for love in poetic, grand gestures; and the Superman who will save you and keep you safe from all "the bad guys."

Once a commitment is made, this Dr. Jekyll turns into Mr. Hyde. He conceals his behavior and becomes angry and silent about his feelings once married, has children, or lives with you. He abandons intimacy and will say one thing while doing another. He will present excuses as to why the relationship will never work and will become abusive and enraged with the woman who "caged" him. He finds fault with that woman in order to make himself feel better and to make her feel the guilt of doing whatever wrong he

Types of Toxic People

imagines that "forced" him to leave. This man says, "Things were great, we just shouldn't have gotten married."

Deep down, he will feel the guilt of abandoning the love he adores, but the relief from anxiety and panic is better than the loss. So guilt ridden, he'll rarely contact his loved one to apologize, and if he actually does call or write, he'll never express remorse as that would be an admission of guilt.

The women these men leave are devastated, shocked and embarrassed. The degree of their pain is intensified by public judgment and her being the one left to explain what happened Intuition may tell a woman right before her man leaves that something is up – he's acting shady, emotionally distant, secretive, or is absent without explanation. As soon as she's on to him and once she turns her back or goes off to work, he drops out of sight, taking everything he owns with him. This pattern is commonly repeated with women throughout his life. And he apologizes to none of them.

There are four stages of leaving:

1. directly after a great first date,
2. soon after an amazing night of sexual intimacy,
3. right when the woman talks about wanting to get engaged or married, and
4. after the marriage.

It's the fourth stage, after the marriage that is the most emotionally devastating. He took sacred vows in front of your family and friends, which meant nothing to him. This is a sign of sociopathic behavior. He will nitpick, start major fights, gain weight, complain of heartburn, headaches or stomachaches, and start looking at, or flirting with, other women. He may begin an emotional or physical affair, either live or online, secretly watch porn or engage in another addiction; anything to break the emotional connection to you.

Women involved with this hurry-up-and-run-heartbreak-Harry know instinctively that they did nothing wrong. They're not guilty of breaking their vows, stayed attentive to their man and the relationship, remained sexual and attractive, but their thoughts often turn to what they may have done wrong or neglected to do. Ladies, it is my job to tell you that you've been involved with a sociopathic man with mental health and emotional issues, along with extreme anxiety or panic disorder who is unable to make an honorable commitment to you or anyone else.

His actions are not your fault, but are unfortunately your problem.

First, if you're married, seek an annulment and dissolve the marriage as fast as you can to legally protect yourself and your assets. This is a man who cannot be trusted, and if you wait too long, the time period for annulment will pass. Go to your county courthouse law library and ask the clerk to give you the paperwork for a Pro Se Annulment and to show you the books on case law for annulment. You must have documented proof that your husband engaged in one or more of the listed areas in order to grant an annulment. Winning an annulment is rare, but it can be done acting as your own (Pro Se) attorney. Don't be afraid to go for it, stand up for yourself and your rights to end a fraudulent marriage! If you're afraid you can't handle this yourself, hire an attorney immediately. You will at least have legal documentation of the fraud and deception effected against you to help protect other women in the future.

Second, seek a coach or counselor immediately to help you deal with your feelings of abandonment and grief. Don't start dating right away, stay close with friends and let them be your support system. Don't let your man make you a victim, instead, reinvent yourself to become even more fabulous, accomplished, attractive and kind. Don't let his incapacity to love affect yours. Refuse to assume responsibility and guilt for his outrageous choices and behavior. Know deep in your heart you did everything to love your man with integrity, truth and honor and now is the time to return to a deeply spiritual faith to help heal your emotional wounds.

Third, know the warning signs of the commitment-phobic man.

1. He is highly romantic, fixated on you, moves quickly, will say and buy you anything to win you. (Be very slow to commit and don't immediately get sexually involved.)

2. He'll come on with too much too soon, talk about a fantasy life with you, push for sexual intimacy, or give you constant sales pitches about how great a relationship the two of you could have. If he adds marriage to the pitch, don't believe it. (Stay aware and watch his actions over time. Don't let yourself be fooled by his words.)

3. He has had a few marriages or short-term relationships, which always end because of "her faults." (Ask questions on the first few dates and don't buy into something having been wrong with the other women). There are always two sides to every story. If he treated other women badly, or cheated on them, he will with you too. Once a cheater, always a cheater – it's a fundamental character flaw! If he does put blame on himself, believe those statements.

See if he's remorseful for his poor choices and actions, or entered extensive therapy to change his destructive ways.

4. He will sell himself convincingly to you, your friends and family. This could include buying you nice gifts, throwing you parties, traveling or taking you to fine places and generally doing anything to impress. He wants you to feel special now, but not forever. He's conning you into thinking he would be the perfect partner. Slow down, watch everything, and be knowledgeable about his actions when he's not with you. Can his time be accounted for?

5. He comes across as needy, talks about his emotions and his painful past to try and build a connection. Don't feel sorry for him, and know that if there is a painful past there are likely to be mental health issues. Find out as much as you can, reread this book and pin down the issues you won't want to deal with in the future. If you see one or several danger signs, cut things off immediately to save yourself.

6. He becomes dependent on you by frequently phoning or texting because he wants assurance that you're there for him, and you do make yourself available. You start a pattern of reassuring him so that he is less anxious, yet doesn't give you the same courtesy. Understand that overly dependent texting or calling is obsessive, not flattering!

7. He will speak of the "future" and "forever" so that you believe this will be a life-long, stable relationship. He acts like you're his priority, making you focus on him and building a life together. He tells you what you want and need to hear to build trust so that you'll make a commitment

to him. He will tell you early in dating that he sees marriage in your future.

Don't make an exclusive commitment to any man until he asks you with an engagement ring. Don't live with him or let him move in with you until a ring is on your finger and a marriage date is set. Date others to discover the best man for you. Men get all they want from an exclusive woman without an engagement ring. If you're a woman who desires marriage, early exclusivity without a ring is a huge mistake.

If you do get engaged, maintain your sense of self, your hobbies, friends, work commitments and do the things that make you feel whole and complete. Be aware, after an engagement or marriage takes place, if his attitude turns secretive, disrespectful and hurtful. Notice if he distances himself, becomes quiet, anxious, moody or sullen and less sexual. Then watch out! He could be planning his escape. Your best move is to back off, get involved with your own activities and give him space. Don't get clingy or dote on him excessively as this could begin a cycle of codependency. Don't nag or ask him a lot of questions. If he's mature, he will talk when he's ready. Be sure to live your own life as you did before meeting him.

8. He may be kind and affectionate at home, but in public he may back away as if to deny the relationship. He gives confusing messages. Get to a relationship coach or couples counselor to address these issues. If he won't go, that's another warning sign. Go on your own to help protect yourself from his current or future actions.)

9. He avoids activities with your family and friends because he feels like a con, a fake, and doesn't like the guilt he feels about treating you badly. (Stay close to friends and family, you'll need them when he makes his impulsive plan to leave.)

10. He stops making you a priority in his life, doing things without your knowledge, no longer calling or telling you about his day. (Don't be there for him every time he calls; he's keeping tabs on you so that he can do what he wants. Live your life and stop checking in.)

11. His sexual patterns change; either he becomes aggressive and demanding or he cools down and becomes emotionally withdrawn and not interested, making you feel insecure. (There is nothing wrong with you, but don't nag or become sexually needy. Let him pursue you as you focus on other things. If you look fabulous and feel confident, he will often chase you again. If he doesn't, he may already have someone else on the side.)

12. He wants you to follow his schedule and agenda but resents you having expectations from him. He wants the freedom to come and go as he pleases. Stop counting on him, don't accommodate or make excuses for him, and don't ask anything from him. Don't demand to be treated with respect, it won't come. These are signs to stop seeing him. Keep your own life full of purpose. Attend social events and ask him to join you, but take note if he won't.

13. He finds fault, nags or picks at you, or says and does anything to put you down. He imposes his own guilt on you, saying that you don't love him enough or as much as he

loves you. (Do your soul searching to ensure that you're a great partner. You may now be aware of his mental health issues and intuitively feel that you must move on from this toxic man.)

Now, ask yourself, "Why would I accept this kind of behavior – isn't it time I love myself more?" If he hasn't left yet, know that it may only be a matter of time, as he's showing all the clues that he feels miserable in this commitment. Leave while you can and with the conviction that you deserve a better type of love. Don't get lost thinking that the early days of the relationship could and will return. Staying with him will most likely lead to an emotionally abusive, selfish, one-sided relationship at your expense.

If you break things off, or he left you suddenly, take the time to heal. While grieving and experiencing the pain, acquire a legal divorce or annulment as soon as you can so that you can get busy with your new life. Continue being who you always were, but reinvent yourself by setting new goals for exciting aspirations. With your relationship coach, revisit your goals, make your bucket list of dreams and go for it! Become your best self by reading my previous book, *Live Beyond Your Dreams – from Fear and Doubt to Personal Power, Purpose and Success* and other wonderful books listed in the recommended reading section.

Healthier partners move more slowly, become your friend first, and don't push for sex or put overly romantic moves on you. They're the ones you barely notice at first, and who may seem dull or boring. You may feel things are moving too slowly, or that there is just "no chemistry." Give these types of partners another chance. Start dating many suitors and point out that you're looking to make friends and don't want a serious relationship right now. Take time to build friendships, and do what you weren't able to do while involved. This can be an amazing time of personal growth and accomplishment. Focus on yourself, your business, a new hobby, class, or spiritual growth and enlightenment. Become your best, evolved self to the point of feeling true bliss, inner light, and pure happiness.

Just when you've reached a healing point beyond the loss and are back on your feet, the commitment-phobe is likely to call or text because he misses you. He created the distance that would end his anxiety but his abandonment issue compels him to obsessively reconnect with you. He will often say that you were the best woman in his life, he realizes you really loved him (and you did), and he'll sweet talk you with new promises of romantic vacations, among other things. However, he will rarely apologize for his actions. He may say something like, "If you only did the right things, we never would have split up." No, he immaturely left and he did the wrong things, not you. He will never change his pattern of lies or dysfunction, so don't be swayed again.

Be strong and smart enough to know that if you allow him back into your life, the whole pattern will repeat itself, only faster and more viciously, so move on, and don't pick up that phone! Block his text, phone number and emails. Love yourself more! Get out there and meet many fabulous men – then choose one who could be the new, healthy, loving partner you deserve.

K) The Perfectionistic, Obsessive-Compulsive

Perfectionism is not a quest for the best. It is a pursuit for the worst in ourselves, the part that tells us that nothing we do will ever be good enough – that we should try again. – Julia Cameron

Although the obsessive-compulsive personality disorder (OCPD) is similar to obsessive-compulsive disorder (OCD), which is a repetition of rituals, OCPD is more defined as an unhealthy adherence to perfectionism.

Perfectionism can be defined as a person who sets excessively high standards for themselves. This can be accompanied by overly critical self-evaluation and worry about the perception of others. Sometimes a person's ideal goal can be reached through motivational, adaptive perfectionism, leading to great personal satisfaction and power. However, another type of perfectionist measures self-worth by levels of accomplishment and productivity, which leads to excessive pressure and unrealistic goals, leading to anxiety, stress, disappointment and depression.

There are two distinct types of perfectionists, according to Hamachek, D.E. (1978). Normal perfectionists pursue their goals without compromising their self-esteem because they enjoy the process of their efforts. Neurotic perfectionists strive for unrealistic goals and feel constant anxiety and stress when unable to reach them.

Stoeber and Otto (2006) wrote that perfectionism consisted of perfectionistic strivings, which are positive aspects of perfectionism. However, perfectionistic concerns are psychological issues that can occur, such as anxiety, depression, and maladaptive coping styles. People with high levels of perfectionistic strivings and low levels of concerns showed higher self-esteem, academic success and social confidence.

Greenspon, T.S. (2008) says that what one gives to the meaning of their mistakes determines the difference between striving for excellence and perfectionism. Those that strive for excellence look at their mistakes as an incentive to work harder. Unhealthy perfectionists consider their mistakes a sign of personal defects, giving them anxiety due to potential failure of self.

Narcissists are a type of perfectionist who require being the center of attention and who create scenarios to make sure they get that attention. They seek power in feeling grandiose and better than others. If that fails, they can feel anxiety, jealousy, anger or guilt due to a perceived lack of love and approval from others for their imperfection.

The obsessive-compulsive personality disorder (OCPD) is someone with a preoccupation with orderliness and perfection. According to Pinto, Anthony (2008), twice as many men as women have OCPD. It occurs in about 1% of the general population but in up to 10% of psychiatric outpatients. This chronic, addiction to detail and neatness is a form of extreme perfectionism and control, which requires the need to have power over one's environment as well as the people within it. This causes major stress in relationships and parenting because of deep-rooted inflexibility, a need to control, and excessive detailed attention to normal routines.

People with this disorder usually see their own and others' actions in terms of "black or white." They make "always" and "never" statements. Their rigidity, stubbornness and tendency towards pessimism creates strained relationships, with angry partners feeling they can do nothing right.

The following are characteristics of OCPD:

- Perfectionism with respect to details, rules, order, lists or schedules.

- Tasks are often uncompleted due to excessive doubt, caution or need to be perfect.

- Anger, blame, and unresolved arguments can lead to avoidance and withdrawal from the partner. Distancing is used as a coping mechanism to reduce risk of rejection or criticism.

- Displays of anger occur because he feels he has been wronged, abused or invalidated.

- Constant insistence that his partner follow his way of doing everything; reluctance to allow others to do things as they see fit.

- Persistent and unwelcome impulses and thoughts.

- Often stingy in spending on self and others; money is hoarded.

- Difficulty with trusting others, sharing, compromising, and delegating.

- Obsessively clean, must have things lined up in a certain order or exact spacing between items, with an extreme need for hygiene.

- Often alienates his partner from relationships with others.

It is evident that a person displaying this type of behavior would be a very difficult life partner. You would likely end up severely lacking self-esteem, feeling so controlled and overwhelmed that nothing can be done right in your partner's eyes. Therapy would be important to help start a change process, but the person with OCPD often denies the problem.

If you're already in a relationship with the perfectionist or OCPD, get therapy for yourself and see if your partner will follow. There is medication management that seems to help the OCPD. But he has to begin by wanting the change in his own thinking, behavior and levels of control, as well admit he has a problem. Good luck; remember, he thinks he's perfect!

L) The Habitual Liar

The Promise we made each other haunts me to the end…I know you're out there somewhere, somewhere. (Song) *"I Know You're Out There Somewhere"* – The Moody Blues; Sur La Mer CD (1988).

Deception can be defined as lying, denial of truth, falsely representing oneself or actions, betrayal, fraudulent actions, constantly breaking one's vow or word, living a secret life and hiding significant aspects of one's self or actions, keeping secrets, using deceptive manipulation, presenting a false image, emotional or sexual cheating, and avoiding or preventing the truth about one's self.

If you have been deceived by your life partner, real love can no longer exist as the trust has been broken. Plainly and simply, there is NO relationship without trust. When you uncover deception, overwhelming feelings of betrayal and abandonment emerge suddenly and fiercely. You, the victim, feel shattered by broken dreams and the inability to trust your partner ever again. Even small lies and elements of deception repeated over time whittle away love, trust and intimacy, leaving you feeling jealous and anxious. Your self-esteem is tested as you consistently feel the need to check-up on your partner.

Types of Toxic People

Trust is essential in a healthy relationship and it's impossible to have a romantic, loving, close relationship without it. Trust is easily destroyed by acts of lies and deception. Those who habitually deceive have grown up doing so and tend to be brilliant at it. These are the worst emotional manipulators and are usually sociopathic con artists as well. Once discovered in their deception, they often run the moment you turn your back. Most people are unaware that it's so difficult to catch a deceptive spouse.

I had a woman in a marriage of twenty-five years finally catch her cheating husband who was also addicted to pornography. I was able to help them reconcile using the *forgive-him-this-one-time* method. After they made up, she discovered another round of cheating. Her husband had failed to disclose all the details of his deception and she now has filed for divorce. Despite the pain and difficulty, it's possible to rebuild trust over several months after the first time deception has been uncovered. But a second infraction after a vow to never deceive again is the deal breaker.

Deception remains problematic *even when it's not detected*. When one deceives, there is distance created in the relationship. A hollow emotional connection often sets off suspicion in the healthy partner. The more lies, the less trust. Both tend to feel misunderstood by the other. The guilty partner projects his own shame and deceptive tendencies onto his partner. He, the cheating partner, gets more jealous, controlling and irritable over innocent activities his partner always enjoyed with friends – a sure sign that something is up with him. He often accuses her of cheating because of his paranoia and guilt, and because he *is* actually cheating on her.

Deception, once begun, is hard to stop and he'll start to believe in his own lies and stories. He'll try to convince his partner that she's crazy or couldn't have seen what she actually did witness.

Keep pushing for the truth, and listen to your intuition. When you have the facts, there is nothing more for you to know. Leave this destructive individual as soon as you possibly can. Run, and don't turn back!

M) Abusive Partners

The more you depend on forces outside yourself, the more they dominate you. – Harold Sherman

Any sign of abuse is a sign to stop the relationship. Abuse can be emotional, physical, verbal, sexual, or financial, and can be directed towards you, children, the elderly, or others. The cycle of violence is a well-documented phenomenon, and it's important that you recognize the warning signs that your relationship has become abusive in any way.

One of my best friends in college was brutally murdered by her boyfriend. It was clearly evident that he had been abusive and jealous from the beginning. Her girlfriends, including me, begged her to stop seeing him. Each time they fought, the drama and abuse intensified. After I left college I heard she finally felt ready to leave him, but on that fateful weekend she planned to move out, she ended up dead. At 24 years old, I had lost a best friend to the fateful reality of domestic violence.

The cycle of violence described by *The Domestic Violence Intervention Project from Duluth, Minnesota* is based on years of research. Below is the example of a healthy, loving, equal and nonviolent relationship. There are eight key elements that must be in place to have a safe, evolved relationship.

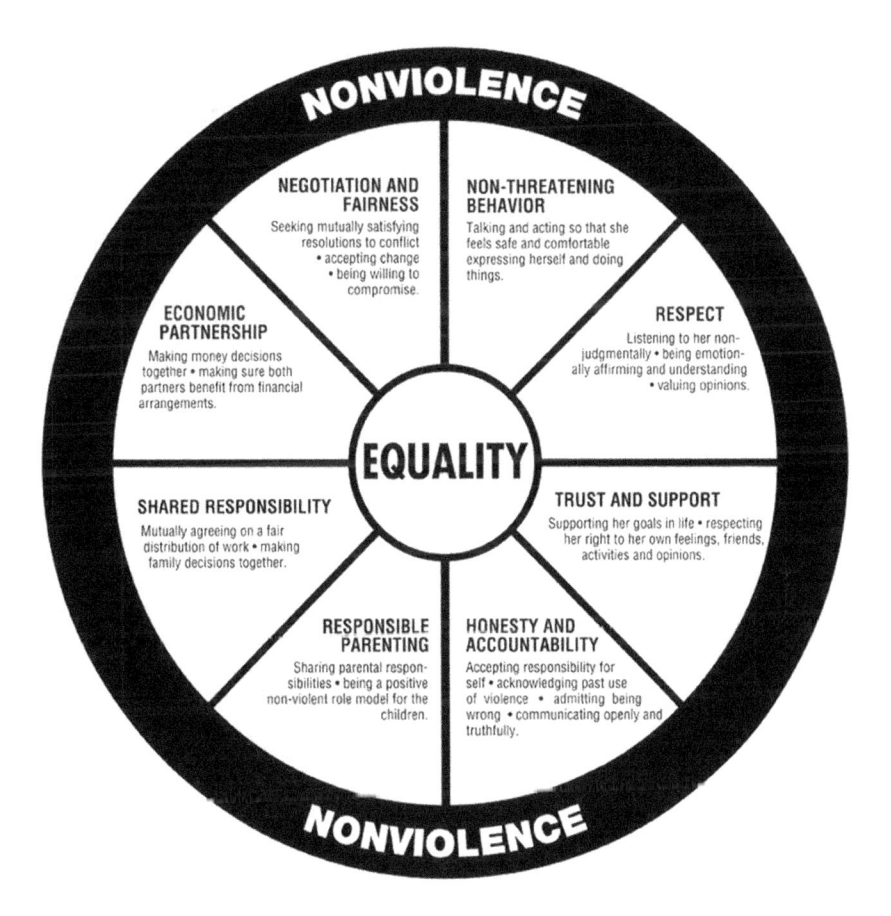

NONVIOLENCE

NEGOTIATION AND FAIRNESS
Seeking mutually satisfying resolutions to conflict • accepting change • being willing to compromise.

NON-THREATENING BEHAVIOR
Talking and acting so that she feels safe and comfortable expressing herself and doing things.

ECONOMIC PARTNERSHIP
Making money decisions together • making sure both partners benefit from financial arrangements.

RESPECT
Listening to her non-judgmentally • being emotionally affirming and understanding • valuing opinions.

EQUALITY

SHARED RESPONSIBILITY
Mutually agreeing on a fair distribution of work • making family decisions together.

TRUST AND SUPPORT
Supporting her goals in life • respecting her right to her own feelings, friends, activities and opinions.

RESPONSIBLE PARENTING
Sharing parental responsibilities • being a positive non-violent role model for the children.

HONESTY AND ACCOUNTABILITY
Accepting responsibility for self • acknowledging past use of violence • admitting being wrong • communicating openly and truthfully.

NONVIOLENCE

Love Beyond Your Dreams

Below is the wheel representing the Power & Control Cycle. Any one of these aspects creates fear, intimidation, and is a reason to leave the relationship.

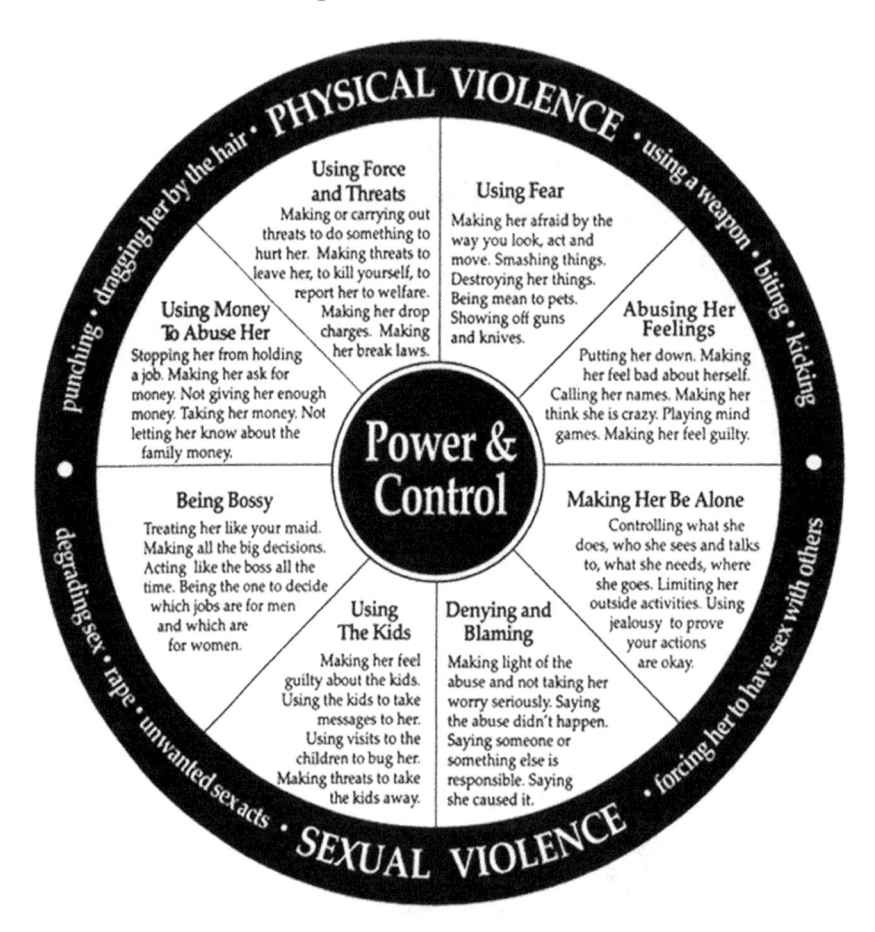

PHYSICAL VIOLENCE · using a weapon · biting · kicking · forcing her to have sex with others · unwanted sex acts · rape · degrading sex · punching · dragging her by the hair · **SEXUAL VIOLENCE**

Power & Control

Using Force and Threats
Making or carrying out threats to do something to hurt her. Making threats to leave her, to kill yourself, to report her to welfare. Making her drop charges. Making her break laws.

Using Fear
Making her afraid by the way you look, act and move. Smashing things. Destroying her things. Being mean to pets. Showing off guns and knives.

Abusing Her Feelings
Putting her down. Making her feel bad about herself. Calling her names. Making her think she is crazy. Playing mind games. Making her feel guilty.

Using Money To Abuse Her
Stopping her from holding a job. Making her ask for money. Not giving her enough money. Taking her money. Not letting her know about the family money.

Being Bossy
Treating her like your maid. Making all the big decisions. Acting like the boss all the time. Being the one to decide which jobs are for men and which are for women.

Using The Kids
Making her feel guilty about the kids. Using the kids to take messages to her. Using visits to the children to bug her. Making threats to take the kids away.

Denying and Blaming
Making light of the abuse and not taking her worry seriously. Saying the abuse didn't happen. Saying someone or something else is responsible. Saying she caused it.

Making Her Be Alone
Controlling what she does, who she sees and talks to, what she needs, where she goes. Limiting her outside activities. Using jealousy to prove your actions are okay.

At the center of the wheel is "Power and Control," which is how the drama begins. There are eight areas where power and control can escalate and lead to physical and sexual violence.

They are:

1. **Intimidation:** He makes you feel afraid by looks, actions, smashing things, hurting pets or displaying weapons.

Types of Toxic People

2. **Emotional abuse:** Calling you names, putting you down, making you feel guilty or that you're crazy, playing mind games or humiliating you.

3. **Isolation:** Controls what you do, who you see and talk to, where you go, how often you see your family or friends, and shows jealousy ("I just love you so much I want you all for myself.")

4. **Minimizing, blaming, and denying:** Not taking seriously your concerns about the abuse, denying its existence or saying you caused the actions to happen.

5. **Use of threats:** Threatening to leave you, to commit suicide if you break up with him, making you drop charges or do something illegal to prove your love for him; or he threatens to do something that will hurt you.

6. **Economic abuse:** Preventing you from getting a job, making you ask for money or an allowance, hiding his income, or taking money from you without asking.

7. **Using male privilege:** He makes all the major decisions, treats you like a housemaid, refusing to help with chores, acts like the "master of the house."

8. **Use of children:** He'll use your children to send you messages, harasses you at visitation time, threatens to take your children away, or makes you feel guilty about how you've raised them.

There are many early warning signs that you may be in an abusive relationship, but if you aren't sure, seek the help of a coach or counselor.

Here are a few common signs to look for:

1. He yells, screams, swears at you, calls you names, orders you around, or insults you in front of others.

2. He criticizes the way you perform domestic chores, or your physical weight, the way you dress, wear your hair or makeup.

3. He continuously brings up the past or throws back at you a cherished secret you shared with him when falling in love.

4. He withholds or demands sex or affection, refuses to talk for days, sulks or is extremely moody or has temper tantrums.

5. He is selfish, stingy with money, doesn't give you enough to manage the household, or uses large sums of money for something he wants without consulting you.

6. He is jealous of your friends or family members. He doesn't allow you to work, go to school, enjoy a hobby, go to the gym, or socialize with your friends. He may restrict your phone use.

7. He blames you when he is upset, never apologizes or shows remorse for his actions. He tries to convince you and others that you're crazy, nasty, unreasonable, and the abusive partner. He constantly threatens to leave or divorce you.

8. He pushes or hits you, threatens to hurt you, hits the children, punches holes in the wall, intimidates by anger, drives recklessly, or shows other signs of physical threats.

Abusive relationships never get better and they only worsen to become more dangerous with time. You will see a pattern of

Types of Toxic People

"hearts and flowers" after the first abusive episode. The abusive partner will want to make up, be romantic with you, and will do anything to keep you with him. Abusers are "good" for a while, only to become abusive again, once they feel you've relaxed and forgiven them.

The time in between these stretches of "love" get shorter. You stay because you believe he'll change. He may go to counseling for a short period of time, claiming he's "fixed" when, actually, his problem demands very long-term therapy. He may need medication management for the rest of his life. The challenge is that few abusers admit they need help. So save yourself and your children and get out of the relationship as soon as possible.

You must have a plan in place before you try to leave an abusive partner. Have money placed aside in a vault box or with a parent or trusted friend. Save enough to rent your own apartment for at least two months, including the security deposit and utilities. If you don't work, ask your parents if you can borrow enough money to get you out on your own, or ask if you can move in with them until you find a job and save enough to move out. Once employed, offer to pay your parents a small rent that they'll save for you so that you can move on to an apartment or home.

Place a suitcase containing enough clothes for several weeks with your parent or a trusted friend. If things get bad late at night, just leave with your purse and go to your safe place. Keep your best jewelry pieces in this bag; if things get really tight, sell what you can to get by. Men often steal the jewelry they've given you if they suspect you're leaving.

If you fear him because of his anger or threats, file a complaint immediately with your local police department, then go to your county courthouse the next day and file for a full restraining order. If you lose the first time in court, file again. There are court advocates dressed in plain clothes who watch women come and go. One of these women approached a female client of mine after she lost her case. The advocate had witnessed her husband saying threatening and abusive things to his wife after she lost her claim for a restraining order. The advocate insisted that my client go and refile, and that she would testify for her in court as to what she witnessed. My client won the second time, and her court advocate appeared "by telephone," with the judge giving full recognition to her testimony.

If you choose to move out, have two male witnesses there for protection. If your situation is exceptionally bad, hire a detective, security person, or request a police officer to assist you. If things get rough as you're moving out, your witnesses can call 911 and get the police there to help. Don't attempt to move out without help!

If you own the house, pack up all his things in large trash bags and put them into the garage when he's at work. Arrange for a locksmith to change all the locks. If possible, install an alarm system the same day. Change all the codes that he may know on garage doors or alarm systems. When this is done, call him at work at the end of the day. Calmly tell him the relationship is over and that his things are moved out. Inform him that all the locks and codes have been changed (or that an alarm has been installed). He must come with a friend at an arranged time to pick up his things from the garage. Tell him that if he comes alone, or tries to cause any trouble, you will call the police. You'll have witnesses there to observe his actions. Tell him as well, "This is your last warning. Don't contact me by phone, text or email." Then hang up. Save all his messages if he does write or text you as these can be used in court.

My dear friend Corrine made the mistake of not having anyone with her when she attempted to move out from her abusive boyfriend's house. No one witnessed what actually happened to her, but she was found dead on the side of a road. The story her boyfriend told: "She fell out of the van as it went around a corner." I know that isn't the truth. My heart and soul are always with her, and in her memory, I repeat her story to help others. It is in Corrine's memory that I dedicate partial proceeds of this book to various women's empowerment groups. I've also taken extra training in domestic violence, and worked at a women's safe shelter during one of my college internships. Please don't be another statistic. Do what you must to protect yourself without guilt or remorse for your lover's issues. After all, he abused you. What feelings of love or concern did he have for you?

N) The Overly Anxious

Anxiety is love's greatest killer. It creates the failures. It makes others feel as though you might when a drowning man holds on to you. You want to save him, but you know he will strangle you with his panic.
– Anais Nin

Different forms of anxiety include symptoms of social phobia, panic attacks, obsessive-compulsive disorder, post-traumatic stress disorder, acute stress disorder, substance-induced anxiety, or agoraphobia (anxiety about being in places or situations where escape may be difficult or embarrassing, or where help may not be available).

For this book, I discuss only generalized anxiety disorder and post-traumatic stress disorder. With generalized anxiety, the person finds it difficult to control worry, and it occurs throughout more days than not, for at least six months. This worry could relate to a number of activities such as work, relationship, or school performance. The DSM-IV-TR outlines the following three or more required symptoms that would substantiate a diagnosis:

1. Being easily fatigued.
2. Feeling on edge or keyed up, restless.
3. Irritability.
4. Difficulty concentrating or mind goes blank.
5. Difficultly in falling or staying asleep.
6. Muscle tension.

The disturbance is not related to the use of a substance (medication or drug abuse), and the anxiety causes significant impairment in social, occupation, relationship, or other areas of functioning.

Those with severe anxiety usually have experienced an emotionally, sexually or physically abusive childhood. As an adult, you feel like no one "gets" you and that no one seems to know how to help you. You often are so anxious that you're afraid to speak your mind to communicate your wants, desires and needs. This raises your anger and frustration levels, especially towards your partner. Anxiety makes it difficult to get your basic needs met, including feeling good about yourself, acquiring and keeping friendships, and feeling a sense of security. It negatively affects your ability to love and connect with others.

Anxiety can ruin your relationships because it makes you self-conscious, self-centered, moody, irritable, angry and isolating. Your anxiety frustrates your partner because they don't understand why you're angry, bitter or act out unexpectedly. The anxious person mentally argues constantly about issues felt to be his partner's responsibility to know and understand even without having been told. Expecting a partner to be a mind-reader adds considerable negative strain and pressure to a relationship.

A man must keep an open line of communication with his partner to make the relationship work. He must say what he feels and what he needs to help him relax and dispel his anger. Writing a letter could help him get his thoughts across without interruption. You will need patience and understanding as he explains his thoughts and fears, but you can suggest ways for him to solve his own issues. He shouldn't expect you to have all the answers or to make all the concessions. Ask your partner to attend therapy sessions with you or to read more about anxiety so he better understands what you deal with from day to day.

Don't let him use anxiety as an excuse for undesirable behavior or fighting with you. He needs to be aware of what he says and how he says it. If he isn't careful, he'll frustrate and drive you away by expecting too much from you. Share your feelings and don't expect perfection. If his anxiety has constantly sabotaged his relationships, he should meet with a psychiatrist to see if medication would be helpful. I've seen lives changed and relationships saved with the help of the right medication for this disorder.

Posttraumatic Stress Disorder (PTSD) is an emotional and psychological trauma that is the result of an event or series of events that shatter your feelings of security, making you feel helpless and vulnerable. It can occur in any situation that leaves you feeling overwhelmed, fearful or suddenly alone. Your subjective emotional experience of the event determines whether you are experiencing PTSD.

Among the causes:

1. Intentionally cruel actions shown towards you, your child, or someone you love.

2. A terrifying event that happened repeatedly, suddenly, or unexpectedly. It can involve witnessing a death.

3. Feelings of powerlessness to stop the event.

4. A severe breach of trust by someone you know and/or loved.

5. The sudden, shocking loss of someone you loved.

Often affiliated with those serving in war, or experiencing a sudden death of a loved one, PTSD can also occur with the sudden breakup of a significant relationship or a deeply disappointing, shocking or humiliating experience caused by someone you loved and trusted. If you're currently dealing with overpowering stress, or have experienced a series of losses, these circumstances could signify an emotional overload. If similar stress occurred in childhood, the person is more likely to be traumatized by the new situation.

According to the DSM-IV-TR, PSTD can apply to anyone who has been exposed to a traumatic event in which both of the following conditions are present:

1. The person experienced, witnessed or was confronted with an event that involved actual or threatened death or serious injury, or threat of personal injury or injury to others.

2. The person's response involved intense fear, helplessness, or horror.

The event is repeatedly experienced in one or more of the following ways:

1. Recurrent and distressing recollections of the event through dreams, images, thoughts or perceptions.

2. Acting or feeling as if the event were recurring (the sense of reliving the experience through hallucinations and dissociative flashbacks).

3. Intense psychological distress or physiological reaction on exposure to internal or external cues resembling an aspect of the trauma.

The disturbance causes significant distress or impairment in social, occupational, relationship or other important life areas.

Two or more of the following reactions can also occur:

1. Efforts to avoid thoughts, feelings or conversations associated with the trauma.

2. Efforts to avoid activities, places, or people that stimulate memories of the trauma.

3. Inability to recall certain details of the trauma.

4. Diminished interest or participation in significant events.

5. Restricted affect of emotions.

6. Inability to envision the future, or imagining a shortened future.

7. Persistent feelings in two of the following areas:
   a. difficulty falling or staying asleep
   b. irritability or outbursts of anger
   c. difficulty concentrating
   d. hyper-vigilance
   e. exaggerated startle response.

Many clients present with symptoms of PTSD if they have uncovered an affair or caught their spouse in a deception involving another person. Their world has come crashing down in an instant, along with their dreams, vows and promises, ability to trust, the safety of the relationship they loved, and the realization that the partner they adored isn't the person they thought they knew.

Visuals (movies, letters or photographs), replay in the mind of the traumatized person. Healing takes a long time, and with severe depression, medication may be needed for a period of time during recovery. Therapy is essential to the process of rebuilding overall trust and confidence after such an experience.

If you, a friend, or someone you love has experienced an unexpectedly shocking event, strongly encourage them to get counseling help right away. In the case of a sudden and devastating relationship breakup, I suggest finding a new spiritual sense of faith and healing, read the recommended books that address the particular situation, and do daily meditation. In addition, I encourage starting a new creative project or educational program to help distract the mind from the incident, and to keep you mentally occupied.

With my PTSD clients, we work towards their personal reinvention, rebuilding self-esteem and the creation of new goals for a strong future. We focus on healing mind, body and soul to find a sense of personal safety and rebalance. Medication may also be needed for the severely depressed or traumatized until they feel emotionally stable. There *is* a light at the end of this dark tunnel. Time *does* heal all wounds. Find joy in simple pleasures, stay close to family and friends, and acquire a sense of spirituality for healing.

O) The Peter Pan Syndrome, the Mama's Boy, and the Mother Hater

For a long time I was scared I'd find out I was like my Mother.
– Marilyn Monroe

We all know the type of guy who is referred to as "Peter Pan"; he's the one who lacks maturity, responsibility and refuses to grow up. He acts helpless, disorganized, gives tons of excuses why he can't or won't do something, and procrastinates on everything. He often lacks ambition, has no future goals and lives for today. He can be financially irresponsible, and can exhibit childish temper tantrums when angry. He will rarely apologize, has difficulty talking about his feelings, lies often, overreacts, blames others, is over-sensitive to rejection, and is prone to addiction. Many personality traits of this man fit under the ACOA category.

Dr. Dan Kiley, author of *The Peter Pan Syndrome,* mentions six major symptoms to the disorder.

1. **Irresponsibility** (peak age 11–12): as an adult he is lazy, has messy habits, is forgetful, inept, and blames others.

2. **Anxiety** (peak age 13–14): often caused by parental marital discord and emotionally damaging parents. This creates a negative self-image as an adult and a pattern of magical thinking, using lies to cover bad choices.

3. **Loneliness** (peak age 15–16): the child feels unwanted, estranged from his father, and harbors feelings of guilt and anger towards his mother for needing to step up to protect her. Adult actions are driven by anxiety, panic and impulse.

4. **Sex Role Conflict** (peak age 17–18): sexual attitudes lack warmth, focused primarily on physical satisfaction. As an adult, he often develops a pornography or sexual addiction to help build his lacking ego. Extreme actions make you question *exactly who he is.*

5. **Narcissism/Chauvinism** (peak age 19–20): he craves perfection to cover insecurities, blames others, is reckless and impulsive, repeats mistakes and doesn't see them as his fault. Often has an addiction; uses sexual seduction and emotional distance for control in his relationships.

6. **Crisis: Social Impotence** (early–mid-twenties): all six categories combined produce social ineptness that damages future happiness. Irrational thought and illogical judgment occurs, especially in primary relationships, leading to emotional panic and rage. He somewhat realizes he has problems, but remains in strong denial. He procrastinates, feels self-disgust, hopeless and self-sabotages frequently. He emotionally executes women who love him and runs away from the relationship and his feelings of guilt.

If your man is mad at you, he'll act out passive-aggressively by deliberately not doing something you asked him to do. He'll tell you that he forgot or shuts down emotionally and verbally for hours or days. He lacks control in many areas of his life especially where you're concerned. He mopes if you aren't feeling sexual, and might throw a temper tantrum at these times. He can also act excessively sexual, using conquest behavior to feel manly and to boost self-esteem.

Many of these men are self-absorbed narcissists because they've learned from their mothers that they're more special and important than anyone else. They often appear needy and greedy, and the imbalance of such a relationship feels overwhelming to their caring women. Although these men can behave affectionately, their women often feel resentful of his neediness and lack of support for them.

What is the difference between the two types of men? The Mama's Boy is stuck emotionally at about age 10, and the Peter Pan Man is stuck in the developmental age of late teens to early twenties.

The Mama's Boy is often an only child, and was spoiled by his mom who did everything for him. He refuses to cook, clean, or do his own laundry, believing it's "the woman's role" to perform all the non-gratifying household chores that should be split in today's world. He whines when he's sick and stays in bed all day with a basic cold, wanting to be catered to.

Picture the character Ray Barrone, from the TV comedy show, *Everybody Loves Raymond,* who is the classic Mama's Boy. His mother caters to his every whim, making his wife Debra feel her care for him and their family is sub-standard. Ray's mother is overly involved and believes her son Ray can do no wrong, leaving Debra angry and frustrated. This TV show was slated as a comedy, but if you're living this nightmare, it's not so funny!

It's up to the man to stand up to his mother and set her straight, defending his wife and their relationship. His mother will eventually get over her feelings of rejection if she wants to stay involved in her son's life. This is the only way he'll grow up and get his clinging mother to back off. If he refuses to confront her early on in your relationship, watch out – he'll always have his mama in the first position – until you're ready to walk out the door.

He will stubbornly keep this pattern because his mother never saw him do anything wrong. So you'll have to be firm, patient, and too busy to do everything around the house. This will encourage him to step up and make some changes. Instead of asking him to do things he should know to do (he'll call this nagging), focus on yourself, get busy with your goals, and stop telling him what to do or worry about his problems. Be gone more often, and take care of yourself.

Consider the following examples to encourage changes:

1. Stop picking up his clothes and towels. Put a wet towel on his side of the bed and tell him it needs to go into the laundry basket.

2. Stop doing his laundry. Of course, if you're throwing in a load you could do his too, but then take his clothes from the dryer and put them on the floor while he lies on the couch and watches TV. Tell him, "Here are your clothes ready to be folded."

3. If he makes a mess in the master bedroom, move all his clothes into the guest room and say you want to keep your shared bedroom neat and romantic. He can get dressed and handle his clothes in the other room. Close the door so you don't have to see the mess.

4. After work for a few days a week, run your errands or go to the gym, and tell him, "You've got dinner tonight. Thanks for having it done by 7pm." If he claims not to "know how to cook" tell him he'll figure it out. Then cook a few nights together and show him exactly how to prepare several meals. He'll learn when he's forced to do so.

5. Make a list of the times and places he should drive the kids to their activities and appointments. Leave the list

on the refrigerator and don't call to remind him. If he forgets, let your children show their disappointment in him. Don't come to his rescue. Remind your children that they can always call you if they need to, and of course, you'll help them.

6. Post a family schedule for the children's homework, bed schedules and other family activities. If you aren't at home, he can read the schedule and follow through on what must be done.

The Peter Pan Man is stuck in late teens or young college-boy party mode. His buddies are more important than you; he's a couch potato addicted to TV, video games, sports, and has too many nights out with the boys. These boys' nights out are not innocent; they normally entail one-upmanship activities, contests of who can come on to whom and "score" the attention of the prettiest girl at the bar. He prefers to be with the boys and engage in male bravado games rather than being with you. He rarely wants just the two of you on a date – there has to be another couple with you or he'll complain and act miserable. Or, if you're out on a date together, he'll obnoxiously notice all the women in the room. He doesn't like to talk to you about anything important, especially your relationship. He often drinks too much, needing to be the life of the party. He shuns adult responsibilities because excitement and fun are his priorities in life. If you criticize his friends, or pressure him to stay home with you, he'll resent you.

His friends are obviously more important than you. He needs to be the center of attention, and will even put you down to get a laugh. However, your attractive looks are very important to him, to the point where you feel like a trophy to show off to his buddies.

The way he loves a woman is to make her a "mother replacement." He requires that his lady behave in a certain way and if she does anything different from his expectations of perfection, he'll become passive-aggressive, emotionally abusive, or throw a temper tantrum. She must always approve of what he says and does or he becomes very destructive. If a woman stands up for herself, or catches him doing something wrong, he often runs away like a child, unable to handle the repercussions of his actions.

You may want to test his degree of loyalty and love by focusing on yourself and getting busy with your own life – and see if he misses you. Set a goal date for yourself to decide how much time you want to spend to see if he's willing and able to make a commitment to you. If you're in a dating relationship and he prefers spending time with his male friends, refuse to become exclusive and start dating other people. He may not be ready for a serious relationship with you, but instead wants you around only when he feels like having you sexually. You deserve better; tell him that you've decided to date other men, and do it.

While testing the relationship, get focused on you, find time and ways to enjoy his friends with him, but don't always be available to him. Don't get nasty, just get busy. Don't complain and insist that he should be with you more – you want him to *choose to be with you*. Date, go out by yourself, or put on your favorite outfit and go out with your girlfriends. Hopefully he'll get the message that he's about to lose you and step up to being a real man.

Initially, these men can be kind, fun and affectionate, and he honestly believes that he treats you well. But after the initial laughs and excitement, you feel unimportant and second in line to his friends, sports and activities. He isn't sensitive to your wants and needs. He doesn't want to talk about them, and gets upset and sees you as demanding and "too sensitive." When you do choose to date others, or break off this relationship, he'll often plead, after a period of time, to have you back and vows that he'll be more attentive to you. Beware! This will be temporary, and after your relationship has settled again, he'll revert to putting himself and his selfish desires first.

To help change the behavior dynamics of both the Mama's Boy and Peter Pan Man, a counselor can shed some light onto this situation by telling them that when a man marries or makes a commitment to a woman, she then should become his first priority. He needs to put his mother and friends in fourth and fifth place, behind his wife, their relationship and their children.

A relationship coach will also inform them that today's men must be equal partners in the house when the wife is out helping to financially support the family. This is not the 1950s! When a man acts like a helpless child that needs to be taken care of, he also needs to know this puts you into a "mothering" role. This significantly diminishes your respect and sexual attraction toward him. He finally will understand why you no longer desire him and this, more than anything, will encourage him to change.

You're looking for an equal partner to share life's responsibilities with. If he wants more sex, he needs to stop acting like a child and be more self-confident, self-reliant and manly.

If you choose to be a full-time, stay-at-home mom, then yes, the agreement you've made is to do more within the household as "your work and contribution" to the house and family. I know this is hard work, and he needs to respect the role you've chosen. However, that still doesn't mean that you're his servant and that he needn't pick up after himself or do anything within the home.

If you are a nurturing, responsible and confident lady, you tend to feel initially attracted to this kind of man. If he's kind to his mother, he tends (initially) to be kind to you. You could be considered the "superwoman" who cares for others and puts everyone's needs ahead of your own. Many of these types of women work in caregiving careers; however, over time, your nurturing behavior can become codependent within your relationship. When he becomes needy, selfish and irresponsible, you step up to handle everything, and the relationship roles become reversed. You feel slighted, overwhelmed, unappreciated, and too much like "the man" in the family. Once that happens, sexual intimacy is affected and the relationship suffers.

Relationship coaching can help restore a better level of love and happiness by creating the necessary balance of the hard-wired, male-female roles. If both partners are willing to try the necessary techniques, this type of relationship can be saved.

Mother Haters

I almost forgot to include this category of man until I had a date with one! Asking my standard first-date questions of Scott uncovered some information that alerted my red flags when he spoke of his parents. He was the fourth child born and described his childhood this way: "When I was born my mom had enough of caring for kids. She opened up a clothing store and I barely saw her. I basically raised myself. I always felt alone and I hated her for a long time because of it. Only in my later years I went to counseling and was able to forgive her."

This alerted me to his abandonment issues and lack of nurturing on the part of his mother. I knew this type of childhood wound runs deep, so was it really settled and forgiven by him? The fact that he acted extremely charming, offering overly flattering statements struck me as a desperate need to be wanted, loved and accepted by a woman he desires. His behavior alerted me to be aware and to watch and listen carefully as our date progressed.

The next day, Scott called to say he was in love with me, and wanted to see me exclusively. Trying to be kind, I admitted that I felt flattered, but that I barely knew him, it was too soon, and that he was moving too fast. I suggested we get to know each other slowly as friends first, and see how things progressed. After trying to win me over, and seeing that I wouldn't change my mind, he became alarmingly mean, controlling, jealous of my dating others, and verbally abusive. What I suspected was right! I also believe he may have been a man with borderline personality disorder with his fast, out-of-control temper. As soon as I rejected him (even in a kind, and rational way) he reacted irrationally and became enraged.

The other information I got on the date all made sense. His second wife had a long-term eating disorder, which usually develops when a woman feels a lack of control and extreme stress. A former girlfriend asked him to leave, saying she wasn't happy after he had moved into her house. All red flags. I owned a home and all the sweetness he showed could well have been meant to manipulate me into letting him move in with me. He did ask to stop by my home the next day with a bottle of wine. I said, "No, no one comes into my home until I'm dating them exclusively for quite a while." My intuition was telling me he wanted to come in to check out my home.

Be protective of your home, meet your dates outside at a specific location for a while, and don't be emotionally manipulated by a fast-talking and swift-moving man.

Scott also seemed unsteady in his career, without possessing a business card, had no profile on LinkedIn or on any social media, nor did he "exist" on a Google search, very rare for someone legitimately in business. Who was this person, really? He was another online, one-and-done date for me and he was gone fast! I did report his abusive, inappropriate verbal comments to the online site.

Knowing the warning signs of personality types to watch for, asking the proper questions on your first or second dates, being aware and listening carefully to his answers, taking things slowly, and staying in tune with your intuition should be your new safeguard to keep you from an emotional manipulator.

When in the dating world, you don't at first always know who people are, but do your best to discover as much as possible on that first date. You need to be self-protective, so don't get emotionally invested or waste precious time with someone who shows toxic signs early on. It will only get worse, so get out early!

Section Two

Stop the Cycle of Dysfunction

Pain is inevitable. Misery is optional.
– Tim Hansel

Chapter 5

Should I Stay or Should I Go?

"You won't have your man while he's busy loving every woman that he can. Say I'm going to leave – 100 times a day, it's easier said than done, I just can't break away…
– Candi Staton, *Young Hearts, Run Free* (1999).

LOVE MEANS DIFFERENT THINGS to different people. A man wants respect and appreciation to feel loved. He likes how he feels when he's with his woman, and the idea of her being with another man makes him crazy! Many women expect a man to be obsessed with her, thinking of her constantly; however, a healthy man doesn't love in this way. It's is important that you understand that a man doesn't love or communicate in the same way a woman does. A woman should not expect a man to make her happy; she has to love herself and take responsibility for her own happiness. The toxic insecurity a woman might have that shows as neediness, and a lack of belief that her man loves her, is the very thing that ruins the relationship. Whatever the case, when fighting or stonewalling becomes a common occurrence, and sexual intimacy is infrequent, a relationship is on the fault line.

Other signs of a dying relationship:

1. He fails to call when he says he will, is late without calling, or if dating, you haven't heard from him in days or weeks.

2. Stupid fights occur too often, or he becomes critical of what you wear or do and nit-picks everything.

3. He's dieting to lose weight, is working out more, has bought new clothes, or suddenly is wearing cologne.

4. He stops coming on to you sexually; there has been no sex for a week or more, and he seems distant and disconnected when you do have sex.

One or several of these episodes indicate that the time has come when you realize you're in a roller-coaster relationship and that you must make a decision to stay or leave. If you're are a strong and financially secure woman with a great support system, you may decide you've had enough emotional confusion and are ready to cut your losses knowing you deserve better. Many other women, however, decide to stay, trying to hang in there while convincing themselves that "it's not so bad," or making other excuses while choosing to ignore their partner's poor behavior or deceptions. At this point, one of two things can occur:

1. You leave the relationship and experience an incredible calm, peace of mind and relief from stress. It's as if a ton of bricks has been lifted from your shoulders. Although you may miss the good times, and initially feel lonely, you

realize there simply weren't enough of those great times to make up for all the dysfunction you had to deal with. You realize it was the best thing you could have done, and you're taking active steps to heal as you realize he never could have fulfilled your relationship expectations.

2. You choose to stay and use every rationalization as to why you should. Unfortunately, you live with a constant state of anxiety, and never quite feel that you're getting the happiness you deserve, or equal dedication and effort from your partner. Unfortunately, the longer you stay, the harder it is to get out. Thinking honestly, you probably saw various red-flag signs when dating but "lust blindness" and the great feeling of falling in love made you ignore them. This is the time to get honest with yourself, and see a relationship coach to discuss your options. Your coach will guide you to create goals that will help you move on if you choose to do so. If he knows you're serious enough to contact a couples coach or therapist, he may decide to join you to help improve his part of the relationship.

If you experience consistently negative emotions of anger, resentment, sadness, frustration, and feel upset on a recurring basis, your emotional requirements and core needs are not being met. These are signs to leave a relationship, as you're doing your best to make things work with someone who doesn't care. The stages of a broken relationship occur over time.

Disillusionment occurs during the first stage when one or both partners realize that their romantic image of one another, and the relationship and future they envisioned, are never going to come to fruition. This is the time to seek counseling or coaching help to establish personal needs and expectations within the relationship. If the partners themselves don't communicate a desire to try and work things out, then the relationship will move into the next stage, referred to as Erosion.

During the **Erosion** stage, a partner represses feelings, wants, needs and desires, which leads to anger, hurt and resentment; invariably leading to a toxic relationship. Subtle emotional abuse cues may start during this stage, such as verbal put-downs or emotional distancing. Partners may seek attention elsewhere, feeling they "deserve" to feel happy. It is still not too late to work on negative feelings and conflicts when two willing partners want to save and renew their relationship. If the couple fails to do this, then the relationship can start to spiral towards the stage of Detachment.

Within the **Detachment** stage, one or both parties demonstrate apathetic behavior and may develop their own personal agenda and make a new independent life for themselves. There is a critical absence of emotion towards the other partner and sex is rarely desired. When a relationship enters this stage, it's very hard to renew the sexual chemistry and love that the couple once shared.

Stage four is **Physical Separation**, often the most traumatic stage due to the loss or "death" of the relationship. It's always difficult to say goodbye to someone loved so deeply for a long time. A best friendship, and a romantic, passionate love relationship are suddenly seen as a sham! With the loss of the relationship go the hopes and plans of your idealized future together.

It helps to remember the good times and to thank your partner for the many valued memories shared. However, in order to begin the healing process, you should write in a journal the negative aspects of the relationship so that, hopefully, they won't reoccur in a future partnering. Make a list of negative behaviors acted out against you so that "lust blindness" from the beginning of the relationship won't soften your emotional pain enough to return to the toxic partner. Feelings of overwhelming sadness and the shattering of your relationship expectations are part of the bereavement process. Consciously, you know you must put the toxic partner out of your life; but you may continue to fight unconscious urges and deep-rooted negative relationship patterns that result from childhood wounds and take time to overcome.

A wise man once told me, "Your partner is either a thoroughbred horse, or a donkey. The donkey, no matter how much he tries, will never be a race horse. You cannot expect the donkey to deliver the top-shelf behavior of a thoroughbred horse. You fell in love with *who you thought he could be*, based on what he led you to believe. In the end, the donkey will always be an ass, and will never be a thoroughbred."

That made a lot of sense to me, and reminded me of a coaching client. A very pretty and successful woman, Sylvia, age 51, described the sad story of the sudden end to her marriage. She had married a handsome, charming man with a history of childhood emotional trauma and physical abuse from an alcoholic father. Her husband, Joe, had an overbearing, needy and dependent mother who favored her older son. He learned to be charming, outgoing, humorous and a "people pleaser" to get his mother's attention and then became her emotional caregiver. It also helped him to survive his father's punishing wrath. Internally, his ACOA anxiety remained constant; he had a secret life of sexual addiction, seeking attention from other women and using sexual conquests to boost his severely injured self-esteem. Joe never felt loved enough, and once married, his perfectionistic demands on Sylvia were exhausting for her.

While they were engaged, Joe's anxiety, impulsivity and pornography addiction (which Sylvia was not aware of) made him lose his high-powered, six-figure job. Sylvia felt like she had become his mother, trying to help him get back on his feet by finding him work, helping to overcome his bad choices, and picking up the slack caused by his emotional baggage. Joe's selfish immaturity, together with the need for the women of pornography in order to feel manly, left him emotionally distant from Sylvia. This addiction and lack of a commitment to finding employment to rebuild his life brought about Sylvia's diminished respect and sexual desire for him.

After many months, Sylvia could no longer endure the stress and broke her engagement with Joe, who then went to live with his mother. Although Sylvia loved him, she was advised to try a therapeutic separation to see if Joe could restructure his life on his own. He did report that he went to counseling. Looking back, Sylvia now knows that he was narcissistic, a deceitful sociopath, an ACOA, and had borderline and anti-social personality disorder. Sylvia wasn't sure how long he actually had committed to his therapy because she couldn't believe anything he said. During their separation of several months, Joe wrote Sylvia many romantic and passionate love letters and asking for another chance to prove that he was the man she loved and that he could again be "her knight in shining armor."

Joe reluctantly finally admitted at that time that he had a pornography addiction but assured Sylvia he would never use it again. He said he understood it to be the major addiction that had ruined his life, his love relationship, his financial security, employment, and his reputation in the community. Sylvia decided to forgive him this one time. When they got back together, she set strong boundaries and told Joe clearly that if she caught him engaging in pornography, or in any sexual addiction, telling lies or acting deceitful again, she would end the relationship.

Joe moved back into Sylvia's home, they got reengaged, and she worked very hard at reestablishing her trust for him. They were able to repair their love relationship over two years. She was patient as Joe found part-time work and seemed more stable and confident, so they did proceed to get married.

However, after only a few months, Joe lost his first, full-time job, acquired after his initial firing, and became moody, anxious, passive-aggressive and secretive. Sylvia got suspicious and discovered that Joe's pornography addiction had reemerged and plunged him into a secret world where he distanced himself from her. While she worked hard to pay household expenses, he indulged in Internet pornography sites and chat rooms, spending money he didn't have to get his ego stroked. She found he had spent $2,000 over a one-year period secretly purchasing pornography and visiting online chat rooms while still not gainfully employed. Sylvia was devastated that he had broken her trust a second time. He had self-sabotaged their relationship again and this time, broke his marital vows taken only five months before.

Rather than show remorse for the damage done by his deception and lies, Joe never even apologized to Sylvia for the severe damage he had done. His narcissism allowed him to blame her for everything. It was then that his passive-aggressive anger, sociopathic tendencies and lack of empathy or remorse for his actions became clearly apparent to Sylvia. He moved out while she was hard at work, leaving an irrational note about "saving some chicken for dinner" for him. Sylvia knew then he was mentally ill and possibly dangerous because he could not see the callousness of his actions. I encouraged her to change the locks immediately and file for a restraining order. She chose to love herself more, and got out of the relationship, annulling their marriage. Thank goodness she had a prenuptial agreement in place and didn't lose any of the assets she had worked so hard to acquire before their marriage.

Forgiveness, at least the first time, was the spiritual path Sylvia chose to take, to give him another change. We're all human beings who can make serious mistakes. It was extremely difficult for her to regain the trust for the man she so deeply loved after his firing due to watching pornography at work, but she was determined to do so to save their relationship. She believed that they could rebuild a new future, leaving behind the past toxicity. Still, Sylvia came to realize that Joe was a donkey and not a thoroughbred; thus, he would never be able to meet her expectations of integrity in their relationship. Joe was the type of man who is a toxic, emotional manipulator who would always let her down and break her heart.

This in no way means that she stopped loving him right away. It took over a year, for her symptoms of PTSD, sadness and depression to heal. Her life and love, dreams of a future together in retirement, and assumption that Joe was a good, successful man of character; all had been shattered. With coaching and counseling, she worked hard to reinvent herself and took on many activities that she had put on hold for years. She realized that she had lost herself in trying to help Joe get back on his feet and by over doing to prove her love for him, despite his faulty thinking that she never loved him enough.

She felt proud of the new woman she had become and realized she had fallen in love with the charming image he so expertly projected to the world (Dr. Jekyll), while the true sociopathic inner person (Mr. Hyde) was a selfish, angry, anxious, addicted, narcissistic, paranoid, jealous, self-loathing man. Joe looked for a woman of means to support him after he had messed up his prior life. Sylvia was the thoroughbred horse who went on to win many races in her life!

I often hear these words in my counseling center: "If my spouse could only be who I met in the beginning, then our love would last forever." The emotional manipulator is charming, affectionate, giving, passionate, romantic and almost perfect in the beginning of a relationship. Then, at around the 90-day-to-6-month period (though the deception could go on for years), small signs of emotional or physical abuse, fraud, addiction, narcissism, and sociopathic tendencies begin to emerge. Remember that this person's true character is hidden by brilliant emotional manipulation and lies.

Addictions, cheating, lies and sociopathic character flaws take a long time to emerge fully. It's important that people know that they've done their best to love their partner. When certain that they acted with integrity while their partner chose to live a life of deceit, they'll come to the realization that this wasn't the love they deserve.

Affairs

The longer a couple is married, the greater the chance an affair will occur. As discussed in Dr. Scott Haltzman's webcast, "Preventing and Surviving Infidelity," 40% of couples experience the emotional devastation of infidelity, and more than half who do will try to save their marriage, with many successfully doing so. With all trust destroyed, the victim is left wondering who their partner really is. Today, over 65% of people having affairs use electronics to make connections, compared to only 6% in 2002.

A couple's counselor is essential to help rebuild the trust back. Although the guilty partner wants forgiveness and "things to go back to normal" immediately, this is as impossible as it is unrealistic. The partner must stop all contact and communication with the lover who is often idealized by him. He must recognize the degree of wrong done, admit to the lies he told and to the many ways he chose to break your trust. You deserve a full and honest summary of what was done. You also should have open access to all security codes, email, cell phone and texts. Then both of you must agree to an honest exchange of needs and desires within the relationship to see whether it can be fixed or is beyond repair.

If you suspect your partner is having an affair, trust your instincts. When confronted, he likely will lie so you need evidence before confrontation. He may only admit to what you know, and no more, so be thorough. It's very easy to discover if your man is cheating by looking into email, texts, cell phone bills, Skype contacts, and other Internet-related information.

There are three underlying considerations at play throughout an affair:

1. Opportunity: to cheat (Internet, gym, workplace).

2. Need: a man receives special attention and admiration from an affair that he feels he isn't getting at home; or may be getting from his partner but desires more.

3. The lack of character and maturity to suppress impulses and the inability to say "no." This type of man often has a personality disorder that makes him crave attention and be prone to addictions, in addition to having a history of impulsivity and poor choices.

I have had many male therapy clients defend their female friends' feelings over their partner's; if this occurs, know that there exists an emotional connection stronger than your marriage. Any relationship hidden from you is wrong. Friends of the opposite sex should be friends with both you and your spouse. No secrets should be kept from your partner, who should always be held in high esteem to all your friends. You must break off contacts with friends of the opposite sex if you feel that they're becoming too emotionally close to you. Emotional connection and closeness causes friendships to become affairs, so cut these ties if your intuition warns that a friendship has become too involved and not so innocent.

Many relationships will go through trust or integrity issues that lead to feelings of betrayal. This must be addressed and dealt with. Important questions to ask during this process:

1. What exactly happened? What are the facts according to each person in the relationship?

2. How did each person react and how does each now feel about the other?

3. What past triggers did this bring up? Describe childhood traumas that this event connects to.

4. Who did what? What is each of your parts that may have led to this situation?

5. What personal triggers need to be addressed and healed?

6. Where does this event fall on each partner's requirement, needs, wants and desires lists? Is it made unsolvable by breaking the core values of one of the partners?

7. What does each person need from the other to move forward, forgive, and try again? What is the new vision for your future?

8. What is your action plan (individually and together) to create that future vision and rebuild trust?

9. What new behaviors and actions should now be sought (therapy, coaching, self-care, and other changes)?

10. What valuable lessons can be learned to make this experience a positive change in your life? Try to view your problem as an opportunity to build a more loving, open and trusting bond.

An affair not only causes expectations to be ruined, it can create great fear when trying to start dating and trusting another man. You may wait to become involved with someone else because you may hope your spouse will change "when he realizes how much he misses me." Don't put your life on hold or expect him to alter his basic character.

Of course, as a therapist I believe most people can change, but they *really must want to* and must be willing to spend years working on changing negative, toxic patterns. There must be sincere remorse felt, full acknowledgement and ownership of faults, and a willingness to enter into long-term counseling to understand unconscious, impulsive and toxic survival mechanisms.

Processing the Pros and Cons

Compile a list that outlines the pros and cons of your relationship. Brainstorm without interruption before reading your list. Do your pros or cons fit into the should-I-leave or should-I-go category? You'll add to this list throughout the week, so go back to it often. Be uncompromisingly honest about your partner's positive and negative characteristics. Then discuss the list contents with your relationship coach.

Should I Stay or Should I Go?

Should I Leave?

Did you ever stay in a relationship much too long, hoping and praying it would work and doing anything in your power to try to make it work? Many people make the mistake of staying in a toxic, dysfunctional relationship too long. Learning the warning signs summarized in this book will give you the confidence to decide to leave a horrible relationship. After asking my clients, "Can you see living another twenty, thirty, or forty years like this?" most say no, and realize they must take steps to end it.

Statistics show that people rarely change deeply embedded character flaws, and those with personality disorders rarely get better with time. Expecting a man to change sets you up for unhappiness. Honor yourself by seeing the truth in your partner's actions. Observe clearly how he treats you. Many women continually choose not to see the dysfunction and then complain that they feel so unhappy. Ask yourself how you're *feeling* – are you anxious, exhausted, depressed, angry, or have resentment? If so, then he's not the right guy for you. Feelings don't lie, and women need to listen to their intuition. If you make excuses for a man who doesn't treat you well, you're only delaying the inevitable.

If you choose to stay with a toxic man, your lack of happiness will remain your fault. Ask yourself, "How are things working for me?" If the response is "Terrible," then you have a choice – stay and hope for change (slim chance) or start a plan to change your life and find healthy love.

What are the deal breakers? When do you decide to leave the relationship? Here are a few causes for break-ups:

1. Constant lies and deceit, destroying your trust and feelings of safety in your relationship.

2. He repeatedly makes impulsive choices that hurt and disappoint you. If he apologizes and promises not to repeat the actions, he may comply for only a brief period. His actions are repeated and will continue.

3. He is physically abusive. This behavior often escalates with time and rarely stops. You never feel safe or secure, and you live in fear of his random temper explosions.

4. He is verbally abusive, humiliating you by name-calling or constant "put-downs" (most often in private). While communicating, does he yell and blame you for everything, especially his mistakes? Do you feel unloved and worthless because of his cutting words?

5. His behavior is psychologically abusive and controlling, and often accompanied by bouts of extreme jealousy or use of emotional manipulation. You feel constant frustration at his inability to express his needs without temper explosions, blame, or put-downs. He distorts your words, making you sound irrational, resulting in the need to defend or explain yourself.

6. Would you have a sense of calm and relief if the relationship suddenly ended?

7. You really don't like him as a person. He is a turn-off to you and you hate to be around him because he's mean-spirited. He shows no respect for your needs, desires or wants.

8. He expects you to pay more than your fair share financially. Worse yet, he'll move in and contribute little but has a lot to say about how you spend your money. He may take

over your parenting role within your home, or pit your children against you. Be cautious of men who become too affectionate with your children or those who abuse your kids while you're away from home. Believe your children if they tell you that your man is abusing them in any way. Children rarely make up such stories, and it takes them a long time to come forward with their fears.

9. The thought of making love to your partner is repulsive. Sex is often the last thing to go, so if you cannot conceive of sharing your body with him, then your relationship is over. Angry, manipulative men often withhold sex or make you feel undesirable.

10. You set a boundary with him concerning a particular, negative behavior or addiction. If it's ignored, you may feel there is no recourse but separation.

11. He's in denial about an addiction and refuses to seek help. It becomes an ongoing problem due to the stress and deceit.

12. He constantly criticizes you, your weight or what and how much you eat. Many women develop anorexia, bulimia, or digestive disorders because of a controlling, perfectionistic man. These manipulative men bully or pick on their women because they themselves have low self-esteem, out-of-control lives or some addiction.

13. Both of you feel there is nothing left in common and sharing time together is awkward. You prefer to be alone rather than with him. The anxiety you experience when around him contributes to your feeling physically and emotionally sick.

14. After a therapeutic separation, you enjoy your peaceful, calm, new life alone without your toxic partner.

15. The relationship is over if there has been an emotional, sexual or Internet affair that he refuses to stop. If your toxic partner blames everyone else and never takes responsibility for his actions or for your pain, then these selfish actions are bound to be repeated.

16. He makes a sudden unilateral move. This could be a move out of state, signing a one-year lease after a sudden separation, buying an expensive item without consultation, or any other "power move." These actions reflect deep-rooted immature and selfish tendencies common to a narcissistic personality. Your needs or feelings are not important to him.

17. He tells you he's in love with someone else.

Regardless of what you wanted and had envisioned for your relationship, it's time to move on. To help this process and end your relationship in the most respectful way, I suggest the following guidelines:

1. Ask him to calmly explain the reasons he feels the relationship is over. Listen without interrupting so you can learn what to do better in your next relationship. However, remember the sociopath will always blame you, so his reason may not be valid. Don't try to argue your point or defend yourself.

2. Apologize sincerely for hurting him in the ways that he felt you did. You may not agree with any of it, but that doesn't matter. He is entitled to his feelings, and it's important

you acknowledge his pain. Hopefully, at this point, he will acknowledge his faults as well, but if he's sociopathic, don't expect him to do so.

3. Thank him for the great times and memories you had together. It's all right to tell him that you're sad things didn't work out, and that you hope he'll find happiness.

4. Try to end the relationship with class and dignity. It's better for your soul to move on in peace and harmony so that forgiveness and healing will come faster for you.

5. Don't try calling, texting or emailing him; don't emotionally chase him in any way hoping he'll change his mind. If he has told you his feelings of love are over, believe him. If he wants to talk to you in the future, he'll let you know.

6. Try not to talk about his wrongdoings to the community. People *will* ask, "Where is so-and-so?" That question is common and hard to face, so have a statement prepared. If he had an addiction, it's fine to speak the truth and tell people you were no longer able to live with his addiction issues – and don't offer details. You could also say, "We wanted different things," or, "We were better off just being friends." Try not to talk bad about him to your friends. If you get back together after people have supported you in your healing, they'll feel awkward. It's always better to vent to your therapist.

Should you Stay?

Here below are some considerations for staying in a troubled relationship and investing the time and effort to improve it:

1. You truly have a lot of fun together. Do you share a mutually enjoyable activity that brings great pleasure such as dancing, camping, travel, or playing golf?

2. Is your partner kind and quick to ask for forgiveness? Does he make an effort to be clean and attractive for you? Are you still sexually attracted to him?

3. Children and strong memories of family time together could be significant enough to keep trying with your partner.

4. Relationship rituals – places and activities you share on a regular basis are important and you look forward to doing them together.

5. Is there open communication? If not, is the willingness there to work on communication issues with a therapist or relationship coach?

6. Is there career support? Is your partner your best friend?

7. Is dating and romance still a very important part of the relationship? Is there still pleasurable love-making and a real sexual connection demonstrated by each partner?

8. Despite the problems that have occurred, are you *both willing to forgive the past, committing together to make the relationship work?* Do both partners cherish the friendship they have as well as appreciate the many fine qualities of the relationship?

9. Would both partners be willing to compromise on several of their less positive behaviors by moderating them to once or twice a week? For example, you dislike that your

partner binge drinks and gets drunk, but you would feel fine about sharing a bottle of wine together at dinner when out on a date. He could also agree to limit himself to two alcoholic drinks when you're out together. Or, if your partner secretly watches pornography and then lies about it, you may feel agreeable to watching some respectable, "couple-oriented," romantically sexual movies together to spice up your sex life. In turn, he agrees to have no secret codes on his computer or to watch pornography in secret. In summary, you both are open to negotiate a new direction with your problem issues.

10. After a therapeutic separation, each having tried dating, both partners are willing to communicate and compromise. They're willing to work through these issues together with a counselor, in hopes of achieving a more peaceful and loving relationship.

11. If there has been an affair or a continued lack of trust, did the toxic partner apologize, show sincere remorse and ask for another chance? Are both partners committed to getting counseling over a long period of time, doing anything necessary to trust each other again? If the hurt, anger, pain, and fear subside after several months, and forgiveness still remains, this relationship may endure. If you love him, give him another chance – it could lead to your best relationship ever.

12. Many partners choose to stay together because of the children or they can't afford to leave and manage financially on their own. Staying together for these reasons alone usually doesn't work, and the relationship can become

very toxic. At this point, couples need to enter counseling to become strong as a pair and as individuals. Both can reinvent themselves with new jobs, hobbies, or educational pursuits.

13. Reset your goals and dreams together for your future.

14. Suggest counseling for both of you. Both should go individually and as a couple. If there is enough love and both want to rectify the problems, then both should commit to counseling. If one or both partners don't care, refuse to go to counseling, or one suddenly decides to leave the relationship, then separation begins. This doesn't necessarily mean the relationship is over and the love is gone, but it does mean counseling should start for both partners.

If love endures, time will heal the wounds for both partners. If you still love him, take your time to decide on a divorce and see if his feelings can be turned around. Some partners run away, then realize after a few months that they really do love you and want you back. But delaying a divorce from a toxic partner can lengthen your misery and time to heal. So don't wait too long, and ask yourself, *do I really want HIM back?*

Guidelines regarding healing time:

There are seven stages of grief (i.e., profound sorrow) that one goes through after suddenly losing a love partner.

1. Shock, disbelief, denial, emotional numbness or unpredictable crying.

2. Emotional pain and guilt, bargaining to get the toxic partner back, blaming of self.

3. Anger, blaming of partner, hostility and ruminating on partner's faults.

4. Depression, sadness, hopelessness, social isolation.

5. Upward turn of emotions, starting to have days of happiness, hope and creativity.

6. Acceptance that the relationship is over; hoping and planning for a better future.

7. Reconstruction and reinvention of oneself; goals made and acquired for growth and change in all areas of life.

General timelines for healing after discovering your partner's emotional or sexual affair:

- **After the first month:** Anger, sadness, and obsessive thoughts about the affair are still apparent in both partners. New topics and experiences should be explored to help you reconnect with your partner. Patience should be exercised by both partners. The guilty partner should do everything to reestablish trust, and should understand the other's fears. All secret codes or passwords should be removed, allowing the hurt partner access at any time to computers, email, Facebook pages or cell phones.

- **From the second to the fourth month:** Calm communication about rebuilding the relationship to ensure that infidelity never happens again. You're both negotiating your needs without anger as intimacy is slowly restored. Both partners are supportive and loving while the pain is processed. Your partner reassures you of his love by showing you he can be trusted.

- **From four months to twelve months:** Your sexual connection is more loving and intense; both partners are starting to relax, trust and share powerful emotions for each other. Sexual passion has been renewed, and improved variety or techniques for both partners emerge because of what has been learned since the affair.

- **After the first year:** Emotional pain has lessened and healing has taken place. The relationship has solidified and rarely does the destructive incident get discussed.

- **From one to three years:** Both partners work hard and take full responsibility to ensure a healthy and happy relationship. Actions of trust speak louder than words. The couple becomes strong again and society sees that they "made it" together. Openness with social media and cell phones remains for both partners for the life of the relationship.

Forgiveness is Essential

Forgiveness is the highest spiritual concept. It's hard to forgive someone who has deeply hurt you with lies, cheating or deception. Yet you must find the strength to forgive for your relationship to have a chance. And it's hardest to forgive someone who hasn't sincerely apologized for a grave misconduct. The inability to apologize is a strong sign of arrogance, narcissism, and weakness of character. In the face of your partner's refusal to apologize, you still want to offer your forgiveness to help your own healing process.

Forgiveness doesn't in any way mean acceptance of deception. Humans make mistakes. Forgiveness releases you from the anger and negativity that perpetuates emotional pain. Being the first to forgive may help your partner realize the extent of your love and understanding and allow him to apologize with dignity and love.

Taking time to think things over during a therapeutic separation is a good idea, as long as you keep the lines of communication open. Let your partner know that you're willing to consider working things through with additional time to heal the wounds. If he refuses to return your messages or letters then he clearly isn't interested and it's time to move on.

Be kind and loving when you tell your partner that you feel it is best to move on with your life and that the relationship is over for you. Wish him much happiness and apologize for any infractions of your own as this will help both of you find closure. Show him respect to acknowledge that there had been genuine love felt for him and sorrow for all harm caused. This will help you both move on in love and peace.

If there are a lot of "reasons to stay" on your list, then you'll have a hard time trying to duplicate your depth of feelings for your spouse with another. All marriages and relationships encounter hard times and emotional pain. True love is hard to find and is worth fighting for! Giving up too easily could be something you'll both deeply regret. If there are more reasons to stay than reasons to leave (excluding physical and emotional abuses), consider going to relationship coaching and rebuild your love relationship into something better than you both had experienced before.

The bottom line here is that if all the problems in the relationship were gone, and you still felt some degree of love, attraction and a new form of trust, would you want to stay?

If you said yes, then the relationship is usually too good to leave. If you *both want it to work*, both admit fault, both extend apologies and forgiveness, agree to get counseling to discuss mistakes made, stop an addiction issue, or correct a history of negative traits, then hang in there, and give it more time.

If the answer is no, and you're too concerned about the history of the relationship or your partner's toxic behaviors, ongoing addiction or personality type, then the relationship is too dysfunctional to stay in it. You'll be happier if you leave. Exit with the final statement, "Goodbye, good luck and God bless."

Chapter 6

Try Coaching and Couples Counseling

If you attack apparent negativity with negativity, you merely feed and inflame the source. It's always best to take the positive in any conflict. If you genuinely love, or at least send kind thoughts to a thing, it will change before your eyes. – John and Lyn St. Clair Thom

---

BEFORE YOU TOTALLY DECIDE to give up on your relationship, it's best to try coaching or counseling first. If your partner won't attend, consider his refusal a bad sign and go yourself. Begging him to get help or trying various ways to talk about fixing the relationship won't work; he will only be repelled by you. You need to understand that you can't force change upon someone else, but you can change yourself and, therefore, the patterns of your marriage. He'll see that you're serious about getting help for yourself as well as the relationship. Hopefully, he'll ask to join you in your counseling sessions.

Changing a bad marital relationship starts by focusing on building your own confidence and joy in life. Start working out, get together with friends; begin a hobby or a new class. Worry less and try to simplify your life; getting rid of massive "to-do" lists. Rediscover your softer, feminine qualities by taking care of yourself and giving him space. Doing things purposely to please him will push him away. He's not responsible for making you happy, so don't demand that he should. Don't attack or nag him. If he does something that pleases you, make sure you show appreciation and thank him with a smile. Exhibiting positive energy for yourself and others, as well as your outlook on life, will make him attracted to you again.

Reevaluate your boundaries and refuse to accept any disrespectful behavior from him. If he does something offensive, tell him plainly that your feelings were badly hurt, and that his behavior wasn't acceptable. Give up trying to figure out what he will do or say next. Don't yell or lecture him, just go about doing whatever makes you happy.

Men of good character like to please their women and make them happy by showing affection, integrity and faithfulness, and spending quality time together. They take pleasure in giving gifts. Your being a positive, confident woman who feels blissful about her happy life will make him attracted to you.

When your partner does something especially hurtful and damaging to your relationship, it's common to ask, "Can I ever forgive him? Should this relationship be over?" Although the previous chapter offers reasons why people choose to stay or leave, I've seen many relationships in the utmost disrepair that I've helped to make happier than ever before. It takes time and patience from both partners, but most importantly, both must want the relationship to work.

Try Coaching and Couples Counseling

If the partner who lied, cheated, or caused the infraction wants instant forgiveness and to see an immediate return to normalcy, this is neither reasonable nor possible. With these clients I ask them to turn the tables and ask themselves, "What if my partner did the same action to me? Would they be so quick to forgive?" However long the addiction or affair lasted (whether months or years) it might easily take the same amount of time to forgive and rebuild lost trust, if at all possible.

Every woman has a different tolerance to the amount of emotional pain she can absorb; she has a certain boundary or limit when she knows her relationship is unfixable or over. Boundaries should be clearly discussed early in the relationship, and again, following a breach of trust. But when there is an isolated incident in a relationship you otherwise consider wonderful most of the time, relationship coaching or couples counseling is surely worth considering before breaking off completely.

Coaching can offer insight into all the wonderful times you do have in your relationship, and into the time you fell in love and cherished your partner. When I have a coaching couple in session, I ask each the following three questions:

1. What made you fall in love with your partner when you first met? Name some qualities and character traits that especially stick out in your mind.

2. What would you like to work on within yourself to help you be a better partner?

3. What are your future dreams and goals for yourself and within your relationship?

These three questions take the couple back to the time of falling in love and make them examine their own responsibilities as to why the relationship fell apart or is challenged. It identifies what they each gave up because of the relationship and what they want to see come to fruition again. It's also helpful for them to define the future they wish to have, individually and with their partner.

The questions also allow for keen insight into how each felt when falling in love and helps define the qualities of their partner. It tells me who is truly invested in wanting to fix the relationship, and who is not. One wife responded slowly to the question about her husband's wonderful qualities. After an extremely long pause, she declared with flat emotion, "He's a good provider." I knew that their marriage was over. Still, the husband tried all he could over six months to rebuild their marriage, doing anything she requested of him, while she did nothing to change. She wanted to party with her friends, and often went out leaving him at home. It was later discovered that she had a secret boyfriend.

Tom is now involved in my coaching program for individuals and has successfully reinvented his image. He looks and feels amazing. We both had known from the start that first night that his wife was not invested in the marriage and appeared already to be halfway out the door. But because he had tried everything he could before filing for divorce, he left the relationship without guilt or remorse and feels good about himself as a person.

For partners who are *both* invested in wanting the relationship to work, I give small assignments for the couple to try together after each session. I also give each partner a personal assignment to work on for their own growth, change, or stress reduction. This helps to make their weekly goals grow quickly into a new, quality relationship. It's interesting to see during the first session, from

Try Coaching and Couples Counseling

body language to the chosen seating arrangement, how the couple relates to one another.

I review communication styles and help them create a new way of speaking to each other. Talking about personal feelings, i.e., "I want, need, feel….," versus blaming, controlling, whining, nagging or yelling, will improve chances of being heard. Poor vocal and non-vocal communication habits take about thirty days to break, so be consciously aware of what you need to do, and practice it daily. Use the term "we" when suggesting change. Ask his opinion on an idea, and be open to compromise. Be complimentary – often! Let him know he makes you happy and that you appreciate his kind gestures. A calm, positive manner is more easily shared. If he feels safe and able to discuss private feelings with you, he'll stay connected to you. Being negative or controlling will push him away. If things get heated, take a break from each other for an hour.

After a few weeks, when I come into the waiting room and see them giggling while sitting together on the couch and holding hands, I know that we've made progress.

Sometimes the hardest part of relationship growth, connection and change is getting the couple to become sexual again after many months of no intimate relations. Usually, once the couple starts dating again (alone; without family or friends) for a period of time, and they progress to a brief trip to another town (at least two nights), I find that their sexual connection and chemistry returns.

The following suggestions are in no way meant to be read as sexist or stereotypical. Reflect on who you were and what you looked like when you met. Be determined to recapture the attraction factor if you want your relationship to work through the years.

1. I do advise the woman to invest in some stylish outfits and accessories, consider a new hairstyle, or do anything else that makes her feel sexy, confident and attractive. Women that "dress comfortably" on a daily basis in sweats and sneakers can slowly lose their sex appeal. Even on a bad day or weekend, go for a sexy-jean look with boots and a pretty top. Weekends are not the time to dress like a slob; rather, it's the key time to be romantic with your mate. The "caveman" or "reptilian old brain" in a male (which emotionally assesses our performance and is based in our evolution and primitive urges), causes a man to fall in love first by visual attraction. If you no longer put any effort into the attraction factor, then your man may no longer want to be sexually intimate with you. What did you look like back in your dating days? *Be that woman again!*

2. This philosophy is exactly the same for men. I advise them to analyze their wardrobe and update it so that they're dressing stylishly for their dates, wearing cologne, appearing clean-shaven with a sexy hairstyle, and they should do anything else that makes them feel and look sexy, masculine and confident.

Women are attracted to a well-groomed, well-dressed man (think about Richard Gere in *American Gigolo,* for example); those Italian loafers, sport jackets, suits, silk ties, fit jeans and leather bomber jackets look amazing! When I was a model and talent school director and agent, I provided a shopping service that helped men "get their look together," because if they hoped to be a male model in my agency, they needed to look the part on a daily basis. Try to get away from baseball caps, sloppy sweatshirts, baggy jeans

Try Coaching and Couples Counseling

and sneakers. YUK. Men, do you want more sex? Remember that women are visual creatures too!

3. Weight loss and getting toned, fit and healthy are subjects also discussed with both partners. I suggest they do it together and support each other to ensure they have equal time at the gym.

Time management, daily routines, financial stress and children's schedules all cause sexual and romantic feelings to be lost or forgotten. Many couples "just exist" to get through their day, and the joy and romance completely leaves their relationship. Together they set new routines that will simplify their lives. Coaching can rekindle their love and reignite sexual passion into the fire they both long for.

Often after the children come, couples focus so completely on the children, their needs and schedules that they put themselves last, as individuals and as a couple. The balance triangle (as described in my book, *Live Beyond Your Dreams – from Fear and Doubt to Personal Power, Purpose and Success*) for a couple should be equal sides of Self, Partner, and Family. If you slight yourself you become resentful and burned out; if you slight your partner, he may look elsewhere for desired attention. If you neglect your children, they won't have the support they need to be confident, successful and independent young adults. It's important to have these three areas in equal balance for yourself.

Setting a weekly date night with your love (Saturday night is recommended for couples), and perhaps having a family game or movie night on Friday will satisfy both your children and your partner. Your kids will adjust to the fact that their parents have a date every Saturday night, and you'll look forward to having that special romantic time with your partner. There are many ideas to help you stay in love or to help you fall in love all over again.

Love is more than a feeling – it's an action. Pay attention to the relationship with daily maintenance. Put your marriage relationship second only to your relationship with God or your faith. With spiritual faith, you have the confidence to feel at your most complete, and to sustain the most honest love for your partner. When trying to rebuild your relationship, speak openly and kindly to one another. Spend quality time together, maintaining your weekly romantic and fun dates to help rekindle the passion you initially felt for one another. Love produces powerful feelings, so give respect, value and honor to your partner and feelings of love will follow. If you drift apart, do what you initially did when you were courting, and confess your wrongdoings with a sincere apology. If a significant infraction occurred in your marriage, consider renewing the vows made to one another.

During relationship coaching, I encourage you to look candidly at your current situation and to discuss your goals and dreams as an individual. Personal balance in life is examined, as well as your life stressors. Nitpicking or blame in a relationship happens when individuals feel unhappy with where they are personally. It's very important for your partner to know what you believe is lacking in your life, and what areas you hope to improve or change. New communication skills are learned so that each feels supported by the other and can speak freely about needs, wants, requirements and desires in order to feel happy and to set goals for the relationship.

Often when communication breaks down, no one feels heard. The toxic person uses the worst approach and screams to make sure you hear him. Anyone being yelled at is going to shut down, not want to listen, feel bullied, and will engage in a personal, silent communication about what a jerk the screamer is.

Try Coaching and Couples Counseling

The way to be heard and hold power in a conversation is to speak calmly and slowly about what's on your mind. Quality, safe communication should be an equal exchange of feelings and thoughts, and speaking and listening.

1. One person should not talk over the other, or monopolize the conversation. Your partner can listen only when feeling safe and not under attack. When both feel listened to and respected, then each will truly feel heard.

2. Learn what to say and what not to say. Turn complaints into a request; clearly communicate your frustrations by keeping positive about the change you would like to see happen. Don't blame, sound negative or bring up the past; it's always hurtful and can never be changed anyway. Don't point out how he failed you or try to fix his mistakes; he will only become angry, anxious or depressed and shut down. Simply tell him your honest feelings and ask for his help. You want him to feel safe so he can directly express his own honest feelings to you. Try to negotiate a win for both of you.

3. Remember that you're each entitled to your feelings, needs and experience; neither one of you "must be right." Accept what you each hear from one another on condition that agreeing to disagree is fine too.

4. Really listen when your partner speaks. Ask him to clarify what you don't understand. You can also ask him, "Is there more?" to make sure he feels he has said everything on the topic.

5. Be truthful and genuine about your thoughts, feelings, needs, wants and boundaries. Intimacy ("In To Me I See")

means having a clear understanding of the character of you and your partner. Start a difficult conversation with "I love you and want us to be happy, but I'm concerned about something – can I ask you about it?" End the conversation with "Thanks for listening, I love you, Hon" (or whatever your pet name may be).

6. When communication is difficult, I often suggest that the couple write love letters to one another. I advise each partner to check their letter to make sure it doesn't sound angry, hurtful or blaming. The letter should be read several times over to ensure the writer says all they want to share. I ask both to go back to the time they fell in love, and tell their partner why they are special to them, and then what they miss from those days. The writer should also suggest several ways to help get back to those "falling-in-love" days.

I advise them to talk about the best romantic and sexy times they enjoyed, and how alive and cherished they both felt. It's important to keep the love letter positive because it will be read several times. I know it's difficult to write such a letter after you've been hurt, or cheated on. But ask what you want more, your pride (a toxic, ego-based trait) or love, peace and understanding? Is it more important to be right, or happy?

If you continue to try to reach your partner who isn't ready to try again, then he may already have moved on to another love relationship. Ask him to be honest and tell you if he sees hope and wants to try with you again, or if has he moved on. Listen to his answer without becoming defensive. You're asking him to clearly tell you if the relationship is over for him. It takes you out

Try Coaching and Couples Counseling

of an ambivalent state and moves you towards healing and the reinvention of yourself. It may not be what you want to hear, but it's better than waiting and wondering if he wants to try again. In this way, however painful, being utterly honest with your partner is a gift.

If you're in coaching by yourself, you may find that you don't want the relationship anymore, and would rather move on. This happens frequently. Initially, the partner who cheated is not sure they want to reconcile, forcing you to hang on to hope. Eventually, you become tired of his lack of love and respect. He can find himself stuck between having you, his lover or his addiction, and wanting all of them. As he continues to show no effort, you decide independently that you're done with the relationship. When you feel second best, it's time to love yourself more and move on to healing, a new way to love, and a better life.

When couples are unsure whether or not they want the relationship, I ask them to allow six months to pass before deciding to leave it. We pick the specific date for them to make a choice. If, on the other hand, they both want to try, I suggest they each give 150% effort to their partner. They need to consciously work on being their best by changing bad habits; e.g., laziness, or a lack of love, affection or respect shown to their partner. If they both try as hard as is necessary, more often than not, their love does return better and stronger than ever. But both partners must dedicate themselves fully to the effort. One partner alone can't make the relationship work, nor convince the other to try. The partner with toxic issues may choose their addiction or an affair over you. This is when you must recognize that you deserve a healthier partner and that it's time to leave and love in a different way.

If you decide to move on, examine some of your childhood issues, relationship patterns, and mistakes you made in the relationship and learn about the toxic types you may be drawn to. Don't jump into dating another person exclusively. Wait until you feel healthy emotionally and ready to love again before dating at all. You must become consciously aware of the past issues you may be bringing into every relationship; be cautious enough not to repeat your mistakes and choose yet another toxic partner. Many of these patterns could exist as a result of past childhood traumatic experiences, so review the ACOA section of traumatic traits in Section One.

The emotional manipulator finds and preys on those who are people-pleasers, codependent, kind and giving or addicted to love. Therefore, it's important to know if you fit into any of these categories. If you believe that you do, get extensive counseling so that you can become aware of your patterns and learn stronger boundaries. The following chapters dig deeper into issues you may be bringing into your relationships.

Chapter 7

Are you Codependent?

Patience has it limits. Take it too far, and its cowardice.
– George Jackson

CODEPENDENT PERSONALITIES ARE particularly vulnerable to the emotional manipulator. They often have low self-esteem, and often deny their own needs. They can be obsessed with fixing or controlling another person's behavior, which tends to affect them in a negative way. The other person usually is a troubled, needy or dependent spouse, partner, parent, child, friend, sibling or someone with an addiction problem.

Codependents are people pleasers who feel the need to control their partner because their partner's life, and then their own, became unmanageable. They feel they're helping and think they know what's best for their partner. They believe that if they force things to happen their way, they can change or transform their toxic partner into a better person. It's important for you to realize that you can never fix or control someone's addiction, compulsive toxic behaviors, emotions, or choices.

The ability to control another is a delusion. People will change when they're ready and willing to change, and not a moment before no matter what you do or threaten to do. You can't love them enough, do enough, and take care of them enough to make them want to change. You must face your fears of losing your relationship and wanting your partner to change. I've seen women suffer for years with toxic, dysfunctional men. Remember, forgive once; after that, if another promise is broken, an addiction reoccurs, or another affair starts, love yourself more, and move on!

The dependent partner often rescues the addicted partner from responsibility by taking care of things, whether involving financial matters, family problems, his emotional well-being, or in making future decisions. When this happens, the codependent later feels used, unappreciated, and angry for not being shown any gratitude. This places the codependent in a parental role of mother or father, severely skews the balance in the relationship and erodes any sexual attraction to the irresponsible, addicted partner.

If your husband is addicted to alcohol, and you have to make sure he wakes up on time, call his boss and lie for him, find a new job for him if he's fired, worry if he can perform professionally when he does go to work, or you need to overcome public humiliation for his drunken actions, then in your eyes, he eventually will lose all sexual power as a man. You slowly feel the need to become the strong, responsible "man of the family," or like his mother, to take care of him and to survive day to day. Rescuing actions can involve the following:

Are you Codependent?

- Doing more work than your partner and picking up his slack; creating a business for him if he's unemployed, doing job searches when he should be looking for work himself.

- Paying more of the bills because of his lack of work; he complains of having no money but will spend on his addictive behavior.

- Trying to calm your partner's feelings, or constantly taking the blame when he's angry or unhappy to keep the peace. Or, you're the one constantly trying to fix and better the relationship while he makes no such effort.

- You constantly give more then you get – emotionally, financially, and with the family. You never feel any appreciation for the actions you take in these matters.

- You suffer due to his addictive actions. You need to "clean up his mess" and walk on eggshells until his next destructive episode occurs.

- Your partner doesn't ask or care about what you want or need. It's always all about him because he's narcissistic or his addiction is the most important thing to him.

- Speaking for or doing the thinking for your partner because the addiction keeps his thinking so cloudy and his anxiety so high that his choices are often bad, impulsive and harmful to the both of you. You feel that if you continue to rescue him, at least you won't suffer from his actions, words, bad choices or thoughts.

- You do things that aren't your responsibility to do and often ignore your own needs and wants, leading to anger and resentment because your partner constantly plays "the victim."

- You're left with these thoughts: "After all I've done for him, why would he treat me like this?"

The codependent woman is overly attached to her "love object" and his problems. She worries excessively about him, feels emotionally dependent upon him, and focuses all her time and energy on him. This behavior leaves her mentally, physically and emotionally exhausted. Intense focus on her man results in loss of her own power and purpose. She continues trying too hard to love, control, or properly react to her man and his actions. She obsesses about why he doesn't call, a certain thing he said or didn't say, a past situation, or if he's gone for hours, she'll become fixated on what he may be doing. These anxiety-ridden preoccupations can easily lead to illness and to a lack of personal control.

Enabling is a destructive form of helping, as summarized in Melody Beattie's book, *Codependent No More*. Anything done to cover the actions of an addicted partner, that helps to avoid consequences and responsibility, or makes it easy to continue drinking, drugging, pornography, gambling, over-eating, or other addictions, is considered enabling.

There is a cycle of rescuer, persecutor and victim. As you enable, he is able to escape the consequences of poor choices; you get angry over the lack of appreciation for your help and lack of time for yourself. You then become the victim when your partner is angry at you for pointing out his incompetency. You feel used, helpless, abused, depressed, anxious, neglected and outraged and take on a self-pity role in quiet despair.

Are you Codependent?

Whether enabling or rescuing, the codependent at some time in her past often was a victim of someone's emotional or physical abuse, abandonment, addiction, neglect, or other trauma. Most feel that rescuing is a good deed and that the desire to be kind and caring makes you a good, spiritual person. Caregiving offers confirmation of self-worth and positive character. Obviously, caring for people and giving of oneself are worthy character traits. However, doing for another who can do for himself won't help if he's already able, or simply too lazy or addicted to do things for himself. Actions done at the expense of your own wellbeing make you codependent.

If you find yourself doing too much for your man, or making yourself permanently available all the time for a distant, uninvolved man, so drastically different from whom he was when you began dating, just stop. Many women start to over-analyze what went wrong, wondering why he has become distant, doesn't call, text or return your messages. Maybe your man is preoccupied with work, a sick family member, a career change or other change in his life. Perhaps he's retreating into his "cave" to think about whether or not he wants this relationship. You need to remove yourself and allow him the space he needs to figure things out. He may have wanted you to be in an exclusive relationship, but then pulled back after you agreed. Be sure that you talk about an engagement before becoming exclusive, because exclusivity without a ring is for his benefit only. You're taking yourself off the dating market for this man so you want to be sure that you've discussed a plan for the future.

If the man you've been dating seems more distant now in comparison to his initial enthusiastic involvement, pull back and start dating others again. Why get angry or wait around for him to make plans? Tell him you're doing this because although you really care for him, he seems preoccupied and appears to need more time. If he does care for you, he'll step up immediately, or keep in contact while he handles whatever matter should be settled before he can devote time and energy to you.

At this point, start focusing on yourself and get busy in your own life. Don't concentrate all your energy on a man, obsessing over what he thinks, feels or does. Instead, do what you love that fulfills your passion in life. An outgoing energy, confidence and enthusiasm shown by living a purpose-filled life will serve as your best attraction factor.

Don't sit around remaining available all the time in case he calls, or wait for him to decide to plan a date or be attentive and get involved as he promised. Doing so gives him power over you and portrays your willingness to settle for whatever scraps he gives you. You need to be circular dating (seeing many) to feel confident you've found the best partner; and don't be intimately involved with any man until you're both excited to be exclusive. Knowing you're out dating other men, he will either be more inclined to give you the attention you want, or lose interest and totally drop the relationship. The latter would tell you he wasn't very serious in the first place, and you'll have other men to consider because you'll be dating. Circular dating boosts your options as well as your confidence. Don't chase the elusive or hot-then-cold man; he's emotionally unavailable and likely to be a commitment-phobe.

While dating others and living a full life that you love, a man will step up and pursue you – you won't have to do any work to win him over. When you stop being too nice, over focused, understanding, or scheduling your life around what he wants and needs, your confidence and self-respect will attract him to you. Ironically, *when he's less important to you, he starts wanting you more.*

Are you Codependent?

Women are often socialized to become caretakers; we're told that it makes us a desirable and loving wife and mother. Men often feel that they must be the breadwinner and caretaker of the family if they're a "good man" and "proper provider." But constant, obsessive helping could be a sign of low self-worth that allows others to take advantage of you. Take care of yourself; don't baby or mother him.

If you are codependent and your relationship ends suddenly, you're left in shock and disbelief over how someone you loved and helped so much could leave you without regard. You feel numb as you look at your personal life and your work and ask, "*Who* am I?" You spent so much time picking up the pieces and getting your partner's life back on track that you took no time for yourself. Now is the time to reinvent yourself and develop stronger boundaries by refusing to rescue anyone again or let someone save you. Be responsible for yourself, and let others be in charge of their own lives so that you'll no longer fall victim to needy people who become too dependent on you.

Remember, you have choices! Choose how you want to feel, behave, act and think. Stop reacting to the bad behavior of others and don't take their moods personally. Remove yourself from being controlled by your partner and don't try to correct his bad choices. If he can't get his life together over a certain period of time, then move on. You don't have to feel embarrassed over your spouse's inappropriate choices and behaviors; it's not a reflection of *who you are*. But realize his bad choices can destroy your financial security, your reputation as a couple, and remain toxic to all your personal areas of success. The sooner you leave, the faster you gain back all that is dear to you.

You need to totally detach and separate from the addictive person to see if he wants to change for his own sake. Some men will immediately take action; others may never stop their compulsive behaviors and destructive acts. Leave them alone, give up and move on to find healthier love. The important part is to set yourself free from trying to help them and start taking care of yourself. Shift your focus onto yourself and the life you want and deserve. You'll be amazed at what you can accomplish by no longer picking up the pieces of a toxic partner's life.

If he has a compulsive addiction, he may say he loves you, but he neither loves you nor respects your needs enough to stop. You *can* choose to stop suffering from his actions. Save yourself, detach from your love object, and move on with your self-esteem and personal power intact. You'll now have the time, peace of mind and positive energy to focus on your own life for a change!

# Chapter 8

Are You a Love Addict?

"I just can't Stop Loving You…
My Life just ain't worth living, if I can't be with you."
– Michael Jackson, duet with Siedah Garrett (1988)

The toxic emotional cycle of the coaddicted relationship is a dependent relationship with your part being either a love addict or an avoidance addict (a commitment-phobe). In her book, *Facing Love Addiction,* Pia Mellody describes the love addict as being focused on the partner and the relationship while the avoidance addict tries to evade intimate connection by engaging in some addiction. This coaddicted relationship has extreme highs and lows.

The love addict experiences compulsive and obsessive thinking, feelings and behaviors and gives her partner too much love, time, and attention while placing a higher value on her partner than herself. She becomes dependent on her partner and the need to please him.

Because she lives with high values, she places unrealistic expectations for unconditional love onto her partner. When he lets her down, she often becomes enraged, suffers extreme disappointment and fear of abandonment. This fear could derive from a lack of nurturing love or some form of childhood abandonment, which can result in the inability to sustain an intimate, healthy relationship.

Very often, she panics and sabotages the relationship to create distance when it becomes too close. The love addict craves intimacy but fears it, and is unable to tolerate a healthy closeness. She will unconsciously choose a partner who is incapable of normal intimacy. The expectations imposed on her partners to love and care for her in the way she always had dreamed becomes overwhelming to the avoidant. The love addict repeatedly feels disappointment because no one can ever satisfy her irrational, unconditional and insatiable longing to be loved.

Like a magnet, the love addict is fiercely attracted to an avoidant, who tends to escape intimacy through addictions to alcohol, work, pornography, or sexual affairs. These addictions often become unmanageable, so the Love Addict often ends up taking care of the Avoidant, which makes her resentful and angry.

She must come to realize her powerlessness in trying to stop the addiction or change her partner "for the better." Her obsessive attempts to control her man results in personal neglect and unmanageability. What initially felt so great and loving has become a compulsion to reconnect with her aloof and emotionally distanced love object. At this point, her desire to be loved, cared for, and safe isn't satisfied. However, she can't leave the relationship because of the intensity of her love and a fear of abandonment. These influences destroy her willpower, consuming her life as she becomes further controlled by obsessive thinking about, desires to talk to, touch, be near and feel loved again by her previously cherished partner.

The love addict searches for someone she can feel safe with and will bond with a partner she believes will fill her pit of loneliness and feelings of inadequacy. She places this imaginary power onto her expectations and onto a delusional image of her partner to make herself feel whole and happy.

The male love addict looks for the super-nurturing woman who ultimately can never love him enough. Unrealistically high expectations are based in delusion and appear as inordinately needy and greedy demands for the woman's constant love and attention. She can never give him enough and when she starts to feel suffocated, she'll pull away to gain some distance. The man then searches outside the relationship to try to satisfy his constant need for admiration, affection and attention. This is a toxic, destructive, vicious cycle.

The Love Addiction Cycle

Here below are signs you may be a love addict wrapped in an addictive cycle with an avoidant:

1. You are attracted to the power, confidence and charm of the avoidance addict.

2. You romanticize and idolize him into being the "perfect spouse," like the prince in the Cinderella fantasy, and you're in denial when his faults or deceptions are uncovered. You fell in love with his potential or the fantasy, refusing to see the real person.

3. The relationship is usually a whirlwind, romantic and passionate fling, with both partners constantly showing

affection and adoration for the other. This allows you to feel valued, loved and complete, relieving you of your childhood abandonment. But if he starts falling in love with you, he'll start to pull away.

4. When the commitment-phobe avoidant distances himself, you ignore the truth and explain away the times he wasn't there for you. You overlook obvious clues that he's sabotaging the relationship while you make excuses, deny or forgive the bad behaviors.

5. Invariably, a specific event or the avoidant partner's leaving occurs, forcing awareness of your present reality. You realize that you had fantasized about your partner's real character and that your expectations of him were illusions. You spiral uncontrollably when you realize that someone or something else is more important to your partner than you and the relationship.

6. This leads to acute fear, insecurity, anger, and intense emotional pain; you then withdraw from everything over the loss of your man and the imagined love relationship you thought was so perfect.

7. You're forced to see your partner and his bad choices and behavior for what they really are. This leads to compulsive, obsessive thoughts on how to get him back. You may engage in destructive, controlling actions to relieve your emotional void (sexually acting out, overeating or drinking).

8. Your anger leads to desire for punishment or getting even with the partner who has caused such deep pain by breaking all the promises he couldn't or wouldn't fulfill.

9. Emotional resistance to facing delusions created about your "perfect partner" is incredibly strong.

10. You want to return to your love object and regain the relationship. When he ignores your attempts, you're exposed to more rejection, lack of respect and low self-esteem. As in childhood, your coping endeavors are dysfunctional in an abusive and self-defeating way and you become even sicker and more depressed with emotional pain.

An addiction is created to remove an intolerable reality in one's life. The love addict would rather have the pain of a dysfunctional relationship than the horrible reality of emptiness, loneliness and abandonment. The love addict's compulsion lies in prompting their love object to tell them they're loved, which involves having obsessive thoughts about their partner. She constantly desires emotional and physical contact and any sort of communication with him. She longs for him "to rescue and take care of me" even though she often can take care of herself quite well. Unconsciously, she tries to satisfy the lack of nurturing from her childhood.

Coming to terms with an addiction begins with the realization that the first step to recovery is to admit the facts and commit to endure the withdrawal from your love object.

Here are some helpful steps through the process:

1. Stop all acting-out behaviors, such as drinking to access, spending, overeating or having sex with inappropriate partners. Take a break from sexual intimacy altogether until you feel emotionally stable.

2. Get support from a counselor and a few close friends who knew of your relationship. Call them when you have the

urge to call him. Keep your mind busy by reading, starting a hobby, taking a course or learning something new to help take your mind off of him.

3. Start reinventing yourself by setting new daily, weekly, monthly and six-month goals. Get busy doing things you gave up long before to cater to him. Eat healthily, exercise and get eight hours of sleep. Take time to rebuild your self-esteem, confidence and attraction levels. Start a new and better relationship with yourself. Read my book, *Live Beyond Your Dreams – from Fear and Doubt to Personal Power, Purpose and Success* to rebuild self-esteem during this difficult transition.

4. Monitor your self-talk, and be sure to keep comments to yourself positive and motivated toward change. Tell yourself you deserve a healthy partner who will commit fully to a loving, balanced, intimate relationship.

5. Pray for personal power and peace. Meditate every morning for fifteen to twenty minutes to calm your nerves and anxiety levels. Start attending religious or spiritual services again. Read motivational, faith-based books that make you feel joy, peace and inspiration.

6. Stop chasing the unresponsive, aloof person who enjoys having control when he rejects you. Instead, call, text, or go out with friends, or try online dating sites to meet new, male friends. With your relationship coach, clearly define the requirements you want in a partner, then write your profile to match that. When alone, read up on how to have a healthy mind-set and relationship.

The commitment-phobe or avoidance addict was described earlier, but let's review. They have a fear of intimacy and close relationships because they hate feeling controlled. Often a loving, long-term, quality relationship explodes if the avoidance addict gets married. Their fear reaction stems from childhood experiences of being sexually, physically, verbally or emotionally abused and/or having an overly protective, strict, and authoritarian parent. This child often has an enmeshed relationship with one parent (usually the abused parent in an alcoholic family). The feelings of being controlled or enmeshed (or both) are what the person runs away from, even though another part of him craves love and connection.

The Avoidance Addict has the following relationship pattern:

1. He is attracted to the neediness and weakness of the love addict.

2. He makes connection through seduction that makes him feel powerful and confident.

3. He feels "high" from the love and attention received from the love addict, but eventually her neediness makes him feel controlled and suffocated.

4. He does something impulsive to sabotage the relationship and to distance himself from the love addict; for example, he'll suddenly leave the relationship or begin an affair. The rush and secret of an affair gives him a sense of power.

5. He returns out of guilt or fear of abandonment and misses the extreme attention, love and passion that the love addict provided. He knows that his partner truly loves him.

He becomes confused and experiences a sense of high anxiety and terror from *what he feels,* not from what you're doing. It's not what you say to him, but *what he is thinking* that wreaks havoc in your relationship.

What makes him run away is the torturous and disillusioned way in which he looks at love and your relationship. There is no way to protect yourself or stop his running away, or understand why he does what he does when he actually does love you. This man is afraid of what love represents – a commitment to one person *forever.* You'll never be able to love him enough, be kind enough, more giving, attractive, sexy or more sympathetic. *It isn't about you; it's about his inability to love you in a healthy, committed way.* Many men have come to fear a confident, strong, and independent woman if they feel unworthy, or lack a healthy ego.

If you're the one with avoidance issues, you can lessen your anxiety by learning the difference between a healthy, loving, intimate relationship and enmeshment (being overly connected). You can learn healthy boundaries and prevention from enmeshment by others by taking personal responsibility and communicating your needs. You'll come to understand that nourishing intimacy is enjoyable and enhances your life.

Childhood experiences of abandonment or enmeshment need not control your life or continue to ruin your future relationships. An avoidance addict or love addict can stop persistent patterns with intensive counseling help and daily conscious awareness. Being consciously aware of choosing not to manipulate or attack your partner and to slow the dating process and not emotionally chase a new prospect can help eliminate fearful automatic and habitual reactions. Refusing to jump into panic, anxiety and pain in response to your partner's actions is a part of healing the coaddictive relationship.

It takes courage, deep spiritual faith, a strong mental mindset and the focused energy that prayer and meditation can bring. It's time to face your relationship reality and move forward from the toxic, aloof and emotionally empty partner you love. Explore childhood issues you may have that keep you stuck in painful relationships.

Recognize the symptoms of codependency, love addiction or avoidance that you may have and read specific books on these subjects. Ask forgiveness for your mistakes in the relationship dysfunction and breakup, then thank your partner for the time you had together. Love yourself more and move on to a place of healing.

Section Three

Save Yourself – The Path to Healing

Every moment that you spend upset, in despair, in anguish, angry or hurt because of the behavior of anybody else is a moment in which you've given up control of your life.
– Dr. Wayne W. Dyer

Chapter 9

Dealing with the Lost Dreams, Anger and Pain

Anger will never disappear as long as thoughts of resentment are cherished in the mind. Anger will disappear just as soon as thoughts of resentment are forgotten. – Buddha

---

STUDIES SHOW THAT 85% of relationships fail. The most traumatic stage of a breakup occurs when physical separation has taken place, by one or both partners deciding to leave. This stage can be marked by shock, disbelief, intense loneliness, anxiety, fear of the future, and rapid mood swings from depression to a sense of relief, peace and freedom. Some common friends are lost in the process and you have to explain the separation to family, friends, coworkers and acquaintances throughout your community. This makes it difficult to escape from being reminded about your partner and the relationship.

The romantic dreams created for the perfect future life together were shattered in an instant when you uncovered your partner's secret, when he left you, or when you mutually broke up. You're now obliged to face the painful reality that your partner is nowhere near the perfect person you fantasized him or her to be. Those prone to being love addicts tend to fall in love *with an idea of who their partner is*, rather than the real person. Sometimes referred to as a "soul-mate," you felt that you had finally found the perfect person who made you feel safe, loved and whole. The notion of the soul-mate and romantic, passionate chemistry is fed into our American culture through movies, music, and romance novels. This idea is neither emphasized nor expected in most other cultures.

The romanticized relationship often starts with a whirlwind courtship and sexual passion, where childhood fantasies of the perfect partner (the knight in shining armor for a woman, or the super-woman providing perfect love for a man) all begins. You're actually falling in love with the expectation of what you feel the ideal relationship should be. You become unconsciously determined to see this romantic relationship come to fruition. You try to get your partner to do and be everything that matches your life-long fantasy. These romantic fantasies were used in your childhood to help you escape the pain of abandonment, lack of love and feelings of insecurity. When your partner "lets you down," you're left with anger, pain and frustration.

Although both love and avoidance addicts have a charming, sensitive, fun and outgoing side to their personalities, the sudden, super-intense sexual and romantic connection is what attracts these two types. This creates the high in their relationship and it eventually must grow into a comfortable friendship and coexistence, or more likely, becomes over-enmeshed by the love addict, which causes the love avoidant to sabotage the relationship and run.

Dealing with the Lost Dreams, Anger and Pain

During the romantic high, you both build a dream-like ideal future, which you both come to believe will bring you great joy. For a while, this fantasy feeds both the needs of the love addict and avoidant. One day your world seems perfect, and the next day there is sudden disillusionment when you discover that the avoidant had been cheating in an affair, or has had an addiction for years without your knowledge. Everything you believed to be true about your partner, and everything you dreamed your relationship to be, has been a lie. As the love addict, you feel angry, deceived, and hate the lies; but you're still madly in love and emotionally connected to the partner who hurt you so badly.

The overwhelming emotional pain of lost dreams feels excruciating and can plummet you into a deep, numbing depression. It's at this time that you must get counseling and call on all your support systems for help. You may need an anti-depressant and/or sleep medication to help you through the early period of your breakup. Sleep is difficult as thoughts of your partner become obsessive and constant, like a form of systematic torture. You might fall asleep early due to exhaustion, but often will awake around 3:00 a.m. and stay awake for hours with disturbing thoughts, anxiety, and fears about the future.

Life as you knew it is gone. Now is the time to heal and reinvent yourself and make your life better than ever. With daily goals, it will take time and effort but you'll have started on a path toward changing your life despite feeling that you're without energy or motivation. With faith and coaching, your life can quickly turn around to be positive and exciting again.

Tony Robbins' four-day seminar program, *Unleash the Power Within,* describes a Triad for Meaning: three critical elements, practiced in combination, to help you determine and control your emotional state. These allied strengths will lead you to face your fears and free you to strive for excellence and success.

1. Physiology: How you use your body movements, breath, posture and energy.

2. Focus: Your emotions are influenced by the focus of your attention. Energy will follow the direction of your feelings. Guide your focus towards what you want.

3. Language: Modify your words to produce a positive and energizing emotional state. Applying language patterns to situations can instill new meaning into how you manage your experiences.

Most people cling to problems that serve them in some way. For example, Tony shows valuable and effective examples of people claiming to feel depressed, yet in an instant, can empower themselves to switch to feelings of elation. As a therapist, I realize there frequently is an underlying biological component in depression; however, learning these techniques can often draw a person out of a negative emotional state if there's an overriding desire to be free of it. For the purpose of this illustration, ask yourself, if you currently feel depressed, whether the situation serves you because you can solicit empathy or attention from others. Does it allow you to work less and have others provide for you? With honest recognition of the advantages your depression might enable, and acknowledgment of the fear of letting go (depression is often a result of childhood trauma), you can alter old behaviors and live a life full of unlimited personal power and happiness.

Tony teaches that people can do anything when they focus on personal control and move toward the most beneficial emotional and physiological states. I had the privilege of learning about emotional and intellectual mind control throughout his presentation. All of us in attendance learned to prepare ourselves to walk on 2200° red-hot coals over a 12-foot path, in bare feet. Consciously, no one possesses enough courage to walk on hot coals or think they wouldn't burn their feet. I love to dance and this was a real fear for me; however, though the coals stayed fiery hot, I was able to guide myself into the emotional and physiological states that I needed to succeed.

"Now make your move!" a voice shouted at me. I mentally and physically psyched myself up, closed my eyes and shouted, "YES!" three times. I pumped my arms with fisted hands and clearly envisioned myself succeeding. Then I bravely walked "the path of destiny," while repeating the words, "cool moss," aloud. After celebrating my accomplishment, I was astounded by how soft and cool the coals had felt. There were no blisters on my feet, or soreness of any kind. Laughing in amazement, I thought of how fast I always run to get to the cooler section of sand at the beach in the summer. But don't try running over burning coals yourself! Tony takes his attendees through 12-hour days, which are filled with experiential education on exactly how to break through fear and turn it into personal power. Everyone should attend a Tony Robbins seminar at least once – and leave on an emotional high, knowing you can face and eliminate your fears, and do anything you choose. I'm now thrilled to be called a "Firewalker!"

Through life and relationship coaching, many singles discover that they unconsciously hold back from having love in their life due to the fear of being hurt, feeling unworthy, or having been abandoned. Couples come to realize that they're sabotaging their marriages by not candidly discussing their needs with their partners. Instead, they search for happiness outside of marriage, or they emotionally shut down in fear of feeling abused, or of losing the relationship even if it's a toxic one. Extraordinarily good life experiences, such as being in love and having a fulfilling, passionate relationship, requires the risk of facing your fears boldly and eliminating them. Uncompromising honesty with yourself and your partner, along with learning alternative behaviors from your Coach, *can* bring dramatically positive changes into all areas of your life.

So say YES! to a fabulous life! Say YES! to falling in love again, say YES! to dedicating yourself to a healthy lifestyle and relationship, say YES! to living in the "now." Set and complete daily, weekly, monthly and yearly goals. Celebrate all your glory when you reach those goals! In my book, *Live Beyond Your Dreams – from Fear and Doubt to Personal Power, Purpose and Success,* the "Watch Me! Mind-set" technique is described, which is very similar to Tony's philosophy in many ways. We teach that with dedication to daily motivational and inspirational reading, fulfillment of defined goals, inclusion of meditation or prayer to focus on life desires (and believing that you can achieve them), giving to others, and empowering yourself by eliminating faulty patterns and belief systems, you *will* feel tremendous bliss and gratitude while living a life and having a love that is beyond your dreams!

Chapter 10

How to Move On

*Destiny is not a matter of chance.
It is a matter of choice.* – William Jennings Bryan

YOU DO HAVE A CHOICE to love in a different way. Teachings from Buddhism say that relationships are brought into our life to teach us something. However, unless you see and understand the childhood patterns that you bring into relationships, you're bound to repeat the same mistakes. Part of healing is taking the time to reflect on what good you brought into the relationship, what past issues or insecurities caused problems, and what you can do better the next time. Realize that your partner had both good and bad qualities and past issues they also brought into the relationship.

Breaking up is hard to do, and it's a process rather than a single event. You probably can recall the beginning of the spiral that led to the relationship ending. Had there been an affair, an addiction, a breach of trust, toxic anger, chronic unemployment, selfishness or a lack of responsibility? As long as it took to reach the final physical departure, it will take as long, if not longer, for him to be gone from your heart, mind and soul.

Usually, the first stage after a breakup is shock, especially if he left you without informing you (the ultimate cowardice). The next stage could be anger or depression or a combination of both. You may even feel some relief, knowing that you no longer will endure his rages, mistakes, addictions, lame lies and excuses. You'll feel anger at his apparent escape from any responsibility after he leaves you to carry on with his destructive habits. While relieved in part, you'll also mourn the loss of your dreams, the death of your relationship and severe bruising of your self-esteem. He lacked integrity and fled, leaving you to explain it all to everyone, his disappearance an admission that he really screwed up and couldn't face your parents, friends, children, or the community.

You may have decided to leave him because of his addiction or toxic behaviors, or for not living up to his promises. The lifestyle you were to share together slowly degenerated as he moved through life "treading water" while you worked twice as hard to make up for his slack. Your dedication to working hard never changed, but his did, making you resentful, stressed, exhausted and angry. You want and deserve more in life as well as a partner who feels the same way, not a child you need to take care of.

During this time, you'll feel emotions that are completely normal: shock, anger, denial, depression, rage, lots of crying at the drop of a hat, pain, planning (solutions to get back together), missing him, and unbearable loneliness. You will not want to go out into the community to "explain what happened" or answer the question, "Where's So-and-So?" when people are so used to seeing you two together. It will be difficult, or impossible, to go to your regular spots, or listen to the music you both once loved and danced to. There will be times when you hate him and wish him dead, love him and want him back, or bargain with him to try again because you'll have weak moments when you think things weren't so bad. The torment of your emotional pendulum is natural and exhausting.

Through the first stage of loss, anger and sadness, I recommend you get busy and clean your environment. Cleaning is a feng shui concept that brings about peace and calm, something you desperately need right now. Cleanse the entire house, throw out anything that belongs to him, empty the garage and attic, wipe down the floors and kitchen cabinets, and clean out the closets. Once you remove all the clutter and anything you no longer want or use, slowly paint or redecorate your home exactly how you want it, starting with new sheets and a beautiful, luxurious bedspread. An excellent guideline for tossing things is to get rid of everything you haven't used in a year – you probably don't need it. You actually may consider a move, so preparing the house now is a good idea. It's still best, though, to stay put for at least a year, and make no quick personal or financial decisions. Realistically, it may be necessary financially to sell your home and downsize your living space. If you decide to stay in your home, consider painting, replacing or rearranging furniture, and purchasing a few new accessory pieces. Be careful not to overspend and get into debt; just purchase a few items that will make you feel renewed.

Some additional benefits of feng shui:

1. It can improve balance in life.

2. It encourages you to think creatively.

3. It helps you get "unstuck" from your current situation, allowing you to think clearly about the new life you desire.

4. It is said that good feng shui can help increase personal wealth.

5. It helps create harmonious relationships with others.

Try learning more about this and other holistic healing methods.

You may find your eating habits drastically changed. Many people admit not being able to eat for days, and others overeat. Be careful to do neither in extreme. If you don't have much of an appetite, eat at least some proteins and healthy foods throughout the day. If you tend to overeat, get motivated to start a healthier eating plan and visit the gym. Looking and feeling sexy again is the best form of personal revenge (but do this for you, not to win him back!).

Eat healthy food. Try what I call "God's Foods Diet": everything that is provided for you on this earth from God is what you should eat. That includes fruits, nuts, steamed fresh vegetables, fish, or lower-level animal meat such as turkey or chicken. Stay away from pasta, white bread, sugar, dairy, large animal red meats (shown to be high in fats and difficult to digest), or man-made or manufactured packaged goods.

For breakfast, have a protein shake with almond or coconut milk, fresh berries, cinnamon, and a spoonful of fiber. At lunch, consider eating two of the following choices: Greek yogurt, avocado, a hard-boiled egg, or fresh green salad with natural nuts, cranberry and light dressing. Throughout the day, drink hot green tea with lemon and unsweetened cranberry juice, or water with lemon. For dinner, eat fish, chicken or turkey with steamed vegetables and a yam. Cook with extra virgin olive oil. Try to eat your dinner before 5:00 p.m., so that your food fully digests by bedtime. Eating later often causes excess pounds. Snacks can include apple slices with low fat peanut butter, or fresh popped air popcorn (or use olive oil). You can often lose a pound a day eating a diet of high protein, steamed vegetables and natural foods. Avoid "whites" including sugar, rice, potatoes and flour.

Start dressing well and present yourself to the world with pride. Now that you're single, you'll soon be available to date (after you heal). Consider a new haircut, color or style; and donate all the clothes you haven't worn, that are out of shape or style, or that you just don't like. The key is to *simplify your life* as much as possible.

The reason I advise all this cleaning is so that you can dispel your hostile energy in as healthy a way as possible. Listen to upbeat music or a motivational recording while doing this task. Exercising or cleaning your whole house will bring fabulous results that you'll love, and at the same time, help get rid of obsessive thoughts and anger. At the end of the day, you should feel exhausted enough to fall asleep.

When going through the aftermath of a shock or sudden breakup, you may often fall asleep only to wake up in the middle of the night with thoughts that keep you awake for hours. In the beginning, a sleeping aid might help but don't use medication for an extended period; try to stop after one or two weeks. A more natural sleep aid is melatonin (found in the vitamin section of your drugstore or health-supplement shop). Take one pill two hours before you want to be asleep. Try saying a prayer as you lay down in bed – for peace and forgiveness, and for you to have a new, healthy love come into your life.

Know that your emotions will go up and down, and the stress will make you feel tired and forgetful. Keeping busy will not only help you frame the time you need to think and dispel your anger, but also will help you set new goals. Your anger can actually push you to excel and create the new life you've always wanted. He's no longer there to tell you that "you can't," or "you can't afford it," or that he "doesn't want you to." So use anger constructively now; let it push you toward your best personal success. Living well is the best revenge! Hate can destroy you if you don't find some good from the bad and use it in a positive, constructive way. It can cause overpowering stress and illness for you and your children. Focus instead on the new life you're creating now. As you cleanse, think about all the blessings you *do* have in life. Be grateful that the toxic, emotional manipulator is out of your life. You've been given an open space for new, caring and loving people to enter your life.

While you're busy cleaning, organizing, and reading motivational and inspirational books, don't isolate yourself. Tell your friends and support system what has happened; don't suffer alone or in silence. Get out to your counselor or to spiritual services, and call a few friends that you know will be supportive. I strongly suggest that you don't date for some time because you'll automatically make comparisons with each new date and more often than not will show disappointment and a negative attitude. Go out with friends instead and enjoy yourself. Plan several ladies' nights out, or consider traveling somewhere beautiful and fun with a good friend.

Stay away from negative people or those not sympathetic to you and your pain. This could possibly include family members or siblings. Be careful not to overload your friends with your pain or with unending stories, as they have their own lives and struggles. Ask about their lives, and share talking time equally with them. Be sure to ask them to be confidential with what you share, as you're still figuring out your own path.

How to Move On

Consider writing out your feelings and sparing your friends from all your obsessive thoughts. Writing is a liberating therapy, so keep a journal or write a book that will inspire or help others. Remember to include your daily blessings! This will help your thoughts move in a more positive direction. Reach out to friends from high school or college through Facebook and get to know each other again. Go to see comedy shows or funny movies – it will feel great to laugh again!

Meditate or pray daily, starting with an "attitude of gratitude" by giving thanks to God for all your life's blessings. Then ask God for what you want, some of which might be peace, energy, a sense of calm in the face of anxiety, stress, or depression, and finally, for healthy love to enter into your life. The latter could appear through several means; female and male friends, mentors, children, and possible future love partners. Don't fixate on falling in love with someone exclusively. Instead, tell potential suitors that you're "in dating mode and not looking for a serious relationship right now." Go out and have fun, smile and laugh a lot. Men love women with positive energy! Get to know these men slowly, and don't sleep around or you'll be known as a player, or worse. Keeping things honest, light, fun and friendly will transform you into a man magnet. With so many choices, your confidence will soar! With time, one special man should emerge who'll let you know he would like to date you exclusively. At that point, you have all the knowledge you need to feel confident that he is a good match for you.

If your ex had an addiction, reach out to the Alanon (alcohol), Naranon (drug/opiates), Gamanon (gambling), SA (sexual addictions) and domestic violence against women support groups. It helps greatly to be around others who have suffered as you have with an addicted spouse. Be open to making new friends, but be cautious not to continue in negativity or ex-bashing, both of which need to end.

Don't attempt to hurt yourself or impose your anger on all men. One man caused you pain, not all of them. Be careful not to spiral and see your whole life as a failure. Don't give away personal power to a toxic mate who isn't worth the effort. Get strong for you and your kids – they need you! If you're feeling suicidal, call 911 and go to your local emergency room for a medication evaluation and a chance to speak with a crisis counselor. Empower yourself to get the help you need. It's OK if you need medication to help you get through the initial pain until you feel more stable. That's what it's made for and you've been through a traumatic episode. Be gentle with yourself during this time of transition.

In the second phase of healing, you may feel ready to date or choose to enter into a temporary, flirtatious romance. This could mean choosing a safe lover who makes you feel sexually vibrant. Just be sure that you both understand that this is a friends-with-benefits or sexual romance. Don't look to this person to be a boyfriend or exclusive mate, and be sure to practice safe sex! This arrangement should be temporary and mutually acceptable; it's clearly not for a long-term, exclusive love relationship. If you choose to have a sexual lover, do so after your anger has dissolved. Remember that this arrangement isn't for everyone. A woman needs to be strong and confident to handle this type of arrangement so that no one gets hurt.

Keep your head clear so that you can move forward with your new goals. This romance will reinforce your physical attraction and sexuality and prove that your ex didn't destroy your feminine power! Make sure that enough time has passed and that you've healed from the breakup. Don't risk emotional pain for either one of you. This can be a fun and fabulous break from the duties that come with a steady relationship. Call your own shots as to when and where you'll see your new friend. Keep it light and infrequent enough so that you feel no obligation during the time that you're still sorting out your new life. Make it quite clear to this man that you're not looking for exclusivity.

Treat yourself to a weekly massage to rid your body of stress toxins. Get a manicure and pedicure and any other spa treatments for a special reward to yourself. Consider getting a treatment to fill in your smile lines or forehead wrinkles. Some ladies go for a tummy tuck or breast implants after a breakup. Do whatever it takes to make you look and feel fabulous. Have no guilt about any of these things but *don't rush into anything impulsively* and do investigate all treatment choices to ensure their safety. It's YOUR life now and you have the freedom to do what you want without asking anyone's permission! Be absolutely certain you're doing these things *for you* and not to win back your ex. Take time with these decisions and choose any or all of these options when you feel emotionally settled. Discuss all major options with your therapist and get at least three opinions on any surgical decision.

When cleaning out things, be sure to throw away all the useless love letters and token gifts he gave you if they're causing you heartache. This lets out old memories and toxic love energy and allows a new path for a superior love into your life. Some women feel fine saving items as a fond memory of the love once shared, and these things can even help in finding forgiveness. For starters, box up the letters and cards and put them away in an attic or someplace where you won't see them daily. You could give old family photos to your children to keep for memories. Whatever you choose to do with mementos, keep the jewelry – you deserved every piece of it! Or get several bids and sell it for the best price to put toward something you really want.

Catch up on all your medical appointments, especially if you're married and may lose your health insurance. Get all your prescriptions filled right up to the date of your divorce. Go to www.esurance.com to find a new and cheaper cost plan that may be better than your COBRA offering (it usually will be).

Do creative things. Write, journal, paint, go to cooking school, dance class, learn a musical instrument, take up photography, or go to a craft class. Creative arts can make you feel calm and you'll enjoy the process as well as your finished product.

Decide to take a period of time to work very hard or to take on an extra job (six months to a year) while you heal and catch up financially. This is best done during the cold, dark winter months if you live in a seasonal climate. Save more free time for the warmer, sunnier months so that you can be outside enjoying yourself.

You may want to adopt a puppy or kitten, plant a new garden, volunteer for a children's organization, or connect with nature and other living things. Eat healthy foods, take vitamins, get regular exercise, and lose any extra weight. Do whatever it takes to feel and look fabulous!

Know that your pain will eventually go away; the busier you stay with new goals, plans, and dreams, the better you'll feel as time passes. After several months to one year, the pain of your lost relationship will subside, and you'll have a gorgeous new home, feel great about your self-esteem and your many new accomplishments!

Remember, this relationship is merely a small part of your life journey. You'll get to a point where you can look back on the painful relationship with some fond memories and minimal regret, as well as a learning experience. You'll grow stronger and finally say, "Look at ME now!" If, directly after the breakup, you did set your daily, weekly and monthly goals to reinvent and love yourself more, you'll be amazed at how far you've come in one or two years' time. You'll know that breaking free from a toxic relationship was the best move you ever made!

By the end of year one, it's important to forgive the toxic person and bless the relationship that had existed. Why? It's important to find the good in the bad, and realize that the breakup may be the very incident that directs you to finding your personal greatness. The relationship may open you to feeling more love and compassion for others in pain. You also will have learned valuable lessons about relationship boundaries and now have the wisdom to recognize dysfunctional personality types before you get emotionally involved.

By becoming so focused on your new life, dreams and goals, you may find that you've radically changed your life for the better. You may have become more peaceful, successful, talented, creative, outgoing, confident, and financially stable. Moving on from your toxic relationship is your opportunity to shine! And isn't that a fabulous blessing?

Chapter 11

Building Support Systems

The greatest discovery of my generation is that human beings can alter their lives by altering their attitudes. – William James

---

When a toxic relationship ends, the love addict or codependent feels decimated when the future they dreamed of is lost. After investing so much time in love and adoration of the toxic partner, there often isn't a strong support system in place for the love addict to turn to. Instead, thought patterns usually involve obsessive planning to get the partner back. Anger aimed at the deeds, lies, cheating or addiction of the avoidant partner becomes all consuming. Often the love addict wants to forget boundaries and forgive the partner, or do anything to get him back. Or, the opposite occurs and the love addict is obsessed with "getting even" or ruining the partner's life.

It's imperative to reach out to supportive family members and good friends. If you lost special friends with this relationship, try calling them, apologizing and reactivating your friendship. Ask for their help, and apologize for not having been a very good friend since your relationship began. Tell them that you'd like to be able to call them more often; ask them to go out with you. Be careful not to make the conversation all about you and your partner and ask about them. To make a good friend, you have to be one.

Start journaling to help process the pain and present your thoughts to your therapist. Meet weekly as this is an important support system to help with your growth and healing. Read as much as you can on the topic of toxic relationships, highlighting the important facts in the book as you may need to read them several times to understand personality types. Discuss openly and candidly with your therapist what you personally may be dealing with from your past. You can't change what you don't understand. Knowing your pattern of choice in men is imperative to loving a healthy partner in the future. Many helpful books are recommended in the back section of this volume to help you continue your education.

If you're married, seek the advice of an Attorney to know and understand your options. You may need to start preparing yourself for a divorce or seek to protect yourself and your financial assets.

Go out to where other singles go; usually Friday night is better than Saturday to meet single people. Find new interests that will attract people of your age. Take cooking or ballroom-dance classes, get a new hobby, join a volunteer organization, go to the gym or join a new exercise class. All these are viable ways to meet other singles and make new friends. Register for a college course to challenge yourself intellectually, or start a new business. Set goals that you're determined to meet using the *"Watch Me!"* mind-set.

Don't be tempted to get into a new relationship right away. With the acute loneliness you may feel following your breakup, another relationship can seem very attractive. Don't rush into a full-time relationship or enter a sexual liaison just to "get back" at your partner. This is an unhealthy step for you and for the person you're using to bandage your anger or jealousy. Instead, get together with friends, and meet healthy people through personal introductions. It's also important that you learn to be by yourself, focus on you, and make new personal goals. You need to learn about healthy relationships, how to get beyond your anger, and to settle your divorce, if you were married. Focus on your children's needs since they too have been through a traumatic loss after a breakup or divorce. Act for yourself and your children and not your ex-partner.

Another excellent support source is a place of worship. Go back to church, temple, or synagogue and start praying or meditating again. Meditation has been proven to quiet the mind and ease stress and anxiety. Create new daily and weekly routines including a Friday night out with friends and a fun adventure day with your children. This creates wonderful, new memories with your kids and a special bonding that will last a lifetime. Routines like this help you feel balanced and give you much to look forward to.

Build friendships with those you date, and take a long time to get sexually involved. If someone is willing to wait for you until you're ready (after at least three months or twelve to fifteen dates); then he's usually serious about you and not sexually obsessed or toxic. After your trust has been broken, you need time to heal and regain the ability to trust someone new again. Take your time. Make your motto the same as Patti Stanger's from *The Millionaire Matchmaker* TV show, "no sex without monogamy" while seriously searching for a life partner. The last thing you need is more rejection – a man having sex with you and then not calling (using you), or setting yourself up for more pain. Realize that you'll probably need at least six to nine months to process your anger (with daily practice in moving toward peace and forgiveness) so that you can meet a healthy, loving partner as well as be one for someone else.

With time and spiritual study, you'll feel more confident and full of positive energy, attracting love to you without even trying. Forgiveness lets you heal and return to a better, healthier self; you will radiate attraction and your inner light when you're truly ready to be in love again.

Chapter 12

Use the "Watch Me!" Mind-set for Change

Most people see what is, and never see what can be. – Albert Einstein

My first book, *Watch Me! The Bold New Motivational Attitude for Personal Success* (2006), and the 2013 release, *Live Beyond Your Dreams – from Fear and Doubt to Personal Power, Purpose and Success,* both teach how to use the *"Watch Me!"* mind-set for personal change and growth during a difficult transition, or in a time of emotional pain and loss. A motivational and inspirational mind-set is essential to learn because your thoughts will either help you grow and heal or keep you wedged between sadness and pain.

The *Live Beyond Your Dreams* book talks about the importance of a personal-life and work balance, spiritual practice, living a purpose-filled life by using the five Ds: Desire, determination, dedication, devotion and dare to dream; goal setting to reach your dreams, learning from life's lessons to pluck the good from the bad, and finding motivation for change.

All these elements are critical to get you through the difficult transition from your addictive or toxic love relationship to a place of personal power, peace, purpose and success. Both those books were written at a critical time in which I needed healing and a rebirth for myself. If you haven't read the first book in this series, *Live Beyond Your Dreams – from Fear and Doubt to Personal Power, Purpose and Success,* please do so after reading this book to help you heal in the fastest way possible.

As Lisa, one of my clients, told me, "Riana, that book saved my life over the holidays." She recently had gone through a divorce and her two children had moved out to have their own lives, leaving her feeling lonely, lost and without purpose or direction. Learning the *"Watch-Me!"* mind-set helped Lisa quiet her fears and find the strength to navigate life independently during her transition period, and to reinvent herself and her new life. She lost 50 pounds in a six-month period using The God Diet and an exercise trainer and looks terrific! She left a demanding job of 32 years to take her dream job in the airline industry, fulfilling her desire to travel the world and see other cultures. Her confidence and sense of happiness has grown more every time I see her.

Part of the *"Watch Me!"* philosophy is to start each day with the attitude of gratitude by saying prayers and thanking your God or Higher Power for all the blessings you do have. Ask for healing, peace, and forgiveness, and a healthy love to enter your life. Say the same prayer again before bed. My motto is, "every day, twice a day."

"Thoughts become things" as quoted in the book and DVD, *The Secret,* by Rhonda Bryne. Do watch this excellent documentary that will also teach you to monitor your thoughts and live consciously in the present. By living a more conscious life, you can remember the real character of the person you loved. You'll come to understand that he had human frailties and dysfunctional coping strategies that may have been deeply ingrained since childhood. Acknowledging your partner was far from perfect serves as the catalyst for forgiveness and change, allowing you the choice to love in a different way. This is the beginning of finding an emotionally healthy partner, one with happy childhood memories and a similar family life, moral code, religious upbringing and economic status to your own. It is best to find a partner with two healthy, loving parents who were active in his life and made him feel secure. However, a single parent who was very attentive, nurturing, loving, consciously aware, and lived in integrity could also raise a very successful child to be an evolved adult. No family is perfect, but make certain there was no parental abuse or addiction. If you're a parent, it's best to choose a man with his own children so that he understands unconditional love, sacrifice and negotiation.

Meditation and spiritual practice are essential components to developing and keeping this mind-set. Meditation calms the mind and brain activity, and can lower blood pressure, stabilize stress hormones and obsessive thinking. Picture *the specific partner and life* that you want. It helps to create a vision board with pictures that you can look at daily to inspire your dream of the life you want. Visualize the place in your mind and see the furnishings, weather, how you're dressed there, your new partner smiling at you, and what you're doing together. Picture however many details that you can imagine. Then pray and meditate on these visions and feelings. This is the law of attraction, "what you think about comes about." That's why it's important to clearly define goals and dreams for a new life.

Chapter 21, "The Law of Attraction for Love," will give you further insight. Remember, the *"Watch Me!"* mind-set is not about anger or revenge, but rather becoming your best, evolved, successful self. By utilizing positive self-talk, spiritual lessons, living your balanced life with defined goals, purpose and values, creating stronger boundaries, reading and taking time to reflect and make goals to reinvent a new life, you'll attract the perfect love.

It begins with focusing on yourself, not your ex. Become strong as you heal by addressing your personal needs, continuing to have faith, writing out your goals and dreams, and following the five Ds of desire, dedication, devotion, determination and dare to dream! Take the time to become the best you yet! Use the anger you feel as the driving force to get more proactive in your new life. Don't worry about meeting someone new – you must take care of YOU now. Heal yourself first and healthy love will come later when you feel ready to attract and receive it! Be open to extending unconditional love to all you meet as you never know what package true love will come in. Trying to look beyond your love map to a more genuine soul, he may not look like anything you previously would have been attracted to. As you date, extend loving friendship to everyone because even if your date is not right for you, he may introduce you to his friend who is.

Remember, the solution for success in your love life is knowing how to make a smarter, healthier choice in a man by evaluating his personal qualities and internal characteristics. By loving and respecting yourself, a good man will honor, cherish and respect all that you are.

Chapter 13

Creating New Goals for a New Life

*You must first clearly see a thing in your mind
before you can do it.* – Alex Morrison

KATHERINE WOODWARD THOMAS, author of *Calling in "The One,"* writes that "the external attributes that we think are so important actually have little to do with the heart of a person or the tone of a relationship, those things that reflect what we call soul. Rarely will the love of your life look the way you think he or she should look. Because we are so attached to our mental fantasies of love, we'll often pass right over that which could be an extraordinary love experience, exactly because the person *doesn't* look the way we think that he should."

She quotes Thomas Moore, "Soulful marriages are often odd on the surface." In her book Paula Robear describes a soul mate as "someone whose way of viewing life is not necessarily the same as yours but complements yours, so that there is not a compromise, there is a complement." Woodward Thomas goes on to write, "You must look for 'the One' with your heart and not with your expectations or hormones. You will feel valued, loved, safe, appreciated and cherished."

Ask yourself if you're making room for love to enter your life. You may say you "want love" but did you empty out a space in your home, clear out old relationship memories, as well as free up your calendar for dating? Are you taking *the actions* you need to meet a man, such as placing a profile on several online dating venues as well as trying new events and activities that open up your world to meeting new friends and a possible partner? When you get busy living your life, you'll exude an attractive energy and you won't feel as lonely or depressed as before. There will be new friendships formed with people who respond to you in a loving way versus staying with a man you can only hope will change his toxic ways. Ideally, be with someone who makes you feel cherished, wanted, heard, and treasured. Someone respectful of your feelings and ideas, and who encourages your individual growth and dreams. Yes, men like this exist! Don't settle for less, and keep dating until you find a man with these traits. By taking full responsibility for what you know you want in a partner, you save time and heartache and will stop dating people who don't have what you spiritually and emotionally need.

"Man cannot discover new oceans until he has courage to lose sight of the shore." This anonymous quote essentially advises letting go of what's behind us. You must let go of your old, toxic relationship to have a chance for a new, healthy, evolved love. Have the courage to change old attraction patterns; open your heart and look deeply into someone's internal qualities and gifts. Slow down to enjoy a special friendship that may lead to soulful love.

Creating New Goals for a New Life

Antoine de St.-Exupery's words sum up this section quite nicely, "It is only with the heart that one can see rightly; what is essential is invisible to the eye." These spiritually-based, deeper characteristics are what you want to find in a healthy, evolved partner.

This chapter introduces the process of deciding what you want and visualizing who you want in your life. It begins with defining your personal and business goals to fully realize happiness in life and love.

Two activities are outlined; first, complete the "Ideal Partner for Me!" checklist below. The following offers how-to instructions for each section:

How to Use the Checklist:

1. The first section – "Must Haves": You must know exactly what you're looking for in a partner so that you'll recognize him when you meet. Brainstorm several options for your own "ideal mate" and pick the top twelve. Be sure to choose excellent qualities and values; for example, honesty, integrity, love and closeness with family, etc. These values and character traits are essential for a great relationship that will endure into the future.

2. The second section – "Would Prefer He/She Have" is about preferences, meaning those hobbies or interests that remain important to you for lifelong compatibility. These could include a partner who loves to dance and travel the world; one who hopes to retire in Florida (because you want to be there); or who loves dogs (because you have two), etc. They can be common interests, activities, or something about his/her appearance. If these things are not present over the long term, you may feel incompatible

and that you had made a bad partner choice. However, you must be willing to negotiate on some of these preferences as your partner will have his, too. The qualities of giving and compromise entail trying new things your partner enjoys.

3. The third section – "Deal Breakers and Red Flag Warning Signs": It's VERY important to be honest with yourself. Examine this list to make sure that you see no red flags. These indicators constitute the very core of toxic relationships and are only a part of the complete list mentioned in this book. There could be more so jot down any other concerns. For example, he's been unemployed for 2 years; he has a large amount of debt or a disturbingly low credit score. Don't make the mistake of falling in love with someone's potential. Examine your new mate for what he is TODAY.

4. List your red flags and concerns and bring this list to your first relationship coaching appointment. It's hard to find someone who is a 100% match. Aim for around 85% and know the most important factors that you won't compromise on. I knew a man that loved to dance, and married a woman who did not, and for twenty years he suffered in a bad, stale relationship, resenting the fact he had neither dance nor music in his life. He missed the cue when dating that she would dance only after having a few drinks (though he realized she wasn't a good dancer and had always felt self-conscious at a night club). Now in his late fifties, he'll ONLY date women who love music and dance as much as he does. That's now one of his "must haves" for happiness.

Creating New Goals for a New Life

Take your time with the list as this is your new roadmap for meeting your ideal partner! Before reading on, please complete the worksheet below.

Good luck, and don't compromise!

The Ideal Partner for Me!©

From: *My Relationship Coach;* Riana Milne, MA, LPC, Cert. Coach

MUST HAVES: (*character traits, internal qualities, values, activities and education level*)

1–

2–

3–

4–

5–

6–

7–

8–

9–

10–

11–

12–

Would Prefer She/He Have:

1–

2–

3–

4–

5–

6–

7–

8–

Deal Breakers and Red Flags:

1– *Any addiction – drugs/alcohol/gambling/sex*

2– *Physically/emotionally/verbally abusive!*

3– *A chronic cheater/cheated w/you*

4– *Any mental health issues as listed in this book*

5– *A chronic liar – can't be trusted, lacks integrity*

6– *Not available – they are married or separated*

7– *A control freak, selfish or jealous, perfectionist*

8– *Mean-spirited, angry or moody temper issues*

Red flags: *List any character flaws, personality disorders, addictions or any behavior that negatively affects and hurts your health, self-esteem, work, or primary relationships (family/kids) that you see in your new partner or spouse.*

Creating New Goals for a New Life

Second, complete the brief "Personal Goals" sheet below from the original *"Watch Me!"* mind-set program, as also presented in *Live Beyond Your Dreams – from Fear and Doubt to Personal Power, Purpose and Success*, and included on the *My Relationship Coach* app. It's very important to define your goals daily, weekly, monthly, and all that you hope to achieve within six months. The goals are broken down into two parts: Personal and Business/School Goals. The following are a few tips on what you'll need to do:

- *Daily:* Each morning, focus on three things you want to accomplish that day.

- *Weekly:* At the beginning of each week (by Sunday night), come up with three personal and three business/school goals you want to have done by the end of the week (the following Sunday night). This helps you define your purpose, drive and focus for the entire week.

- *Monthly:* Have three larger monthly goals for each of your personal and business/school categories.

- *Six-Month:* These three personal and business goals should be a lofty dream you truly hope to reach. If you reach these goals before the end of six months, reward yourself with something special and replace that goal with another.

- *Birthday and New Year's Eve Goals:* Reflect on what you want to achieve for the upcoming year. Reset or adjust goals already made, and make some new ones.

Stop and do the mini Personal Goal sheet now.

MINI-GOALS for PERSONAL GROWTH

This chart will help you achieve your 6 month, 1-year and future goals by defining them into mini-goals for growth.

Daily Goals: Always wake up and plan at least three important things to achieve during this new day.

1.

2.

3.

And if I have time _____

Goals for this Week: The week starts on Monday morning and ends on Sunday night. What do you want to have done by the end of your week?

Business or School Goals:

1.

2.

3.

And if I have time _____

Personal Goals:

1.

2.

3.

And if I have time _____

Creating New Goals for a New Life

Goals for the Month: You can begin your month at the date you start this program, or at the beginning of each month. What lofty goals in both areas do you want done by the end of the month?

Business/School Goals:

1.

2.

3.

And if I have time _____

Personal Goals:

1.

2.

3.

And if I have time _____

Now move on to the Overall Dreams and Goals Vision sheet.

Overall Dreams and Goals Vision sheet for 6 months to 1 year, and from 5 to 10 years ©
From Riana Milne, MA, LPC, LCADC, Certified Relationship Coach

Define where you are now in your life. Identify your sources of happiness and accomplishment. State new dreams you want to reach in your lifetime.

In the following categories list the overall goals and dreams you want to achieve in 5 to 10 years

Personal
   1.
   2.
   3.

Relationship
   1.
   2.
   3.

Parenting – includes goals for your children
   1.
   2.
   3.

Job/Career/School Goals
   1.
   2.
   3.

Now create your vision of where you realistically want to be within six months to one year's time. State the exact date on which you plan reach this goal.

Upcoming goals to reach within 6 months.

Personal:
1.

2.

3.

Business:
1.

2.

3.

Relationship:
1.

2.

3.

Tips for successful goal setting:

- What we focus on we get in life.

- Focus on blessings and what *is* right in your life – *not* on what's wrong!

- Throughout the next thirty days transform negative self-talk into positive reinforcement; consistent practice over thirty days creates a good habit.

- Focus on solutions, not problems.

- Stop judging, blaming and finding faults in others. Be kind to all, and focus on you. Take responsibility for your own actions!

- Find something to appreciate during the challenging time of transition. Be confident that change is for the good!

Write your thoughts and accomplishments in your journal as you go. When you continue this goal-setting system, you'll be amazed at how it transforms your life and how wonderful you'll feel about yourself. Instead of focusing on a partner you have to support and repair, or putting energy into finding the "new love of your life," fall in love again with YOU first. Confidence is sexy and draws love to you like a magnet.

When you love your life on a daily basis, and feel healthy, peaceful, energized and successful, a wonderful partner will find you! Stop "looking for love." By living a full and happy life, you will attract many suitors. Once you see yourself accomplishing so many great goals, reaching your dreams and living beyond them to become even more fabulous, your self-confidence and energy will radiate and magnetize the evolved love you deserve!

Chapter 14

Learning to be Alone

Never be afraid to tread the path alone. Know which is your path and follow it wherever it may lead you; do not feel you have to follow in someone else's footsteps. – Eileen Caddy

---

AFTER A BREAKUP, you'll feel very alone. Part of you will love the relief and freedom from the drama, stress and anxiety; and part of you will feel so lonely that you question everything in your life. Initially, hours and days drag on and depression could set in. Crying comes easily and frequently and without warning. Even when you go out to try and have fun with friends it seems that "everyone is looking at me because they know my story and feel sorry for me" or, you feel invisible and awkward because your self-esteem is shot.

Believe me, it *does* get easier. Start your day with your gratitude prayers for the many blessings you do have in your life. Ask for healing, peace, forgiveness for your anger, and strength to move on. Mentally review the three goals that you want to achieve by the end of the day. You've now started your day with prayer, purpose and direction. The idea is to get focused and stay busy.

Work is good therapy. Now that you're alone, it's the perfect time to start a new, demanding project because you'll have lots of time to commit yourself to it without anyone bothering you! Or, enroll in an educational program that you've been thinking about and putting off. Another option is to take a course to develop new creative skills like cooking, sewing, painting, learning a musical instrument, or photography. Challenge yourself mentally because your healing will begin if you find a purpose to invest time in right now. Watch less TV, which can be a depressant. Now is the perfect time to read healing, inspirational and motivational books like the ones mentioned at the back of this book. Or, attend an empowerment seminar where you meet exciting people also in to self-improvement. I greatly enjoyed Tony Robbins 4-day "Unleash-the-Power-Within" seminar. It really psyches you up for incredible change!

When you write about your feelings, include the good and bad times. Reviewing bad times gives you strength to not return to your partner or get involved with someone similar. Writing about the good times can help you with forgiveness and hold onto valuable, cherished memories of the love you once shared.

Begin a healthy-foods diet and Work-out program. The goal is to feel wonderful about yourself – mind, body, and soul. Set a weight-loss goal, if needed, and get a friend to work out with or eat healthily along with you.

You may have trouble sleeping and may feel exhausted for a period of time. Perhaps you fall asleep quickly but rise around or after midnight and are kept awake by your thoughts and obsessive fears. Start praying again for peace, healing, and for God to provide a healthy love in your life. Trust that God has a plan for you. Pray for direction and what to do next. Try to focus on a dream you put on hold for a long time, a goal you were afraid to set, or a direction you were discouraged to take by your partner. It may not be immediately clear as to what you're supposed to do, but it will come to you when you feel more rested and peaceful. Be patient and not impulsive. Stress shortens your memory and affects your ability to think clearly. Pray and meditate daily; and as you do, the answers will come.

Treat yourself to a vacation where other singles would be – like a Club Med resort. I had a blast doing just that a few years ago and made new friends with whom I've kept in contact. The sun, ocean, and gorgeous surroundings were extraordinarily therapeutic and healed my soul. The men I met while in "vacation mode" were fun, exciting and easy to get along with, without any "relationship" pressure. I repeated solo trips to Cabo San Lucas and Florida several times and these vacation breaks were used for my writing, reflection, goal setting and personal growth. Now you can travel where you want, when you want, and meet many fascinating people from different cultures around the world.

Instead of dreading being alone, you'll welcome the opportunity to eat, do and be what you want, when you want. You won't have to worry about the mess a partner can make and can keep your home in order for days and weeks at a time.

The first thing I ate after a painful breakup was white pasta with clam sauce, a dish I created and loved. I realized that I always gave in to my partner's desire for pasta with red sauce, and hadn't enjoyed this favorite dish of mine for two years. Amazing what we do for love, negotiation, and for our partner, putting ourselves selflessly last. And I wondered if he ever appreciated it. This was one of the first dinners I made for myself after my break up and

I enjoyed every bit of it. It was a celebration dinner of getting my life back and doing what I want, when I want!

Never having pasta with white clam sauce was a crazy revelation of how much I had sacrificed myself for this partner, if only to keep peace and to invest in the relationship. I functioned as the strong, reliable, responsible and financially steady partner, and he had been unable to get his life together. This inability stemmed from a hidden, selfish, toxic addiction. I felt tired of babysitting a grown man, too often needing to step into a maternal role because of his poor, impulsive choices causing us severe problems as a couple. My breaking free from his lies and cheap dramas became a celebration of freedom from endless sacrifice in the name of love. It was also the time of setting new and stronger boundaries to protect myself, my life, my goals, and my dreams.

Perhaps my story will help you see how being alone is a journey you can come to love and not fear. I learned to cherish and use my newly found free time proactively to reinvent myself. Although the breakup happened in mid-April, I wasn't clear about my next major step until summer and took real steps only in August of that year. I set an aggressive 2-year plan for growth, change and creative endeavors I had long desired to do.

I prayed and meditated daily and trusted that I would find the right direction and decide on what steps I should take next. In July, on the beach, I started writing thoughts about how to heal from breakups. I listed the many toxic traits of my ex and the personality types I should avoid. My thoughts turned toward many of my therapy clients who also had been hurt by their partners' toxic, reckless choices and were left looking for answers. I knew that if I could specifically define the toxic behaviors and personality types to watch out for, I could stop a lot of emotional pain and save many people from more heartache, including myself. It became clear to me that I had to write this book in response to my own passion for answers, and to help others heal while inspiring them to move on with personal power, purpose and success.

I set aside a season from late August until May of the following year to complete three major projects. First, I developed an App, *My Relationship Coach*, which launched in December. Then I wrote and published my book, *Live Beyond Your Dreams – from Fear and Doubt to Personal Power, Purpose and Success*, which also came out in December in e-book form and in paperback by February. I went on to finish a required Master's course I needed to sit for the Florida counseling license exam. I passed the LMHC exam, launched a new website, and wrote this book – all within my stated 2-year plan. The final touch – a move to Delray Beach, FL to open my *Therapy by the Sea* coaching and counseling practice. Using my goal setting system, all dreams have been accomplished, and on time!

In addition, I traveled to Florida every other month to write, treat myself to reflection and well-earned time off. I shared lots of quality time with male and female friends, as well as with my beautiful and fabulous grown daughters. It felt refreshing to do what I wanted without hearing complaints that I was working too much or that I couldn't do this or that or anything else. Without another person to worry about, and by being alone at this time, I had unlimited freedom to set goals for my dreams and the ability to make my life unfold exactly as I wanted it to. It felt wonderful to exercise personal control and power and clearly see my dreams come to fruition!

If you are a parent with children at home, they are a top priority and you're not really alone. Encourage them to be a part of a strong team that helps each other through the time of transition. My daughters, Stephana and Alexi, were extremely supportive and we cherished our special time together when I didn't have a partner in my life. Children love their parents and will help you if you ask. Give them that chance, but be strong enough to always be the parent and help them transition confidently. Focus on quality time with them at night and weekends but carve time out for yourself for reading, exercise, and getting out with your friends or dates.

You'll learn to be alone and like it – or LOVE it! Do what you want and prepare yourself for some powerful changes and calculated risks during this transition. Consider personal and relationship coaching at this time to overcome fear, clarify your goals and take concrete steps to reach your dreams. You'll see that this is a huge growth period for you, one that can launch you into your best self ever!

Chapter 15

Relapse and Return to the Love Object

We are the masters of our fate, the captains of our souls, because we have the power to control our thoughts. – Napoleon Hill

RELAPSE AND RETURN TO YOUR love object is common after a breakup. This could mean feeling desperate to reach out by phone, text, email love letters or wanting to see him. The reason for relapse is because you've loved this person for a long time, and no one can go from a history of friendship, passion and love to no loving feelings at all; it's pretty much impossible. For months after your separation you can find your thoughts constantly preoccupied with your ex and trying to come up with ways to make up or get back together.

Don't beat yourself up – this relapse is very common and almost to be expected. Be gentle with yourself and use positive self-talk within your mind as a comforting and coping tool as if coming from a loving parent (e.g., "I know you love him dearly and you probably always will. But now you must love yourself more because you deserve a healthy, evolved, loving partner committed to your relationship as much as you are. You deserve respect, honesty and integrity, just as you give. You know in your heart you loved this man in an honorable way. Thank him for what you had, remember the happy memories, forgive him for his wrongs, and move on to find the wonderful, equal partner that you are worthy of.")

When you first have a breakup, it's important to try to give your partner and yourself some space to think. It's fine to formulate solutions that may work to help bring you back together, but allow some time before you present these ideas. The bottom line is that both partners must want a relationship to work.

If you're willing to go to couples coaching or counseling, but your partner is not, don't force him to change his mind. You should, however, start counseling sessions for yourself and your own healing. Your partner may join in eventually when he realizes that you're serious about getting help. He'll go to therapy if he wants the relationship as much as you do. You may find, though, that he completely refuses to go. With the help of your coach, you may come to realize that your relationship is too dysfunctional and isn't in your best interest to stay or try to reconcile with him.

If you're trying to keep your family together, or are codependent in a toxic or dysfunctional relationship, you may suggest some solutions and a compromise. This usually proves to be futile because the toxic partner continues to blame you, competing to be heard (or yells over your suggestions and doesn't let you speak at all), or presents past issues that supposedly had been forgiven long before.

The toxic partner will remember your smallest infractions from the past, bringing a laundry list of "wrongdoings" into any conversation you try to initiate. His list is of minimal importance compared to his own grave breaches of trust, whether from lies, cheating or deception. It feels like a losing battle, and it is. A toxic partner may also say, "I can never forgive you" when you've done essentially nothing wrong. Without the capacity to forgive, an inability to apologize for any mistake, and no willingness to work out a solution with a professional counselor or coach, it becomes imperative that you get out. This type of toxic personality can never contribute to a happy relationship with you or anyone else.

Toxic relationships are full of unrealized hopes and a significant lack of respect. The emotional manipulator will provide just enough compliments and random acts of kindness to keep the relationship limping along. A "Pavlov's dog" mentality is what feeds the addiction to a toxic person and distorts your own reality. Both then become steadily dependent on the other with an unspoken agreement that neither will change, grow, nor discuss the other's faults. They both stay despite the incessant bad habits, and continue to blame one another. Toxic men are difficult and women sometimes idealize any good they see in order to overcome the negative and try to keep their marriage together.

The emotional manipulator that attracts you with charm, passion and romance, will emerge months later as someone you barely know. This is a sign of the sociopath, narcissist, ACOA, or someone who could have a bipolar or borderline personality disorder. The problem that occurs within these relationships is that initially you fell in love with an attentive, fun, emotional, loving person who couldn't do enough to please you and showed you dedication, devotion and lots of affection. This is whom you desire to have back in your life. Significant early signs to watch for are those actions played to extreme, as in numerous daily texts or phone calls, wanting sex daily (or even several times a day), needing you constantly, showing jealousy over your friendships or complaining when you spend time with friends or family.

The memory of falling in love is so strong that you often forget the horrific ways he treated you, the many lies he told, or the relapses into his addiction. The memories of your romantic courtship and love are what keep you hanging on. What you perceived to be a loving, honest partner is nowhere near reality. You must be consciously aware of his behavior by watching what he does on a daily basis. Don't believe the words or promises he offers; instead, *look at his actions.* Ask yourself, "Can I live like this for the next thirty or forty years?" If the answer is "No" and you feel overcome by a sense of panic, your intuition is saying "Get Out!" Free yourself so that you can meet someone healthy and loving.

Pia Mellody wrote a book I often recommend entitled *Facing Love Addiction*. She describes the emotional cycle of the love addict that makes them want to return to the dysfunctional relationship. Here is a brief summary of the nine stages:

1. At first, the love addict (codependent) is fiercely attracted to the power and charm of the avoidance addict (toxic partner).

2. Delusional fantasy and the love-map attraction from childhood is triggered, which in turn creates a mental state composed, in part, of engulfing admiration and euphoric feelings toward the avoidance addict.

3. The love addict surrenders to these uncontrollable emotions as they relieve the pain of loneliness.

4. Neediness increases, obliging the love addict to ignore or deny the reality of the avoidant's pattern of pulling away.

5. The denial ends only with a severe breach of trust or a breakup, at which time the love addict is forced into an awareness of the partner's aloofness and abandoning behaviors.

6. The love addict enters the withdrawal stage, becoming anxious or depressed, unable to eat or sleep and feeling consumed by the sense of loneliness and fear.

7. Obsessive thoughts arise on how to get back together, or how to wreak revenge against all the bad done to them. This often involves contact by text, phone or letter. The love addict is suffering through a horrible withdrawal and finds it impossible to stop contacting the ex-partner. This would mean giving up hope or the dream of a future together. The emotional pull toward returning to the way things were can last many months, but hopefully, around the one-year post-breakup mark, you'll have reinvented yourself into a more confident and healthier state of being and personal power. By this time you should be dating, have met new friends, enjoying plenty of activities, accomplishing new career and personal goals, and creating new dreams for yourself.

8. This pattern can repeat itself if the avoidance addict comes back to you or has moved on to a new partner.

Be sure you have a good counselor and relationship coach as well as one or two friends that keep you grounded in reality. The love addiction habit has been compared to withdrawing from cocaine, as it affects many chemicals in the brain that crashed upon the loss of your lover. It's extremely hard to overcome but not impossible and will subside with time. If you can't stop reaching out to toxic partners, you're most likely codependent or love addicted and need to address these issues in counseling over an extensive period of time to break unhealthy patterns. The busier your mind, the easier it is to forget. Call your friends when you feel compelled to call or text your ex. Recall and list all his hurtful actions aimed at you; when you feel an urge to call, read your notes again and remember the facts, not the fantasy of the beginning stages of the relationship.

Get professional help so that you don't continue to relapse into conversing with your partner or persist in trying to make up. These relationships get worse and more abusive with time. If you keep going back, this partner will take advantage of your weakness and kind heart and will attempt to control you further. So stay strong! It's time to feel safe by detaching yourself from a painful person who hurts you. Redefine what turns you on, and be determined to break the old childhood patterns that attract you to toxic men. Emotionally unavailable men who act distant, aggressive, belittle or make you feel defensive and anxious take away your personal power. Do you instinctively feel these internal cues?

- The problems in the relationship are my fault.
- You need to work hard to get what you want.
- You need to do more than your fair share to prove your love.
- You should be seen and not heard.

These faulty belief patterns emerged as you grew up, ingraining feelings of deprivation, not being good enough, or lacking attention from one or both parents. Your subconscious mind now

Relapse and Return to the Love Object

wants to maintain what you've known and felt since childhood and prefers to reject and resist change and new information. There is a mental "gatekeeper" that acts as a critical factor in what the conscious mind is thinking; it seeks approval from the subconscious mind before it acts. It's as if we have two minds. Will power rarely works so you simply repeat the same things or choose the same type of partner, while hoping for a different result.

You must change your subconscious to agree with your conscious intentions. That's why meditating daily on what you want, and working with a coach helps override and replace the defective, subconscious belief system. You'll come to know the bliss of living in the present (the "now") and the past will start to disappear along with negative thoughts and choice patterns. Only then will you know and feel happiness. With meditation and living consciously in the now, simple things will bring great bliss – music, art, creation, the beauty of nature, silence, and slowly getting to know the heart, mind and soul of another.

Mental and spiritual happiness enriches feelings of pure peace and joy. In the state of bliss as described by Buddha there is no darkness, only light. Without ego, all anxiety, anguish and tensions are gone because there is no past to hurt you. You feel contentment living in present mindfulness and enjoying life's simple occurrences.

Physical pleasure can keep you enchained, is a superficial state and can become an obsession. A constant need of wanting more turns desire into demand, and the more you want, the greater the fear that it can be taken away. The self becomes hollow. Buddha teaches, "The man who seeks pleasure remains at the mercy of accidents. Happiness frees you and bliss is the ultimate freedom of pure joy and light." Gautam Buddha summarizes,

"There is pleasure and there is bliss. Forgo the first to possess the second."

There *is* life and love beyond toxic relationships. It begins with faith, by knowing the world is abundant and that God has a better plan and partner for you.

Chapter 16

Healing through Spirituality and Reinventing Yourself

We are what we imagine ourselves to be. – Kurt Vonnegut, Jr.

MANY OF THE TIPS IN THE previous chapters help with emotional healing. As you continue with those activities, I also want you to focus on what you may want to do to reinvent yourself. Define who you are, what you do for work, your parenting views, how you balance your time, where you live, how you look, act, think and present yourself to the world. It's time for a full, honest evaluation and complete makeover!

When you're forced to be alone, it's best to concentrate on yourself and not have obsessive thoughts about getting your partner back. Turn all your attention back to YOU. With the time you now have to do what you want, when you want, what would you like become? Your dreams got pushed to the side in a toxic relationship because all your attention remained on trying to fix him and make the relationship work. All your energy went into getting your partner emotionally balanced, clean from an addiction, financially sound, or reemployed. You're not used to thinking about YOU and your needs, but now it's time to do so.

After a breakup, pray for healing, healthy love, peace and to have the power to move on and forgive. Pray for guidance on what to do next to find your purpose in life. The answers will come, I promise you. Meditate each day for fifteen to twenty minutes and envision the new life and love you want. What you think about comes about, so think and feel positive thoughts and see the life you want for yourself.

How does one begin to heal from such bottomless pain and reinvent oneself to be confident and ready to try love again? First, know that it takes time, a long time. At least six months to two years is the normal healing time.

Many suggestions for healing from a break up already have been discussed in previous chapters. Below are a few more tips to help your healing process:

1. Start attending your place of worship again. If you don't have one, try a few to see which service you feel connected to. This will help you make new friends, while receiving the spiritual lessons needed for healing.

2. Fill your mind with positive thoughts and lessons to distract your mind. At your library, find books in the new-age religion, psychology or self-help sections. Read a lot about healing from a break-up! Watch less TV, which can act as a depressant at this time and gives minimal value to your healing. If you do watch, choose a comedy show or TV minister whose words are inspirational and healing. My own favorite is Joel Osteen and I watch him every Sunday.

3. Buy the DVD of *The Secret* by Rhonda Byrne to learn about the Law of Attraction. It is crucial to your healing and reinvention of self for you to discover and understand the principles described. It explains the importance of positive thinking, growth, and healing.

4. Read my earlier book, *Live Beyond Your Dreams – from Fear and Doubt to Personal Power, Purpose and Success* to help jumpstart your emotional healing and reinvention.

5. Be sure to immediately hire a counselor or relationship coach who specializes in healing and transformational tools to help you move on and change your life for the better.

6. Go out with friends to social events that attract singles your age. Look smashing; wear fitted outfits that make you feel terrific and sexy.

7. Attend business networking events to promote the business you're involved with while meeting other successful people. Travel to various seminars and conventions to meet people with common interests who live outside of your local area. The energy of positive, motivated people transformed into self-growth is fantastic!

8. Write or journal your feelings, goals and dreams. Put your thoughts on paper and discuss them with your coach. Start or expand a business, or plan a trip to see a favorite place or friend.

9. Read in detail about the addiction your partner had and about codependency to discover if you're a love addict or avoidant. Learn more about the emotional manipulator or specific problem personality type of your previous

partner. Be able to identify the characteristics of your toxic partner so that you'll forever avoid this type of person. Your reading will reassure you that your life will be better without the toxic relationship.

10. When you have an urge to talk to your ex-partner, call your friends instead, watch a movie, go out for a walk; write, or read. Keep yourself busy. Start a new home project, hobby or work endeavor. Work can be good therapy and a way to take your mind off your partner.

11. Do everything possible to simplify your life. Become debt free, and start saving your money for your future so that you can retire with security.

12. Join a gym and exercise regularly. It helps raise the dopamine and serotonin levels of the brain that naturally improve depression. Go three or four times a week; aim to work out for thirty to forty-five minutes. Do twenty minutes of cardio and twenty minutes of weights for toning and building muscle.

13. Use vitamins to support your immune system and energy. Take a daily multiple-vitamin, fish oil for your heart, B-complex for energy, and D for memory and to help alleviate depression. Vitamin C is good for the immune system, and COQ-10 has powerful antioxidants. Talk to your doctor before taking any vitamins or herbal supplements. Read more about nutrition to improve your overall health.

14. Stop any addictive behavior you might have employed for coping with your toxic partner such as overspending,

eating, consuming alcohol, pot, pills or any other drugs, gambling, watching pornography, having casual sex, or engaging in any other destructive behavior.

15. Think mind-body-soul healing. Be sure to eat a healthy diet high in proteins. Consider a weight-loss goal and stick to it. You want to feel wonderful about your health and the way you look, which will lead to emotional healing, confidence and enhanced self-esteem.

16. Be patient and loving with yourself. Think of all your wonderful qualities and everything you did right in the relationship. Use an affirmation motto when your thoughts fall into fear, such as, "I deserve healthy love in my life and I have everything I need to attract it to me."

17. Pray every day, twice a day, starting with an attitude of gratitude and remembering all the blessings you have. Ask for healing and to have a wonderful, new love enter your life.

18. Meditate every day for fifteen to twenty minutes.

How to meditate – set your alarm to awaken with a calm and lovely sound, like a harp. Sit erect with legs folded, one hand in the other and connecting at the thumbs for energy. Close your eyes and breathe in deeply to a count of seven. Hold the breath in for a count of seven then exhale to a count of seven. Repeat seven times.

Envision a "happy picture" in your mind. This can be a favorite photo or a blissful memory of a beautiful scene. Watch your thoughts as you would the screen in a small movie theater.

I often use the Law of Attraction to visualize and feel myself engaging in the things I want: a loving partner on a balcony with me, looking out at a turquoise ocean while sharing a chilled glass of Chardonnay. Or, I see myself giving an inspiring motivational speech that stirs my audience.

If my thoughts turn sad or negative, I revisit my balcony-and-ocean scene. I like to begin my meditation time with prayers as well. You'll soon find the fifteen-minute session going by very quickly. These daily meditation exercises will help you to foresee the life you want. Remember: What you think about comes about. Be sure to *feel* exactly what you hope to attract into your life.

The success of this process can be explained by science and the strength of the unconscious mind:

- Quantum physics and neuroscience have discovered neuroplasticity – the fact that we make new brain cells and neural connections all the time; no matter your age, your brain is capable of creating new neural connections.

- We can override and rewrite our genetic code, as well as flaws in our upbringing where attitudes, beliefs, and established thought patterns are stored. We can augment our creativity, intelligence and capacity for change and achievement throughout our lives.

- The reticular activating system or RAS (another part of the brain) acts as a filter for cerebral sensory input and draws from your external world. Anything you see, hear, feel, taste, or smell passes through this delicate network.

- No matter what specific idea or goal you place into your RAS, or whether you're asleep or awake, the RAS will do its job to find exactly what you've asked it to find (the best reason for composing a vision board that portrays, with photos, your desired wishes, goals and dreams). When you create a clear, focused picture of what you want, this part of your brain kicks into high gear and won't stop until it finds it for you.

- Here's the trick, if your RAS is NOT programmed for what you really want, then however diligently you pursue a goal, you'll miss all the cues in your environment and overlook all the resources and connections that would help you realize that goal.

- Lastly, the RAS can work against you. This happens to *most* people, because by focusing on negativity, *and what you don't want,* you create thoughts around that feeling ("I'll never find a partner," "I'm not pretty enough, good enough, successful enough"…etc.); thus generating the outcome you most dread.

- This is why most people make the same mistakes over and over in life, whether in choosing a love partner, making business decisions, or having enough money. They self-sabotage a positive outcome.

- Beliefs and habits are a thousand times stronger than desires to the unconscious mind, so a negative belief becomes self-fulfilling and true for you. And you can't *fake* positive thoughts; you have to *feel* them for this to work. Know the importance of loving yourself in *all* your life spheres and focusing on solutions and goals, never on the problem!

It's important to also understand that your toxic partner carried a lot of internal issues, and that his or her leaving you is likely not even about you. It's about their inability to connect intimately with anyone for an extended period of time. This is especially true if they fled from the relationship. Don't take their unhealthy emotional baggage personally. Your counselor can help you understand how their past childhood experiences affects their adult relationships.

Yes, you want to do some soul-searching to see what you need to correct within yourself, or consider why you may need to apologize to your partner. Take the time to correct any negative patterns or behaviors. Before involving yourself with another person, work on making your life healthy enough to feel alive and vibrant.

When you feel that you've reached beyond the pain and sadness of your breakup and are ready to date, ask your friends to introduce you to someone suitable, and look for the many opportunities that present themselves to meet someone new on a daily basis. Say hello to everyone you meet, and be happy and approachable. I've met fabulous people who have become good friends simply by saying hello. If you decide to try the online dating sites, be particular when you write your profile and who you choose to date. Get full names, phone numbers and city in which the person lives before meeting anyone for a date, and follow all the other online dating safety rules. I suggest a LinkedIn and Google search to make sure they are who they say they are. Amazing information – bad and good – can be found through searches. Also, tell a friend or family member who you're meeting and where.

This renewal stage is marked by both relief and a sense of freedom from past toxicity. While reinventing and getting to know yourself again, reassess your values and belief systems. Become strong in your dating rules and boundaries. When you feel you've adjusted to life without your ex-partner and have a clear vision of who you are and exactly what you want in life and a relationship, only then is it time to venture into dating again.

Chapter 17

Letting Go – Forgiveness and the Goodbye Letter

Forgiveness breaks the self-defeating cycle of anger and resentment, which only hold us back. We learn to forgive so we can overcome these demons, experience the emotional relief, and move on with our lives.
– Sarah Buckley, M.D.

Mourning the relationship is a necessary stage of a breakup. The relationship has died, and each will process the loss in his or her own way. There is no doubt your emotional reactions will be felt for a very long time. You might go through different stages of anger, hurt, sadness, helplessness, fear, depression, guilt, remorse, and fantasizing about reconciliation.

You can absolutely hate what he did to you, but it's still important that you forgive the person. Forgiveness doesn't mean that what he did to you was acceptable. Instead, it relieves you of the anger you hold inside so that it doesn't make you sick.

Forgiving yourself is imperative to your health and healing. You may feel angry and believe you didn't "try hard enough" or could have "done something differently" or feel that you're a failure because your marriage didn't work out. With a toxic partner who is also an emotional manipulator and/or addict, you must come to realize that you did all you could do to make the relationship work. His mental health issues are not within your control.

You might feel angry for several reasons, having missed the signs that he had a toxic personality, making excuses and covering up for his bad behavior, or giving him too many chances when you could have left a long time ago, all leading him to manipulate you consistently. You might also feel anger for all the years you wasted trying to fix and change him. You feel frustrated, thinking you could have been with someone more emotionally healthy. If you're near retirement, this resentment usually includes the fear of being alone as you grow older.

What is done, is done, the important thing is not to waste another second of time. Forgiving it all gives you the energy to create and achieve your new dreams for the future.

As you learn to become a more positive individual, you may encounter friends, family members or acquaintances who can make you feel guilty for wanting to end the relationship with "such a great guy." Remember, your partner put their fun-loving, super friendly face on only for the outside world, and not for you. No one knows what you endured nor would anyone understand. If people say, "Wow! Everyone loved Tom!" you can respond, "Yes, I loved him too, and we're all shocked by his behavior," and leave it at that. No one needs to know the details of why he wasn't an honorable man in the marriage or relationship. Stop spending time with negative people who don't support you and your healing.

Letting Go – Forgiveness and the Goodbye Letter

Forgive your past choices, and be keenly dedicated to reinventing yourself now. Since reading this book, you're now smarter about what to watch for in a toxic person. Promise yourself that you'll ask a lot more questions when dating, take things slowly, and keep stronger boundaries. Don't get emotionally or sexually involved too quickly. At the first sign of toxicity, revisit the book, and make an informed decision to protect yourself and break things off. Listen to your intuition. You'll feel anxious when you meet someone toxic. Respect your gut and stop dating or talking to them immediately. Refusing to date toxic people leaves you free to find someone who is not.

Keeping the pro and con list of your partner's character traits may help you remember the good he brought into your life, and forgive – but not forget – the bad. You may always feel hatred and anger toward his lies and destructive actions, and this will stop you from wanting to return to him. But by holding on to the good memories, you'll have something to cherish about him as a person that allows the shared loving time count for something positive. Trying to remember the good times will help to heal your heart and help you to move on. You want to have positive energy for your new life; meditation and prayer that center on letting go with forgiveness toward yourself and your ex is essential. The second part of your prayer should focus on the significant changes you'll make for and within yourself.

Once you feel a sense of forgiveness, and strong enough to leave everything behind you, write the goodbye letter. Closure is an important part of healing. Write the letter in the Word program on your computer and revisit it several times to edit it so that it says all that you want said. Thank him for the good memories, and list a few. Tell him kindly, without blame, how disappointed you feel that things didn't work out. Don't threaten him in any way, or do anything that could legally get you into trouble. Don't suggest a meeting or the possibility of trying again, and *don't expect a response* (sociopaths have long moved on and don't care much about you, your pain, and won't ever sincerely apologize).

So this isn't about getting a response from him, or an apology, or a kind thought in return. This letter is for YOU, and your release from the binds that nearly strangled you. Say what you want in the letter, but remember that he may show others, or try to hold it against you in some way. Choose your words carefully so that can't happen.

End the letter with the spiritual sign off – Goodbye, good luck and God bless. This statement solidifies in your heart and mind that this relationship is now done and you can let go with forgiveness. Signing off in this kind and loving way shows that you have faith that God will bless you with great love the next time. The letter will serve as the closure you need to move on with confidence and in preparation for being the best you – and with the energized focus to find Love Beyond your Dreams.

Section Four

Having Love Beyond Your Dreams!

80% of Life's satisfaction comes from Meaningful Relationships.
– Brian Tracey

Chapter 18

What is an Evolved Relationship?

If you know you want it, Have it. – Gita Bellin

THE SECRET OF AN EVOLVED RELATIONSHIP is that both partners have and practice these nine qualities: Empathy, honesty, integrity, kindness, patience, humility, responsibility, generosity of spirit, and forgiveness.

Spiritually evolved people know that insight into human nature and the ability to see good in all people can build and maintain positive friendships. They are careful not to judge or be critical toward others, extending unconditional love and carefully choosing words and actions that are for the good of all concerned.

Those with a spiritual mission to live each day consciously in "the now" and who approach each person with kindness are more open to receiving all that cross their path. Remain open to meeting a potential partner in any place or time. That perfect match could be right in front of you but if your mind is rooted in your "to do" list, or worried about a past event or bad relationship, you're not open to seeing or receiving the new person into your life.

Love Beyond Your Dreams means having a healthy, evolved relationship that will comprise the following qualities for both parties:

- Solid foundation: The ability to trust and be trusted; confidence in who they are individually and as a couple, and shared moral values.

- Flexibility: Open-mindedness, caring, easy going, patient, understanding, emotionally open, allowing for safe and loving conversations.

- Fidelity: Honesty, loyalty and integrity.

- Friendship: Respect, reliability, kindness, thoughtfulness, and acting as a best friend.

- Intimacy: A balance of love, deep friendship, sexual passion, daily affection and fulfilling romance.

- Fun: Common interests, hobbies and shared activities.

- Compromise: Negotiate differences, acceptance, a willingness to apologize and to offer forgiveness without imposing blame.

- Balanced Individuals: Both partners enjoy healthy self-esteem and boundaries, find purpose and gratification in their work, and have quality relationships with family and friends.

- Spirituality: Belief and faith in something greater than self that provides guidance and demands accountability.

What is an Evolved Relationship?

Intimacy can only come when both partners feel safe to risk and share who they are without being controlled, put-down or criticized. A healthy, evolved relationship will contain all the components outlined above.

In Tony Robbins' audio-video presentation, *Love & Passion: The Ultimate Relationship Program,* he discusses the six basic human needs for sustained happiness in a relationship. He fervently believes that you can transform any relationship by understanding and applying these techniques, especially if you realize which needs are the most important to your partner. Couples tend to stay together when they know how to meet each other's fundamental desires, which are summarized as follows:

1. Certainty: The secure belief that your partner loves you and has your best interests at heart.

2. Variety/Uncertainty: Keeping variety alive makes life exciting and playful.

3. Significance: Your partner feels important, worthy, special, wanted and needed.

4. Love/Connection: Everyone needs to feel loved and most people do desire a true love connection with a special partner.

5. Growth: Each partner experiences the need for continuous emotional, spiritual and intellectual growth, and each should support the other's efforts and progression.

6. Contribution: It's important to give to others beyond one's own needs and to believe that everyone can make a difference in the world.

Tony outlines the seven master skills essential to maintaining relationships and how they should be practiced on a daily basis. By fully understanding the needs and feelings of your partner and yourself, you can create an extraordinary and loving relationship. The expression of these skills should include:

1. Heartfelt Understanding: Putting your partner first by showing emotional empathy, allowing for a strongly supportive connection.

2. Giving to your partner what they genuinely need: It's important to give your partner love instead of focusing on what you feel you're not getting. Understand that you need to love your partner, no matter what; offer praise and show adoration often.

3. Creating and Building Trust and Respect: Trust grows when your partner can count on you, knowing that you'll remain emotionally open, honest and available. Trust and respect will continue to flourish when you show positive intent with a true commitment to meeting your partner's needs. Forgive easily and forget past errors.

4. Reclaiming Playfulness, Presence and Passion: Be present for your partner and show affection daily. Keep your heart open to full emotional engagement without holding anything back.

5. Harnessing Courage and Embracing Honesty: Holding back from communicating your needs and wants leads to a loss of passion. It's essential that you break through your fears and let yourself become wholly honest and vulnerable with your partner; talk about all that you feel as you feel it.

What is an Evolved Relationship?

6. Creating Alignment: It's important that each partner continues to grow and share advancement toward a higher meaning to life. Appreciate one another and be aware of the power of gratitude and giving to others in need.

7. Living Consciously and Being an Example: Creating a life that exemplifies the best in character to your partner, family, and the world.

I believe in the great worth of this program and would strongly recommend that you acquire it to help you continue to improve your relationship skills, or to awaken a positive change in your relationship, especially during times of uncertainty, anger, stress, or life transition. Relationship skills have not been taught to most of us; rather, we must take the time to learn them and stay open to improving them in order to have a passionate, enduring relationship that lasts.

With personal integrity and accountability, you will most likely enjoy a healthy, loving and trusting relationship. It's your responsibility to open a conversation about your needs, wants, fears, and desires and not let them fester and build resentment. State clearly your need and desire for support and intimacy. Ask for support, don't demand it. I suggest a formula:

Compliment, compliment – ask.

Suppose you're upset because you and your husband have little or no quality time together, and your husband isn't making time for you. Rather than blaming him or using a negative tone, try another approach, for example:

"Hon, I have so much fun when we're out together and I've missed being with you. Can we make a plan for a special night out?"

He is more likely to hear you with these words as opposed to hearing you blame, complain and demand. He'll pretty much shut down if you say, "We never spend any time together – all you want to do is golf or be with your friends and I'm sick of it. You always make me your last priority so we'd better start going out or I'm leaving this relationship."

It takes practice to achieve positive and easy communication. Focus daily on speaking in a positive way. After one or two months, this will be a new, healthy pattern for you, which is essential for a loving relationship.

Stay open-minded and listen when your partner comes to you with a concern. Become an active listener, asking him questions that show you truly want to understand his concern. Then summarize what he told you so that you're both confident that you're on the same page. Try not to take things personally, or automatically refute his worry. Great communication skills are vital and a huge part of a successful relationship. Try not to fight or discuss serious topics in front of the children or in the bedroom, the room meant for closeness and intimacy. Leave serious discussions to another part of the house.

In real love you want the other person's good. In romantic love, you want the other person. – Margaret Anderson

In an evolved relationship, you and your partner will bring out the best in one another. Both are honest, confident, exercise integrity and enjoy their respective lives. An exclusive relationship with you is seen as a bonus to an already happy life.

Ask yourself the following about your partner:

1. Do I feel loved, cherished, and secure?

What is an Evolved Relationship?

2. Are we equally balanced in our concerns, thoughts and affections toward each other?

3. Do I feel that he's supportive, loyal and has my best interests in mind?

4. Do I feel recognized and appreciated for what I bring to the relationship? Does he express pride in having me as his mate?

5. Do I respect his daily efforts at home, work, and in the community?

6. Do I feel that I'm my absolute best with him; that it's easy to "be the full, authentic me" without having to act outside my comfort zone?

7. Are we mutually attracted to each other and have the energy and desire to be with one another intimately and sexually?

8. Does he treat me the way a gentleman should? Is he polite, respectful and generous with his efforts and income; does he provide for me (even if it means sacrificing) and take my needs into consideration when fulfilling his own?

9. Do I feel that he's attentive enough without being needy, overbearing, codependent, controlling or disinterested?

10. When we're together, does he offer his full time and attention and avoid distractions like TV, social media, his phone, computer or looking around the room at others? While away, is his first choice of communication the phone, rather than text? Does he respond to your calls and texts in a timely manner?

11. Is he of good character: sincere, kind, patient, responsible, and true to his word?

12. Does he try his best to remain positive, calm, and centered when addressing stressful situations?

13. Do I feel any doubts or concerns with his behavior? Has he given me any reason to doubt what he says as the truth? Do I trust him implicitly?

14. Am I proud of the way he presents himself in a crowd and as he communicates with others? Is he socially confident, non-judgmental and friendly to most people?

15. Is there balanced communication so he doesn't keep the topic of conversation restricted to him? Is he a great listener, shows a good sense of humor and isn't sarcastic at the expense of you or others?

16. Is his communication with me open and balanced, both in listening and sharing his feelings? Is it respectful, interesting and entertaining to me? Can he share his emotions and concerns without distancing himself or shutting down?

Take a moment to think about your answers to these questions and decide which ones resonate with you. These qualities should be your focal point for growth with your current partner. Review the qualities of an evolved relationship again to ensure that you're offering as much as you're receiving from your relationship; identify areas of opportunity to do better. Discuss a plan with your partner to move your relationship to a place where you both feel equally loved.

What is an Evolved Relationship?

Within sixty to ninety days of meeting someone new, you should feel that you are either heading toward an evolved relationship, or you're seeing signs of trouble. Keep strong boundaries and high standards, and approach your partner in a kind and loving way to discuss your concerns. Hopefully, he'll also want to work with you to develop your relationship further. But, if he refuses to address your concerns or exhibits signs of toxic behavior, then you must remind yourself that you deserve a more evolved partner.

Al Ritter explains a 100/0 Principle for successful relationships. Here are the main concepts:

1. You take 100% responsibility for the relationship by showing respect and kindness, even if the partner doesn't deserve it.
2. Don't expect anything in return.
3. Be persistent with your kindness and graciousness.
4. The other person starts showing 100% effort as well.
5. This is about giving from the heart and not taking or overthinking.
6. The main concept is to show kindness, respect and patience, and to not give up. Ritter believes most people give up too soon.

I think this approach has a lot of merit. Instead of getting involved in a fight, stay peaceful and positive. It takes a great amount of self-control. But you'll find that your partner backs down when you say loving things and are careful not to insult the person. An important point to remember about Al Ritter's concept is that the process won't work in an abusive relationship and you must monitor that you are not being codependent. In no way should you accept disrespect or abuse of any kind.

If you want to continue working with your new partner, consider couples counseling or coaching to move through your existing issues. If you're single, you now know what qualities you want to cultivate within yourself and share with a healthy partner.

The next chapter discusses how to attract a healthy, evolved partner.

Chapter 19

How to Meet a Healthy Partner

Life is full and overflowing with the new. But it is necessary to empty out the old to make room for the new to enter. – Eileen Caddy

---

BEFORE STARTING TO DATE, realize that you're not looking to find, or have, a relationship, but rather, you're looking to cocreate a partnership based on honest friendship, positive and open communication, and sharing of time and energy to get to know each other. You must be a happy, evolved person with success in every life sphere – emotional, physical, financial, spiritual, legal, and within your career, family and friends. Being ready for a relationship means you're done and healed from a breakup or divorce, have no financial troubles or outstanding debts (other than a manageable mortgage and perhaps a car loan), no addictions or mental health issues. Your career is secure and enjoyable and there are no family or physical health issues that haven't been addressed.

You want to share positive love with someone who meets your requirements, wants, needs and desires. You hope to form an interpersonal relationship based on comfortable friendship, positive trust, integrity, slow-developing intimacy and, only then, selected exclusivity. There is a comfortable balance between the relationship with self and the love partner. No one needs to give up themselves for the good of the relationship.

The diagram below looks like three equal circles, signifying You, Me and Us. The "Us" is intertwined with who we are, but doesn't consume either of us. As individuals, we share parts of ourselves with our partner, but don't totally give ourselves away or lose our personal power or purpose in life. Thus, we each have a full, happy life, and choose to share that with our partner.

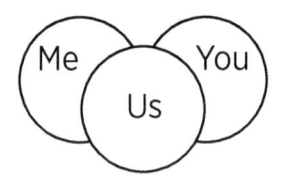

You need to be clear about your happiness requirements in a relationship so that you can recognize a partner who is right for you and to quickly identify who is wrong. When you can move on from those not emotionally healthy as soon as you see or hear red flags, relationship drama becomes non-existent. This opens the path and your time to meet a healthy person.

It's important to enter into dating with a positive attitude and an open mind. Don't go in seeking "the one" but instead, look at it as a chance to meet many new friends. Take your time to look your best, be kind, polite, punctual, and appreciative of the time spent with you. Refuse to focus on the shallow traits of looks, body type, wealth, material possessions or job status (referred to as "packaging"). I understand that there must be some physical attraction; but you really want to look deeper into internal qualities, character, and behavior.

Ask questions before getting romantically or sexually involved. If you feel pushed into sexual activity that's the first red flag signal to get out of a dating relationship. The best love relationships start slowly through friendship and getting to know one another other. Love and avoidant addicts find this approach uncomfortable and unnatural since they equate falling in love with feeling the high of immediate sexual attraction.

Sometimes the easiest way to find a healthy partner is to ask your friends to recommend other singles they know. They would know both you and the other person well enough to believe whether there could be a good match. I've personally introduced four couples that have since married and stayed together in a healthy, happy and loving relationship for years.

It's also important while dating to talk about what each person expects from the other in terms of a healthy relationship, and to share an understanding on the meaning of sexual fidelity. Many people question whether a computer-based sexually oriented chat-room affair is cheating. Most people feel that such an activity does entail cheating and this must be defined as a couple. Anyone to whom you give your time, attention, sexual and/or emotional energy is usually considered an affair outside of the marriage. Couples should enjoy a feeling of "you and me against the world," which would include keeping other suitors out of the relationship. It's up to both partners to protect the relationship and make each other feel safe and cherished.

Keep in mind that no one is perfect. Every person will have positive and negative traits, and it is unrealistic to think any relationship will be wonderful all the time. Be careful not to project a childhood fantasy onto your new dating partner and expect perfection. If you both do the things that make each a good, loving, responsible partner on a daily basis, that's a great start. Make well-thought out, rational (not impulsive) decisions knowing that your choices affect both of you. Problems will arise, but the key is how you communicate through tough times.

Sometimes finding a healthy partner begins by dating and quickly weeding out toxic men who could break your heart. You'll be surprised at how many toxic people are in the dating pool. Even though you live an honest life, you could fall for a sociopath. You may believe their excuses or deceptive stories early on so be consciously aware when dating. It will help to meet their friends, children, and family members, and listen to what they tell you about your partner's past. You have the right to feel suspicious if he chooses not to introduce you to his close friends or family. Many sociopaths have broken family relationships and few close friends. Before getting too involved, check his background history online and confirm where he says he works by doing a Google search. Examine public records for negative press about him or his behaviors. It's hard to hide acts of grave dishonesty at work or within the community as there will be a trail online or in the court system.

The unfortunate reality is that we have to engage in these methods of information gathering. So many people, especially opportunists, lie about themselves and their past. If you're a woman of means, avoid marrying quickly and allow your new relationship to stand the test of time. Protect your retirement and your children's interests in case of divorce. I suggest a prenup for anyone (male or female) entering into a relationship in older years. Do provide the gift of a life insurance policy for each other. After the wedding, whatever you build together should be yours to share together as long as you both contribute toward it. If you buy something solely with your own earnings, or money from an inheritance, and he contributes nothing, this asset should be yours alone to Will as you like. Actively avoid men looking to go along for the financial ride available from your hard work, savings or your family's inheritance gift to you alone, and who will thereafter, use marriage laws to get half.

The best way to find a healthy partner is *to be a healthy person.* Start by splitting the day into thirds and think about being the best you can be within these time periods: from waking to lunch, lunch to dinner, and from dinner until bedtime. Check between each segment of time and hold yourself accountable to being the best you possible and note if there is a need for some personal improvement. This will help you live consciously, making good decisions for your own benefit and that of your future partner.

If you're in a dating relationship, don't try to control, manipulate or convince your new partner to be a certain way so that you feel comfortable. It is also important to always be your authentic self – you can't keep up a pretense if the relationship continues and become serious. Take care of yourself, but schedule quality time to be available for your dating partner. Sit and talk, listen to music, have a glass of wine or enjoy an activity together. Invest the time early on to learn as much as possible about your dating partner.

Use the first date to identify the positive traits of a healthy partner. With the right questions during your dating time you'll quickly be able to sense whether or not this person is your type and worth more time with you. Keep these questions light and conversational. Share your past as well and don't sound like you're conducting a job interview. Listen more than you speak and be your authentic self.

Inquire and learn more about the person's life and views. For example:

1. Tell me about your parents and where did you grow up?

You're hoping to hear that he had two loving, intelligent, responsible parents who were kind, supportive, fair in discipline, and who encouraged him to do his best. Ideally, they would have a long, loving marriage, but if divorced, they remained somewhat friendly and civil and both stayed involved with their children. If they remarried, ask if he gets along with his step-parents. Parental involvement should include his sports, arts or school activities, and the quality time spent with him. He speaks of fond memories, funny stories, traditions and rituals, and family vacations.

Be careful to listen for any signs of alcohol or drug-abusing parents, neglect, lack of affection, abandonment, physical, verbal, sexual or emotional abuse, financial struggle or poverty. Ask about educational and career choices of his parents, and how his parents got along in general.

2. Do you have brothers and sisters? Are they older or younger than you?

Sibling respect and affection, and a well-balanced family life are always a good sign. The siblings can all be very different as long as they respect each other's differences. He should speak affectionately and kindly of his siblings, describing a close relationship. Continue your interest and ask what they're doing now. Successful, happy stories would certainly serve as a great sign.

If a male were the oldest child, he would tend to be more responsible. If the youngest, he might be more spoiled. If he's the middle child, he has learned to negotiate for what he needs, or could have been shy and withdrawn, or sought attention by acting as the class clown or by being the "trouble child." Listen for any signs of extreme sibling rivalry or fighting.

3. What are your happiest and saddest memories?

If he seems to have excelled in school, sports, music, the arts or other activities, talked of good friends, favorite teachers/coaches, had a happy school life and teen experience, he should be well-balanced.

Listen for any signs of bullying, peer rejection or fighting, struggling socially or with grades at school, or with loneliness, anxiety or depression. This could have led to a lack of self-esteem as an adult, and he could be a man seeking female attention to build his ego.

4. Tell me about your last long relationship (or ask if they have been married). Ask him why he thinks it ended.

If the breakup had been due to a specific circumstance (like his wife having an affair), a girlfriend having had an addiction or other toxic issue that he could no longer endure, or he experienced the death of a life-long partner, these are all understandable circumstances for a relationship to end. Do ask for him to expand his answer to get more information. Remember, as you ask these questions keep it very light and conversational. You do want to know if someone is emotionally available and healed from a breakup, and you need some important relationship history to determine if this date could be a good fit for you.

However, if he admits to you that he cheated, move on and don't look back. Cheaters often repeat this pattern of behavior because of low moral integrity and a lack of strong boundaries.

No concern is shown for their partner's feelings, they have difficulty communicating their problems, and they possess an easy willingness and ability to engage in deceitful behavior. Your new dating partner should keep the answers short and admit some good qualities about his previous partner. You don't want to over-investigate his past relationship early on.

If he asks you this question, don't talk a long time about your ex or elaborate on any messy details. Instead, you can say, "I learned a lot. We had some wonderful times and all has been forgiven. We've both moved on, and I hope that he's happy." Don't be negative or bitter and don't share endless amounts of information about your past either.

5. If you're near or considering retirement, and he has at least one divorce in his history, ask how the divorce settlement went. Is he stuck with life-time alimony? You're trying to figure out if he's in a lot of debt or lost half his pension, his home and much of his assets. Has he rebuilt his life since the divorce? As time goes on, you can get more details in this area.

Although you may think these questions are too personal, you *need* to know the answers. Many men and women are crushed financially after a divorce, and with you planning your retirement, you should avoid being with someone who may rely on you for their financial support. You want a partner with a regular income, no debt, alimony or loans (except perhaps a small mortgage), has some investments, and either owns a home/condo, or has the savings to buy one with a future partner. In general, he has his financial act together and has an excellent credit score over 750. You are looking for someone who has his life together. Anyone who does is looking for the same in a partner, so make sure you're financially sound as well before dating. Once things get serious, you could offer the fact that you have no debt, where you credit score is, and see if he offers the same information.

6. Do you see yourself remarrying again?

If you want marriage, you're looking for a "yes" or "I would definitely consider doing that if I met the right lady." This man is seriously looking for a life-long partner. If he says that he isn't sure but would like a companion or an exclusive relationship, then that's an honest answer but one that probably won't lead to marriage.

If the answer is "no," ask why not. Perhaps this man is older and wants a life partner and exclusive relationship but without the legal ties. He may want an exclusive commitment without marriage or to live together, sharing both his and your home, but keeping assets separate. Or, he may say he was tied down for too long and just wants to date and have fun. Avoid this last one, he could break your heart, and you won't convert him.

It's up to you to decide what you're looking for, but don't imagine after he says that he won't marry you that you can convince him otherwise. Believe whatever he says. If you feel this man is just looking for sex or a good time, you should move on. You've probably already met enough of those!

7. If he has children ask, "How old are your children, and how is your relationship with them? Do you see them often, and what are they doing with their lives?"

You should know if he's an involved loving father, emotionally supportive, and who has positive, open and regular communication with his children. You're looking for fond memories and a sense of pride for who his children are. He should make an effort to visit with them if they're grown or if he's divorced. If his children are over age twenty-one, they should be in college, working or on their own and starting to have some personal successes. Be careful if his adult children are still living at home, in rehab, are unemployed, or just don't have their life together.

If the children are teens, ask what their future plan is (like college) and if it's already financially arranged and/or planned for. You're carefully looking to see if they're still being supported, how much child support is paid each month, if there are college bills (now or in the future), and if the children have problems, addictions or mental health issues. Ask why any adult children aren't able to leave home, if they're broke and living off their parents, or have a strained relationship with their dad.

8. What are your hobbies? Do you like to travel? Do you like to dance, see concerts or shows, attend sporting events, etc.?

You're trying to see if you'll have fun with this person. You want someone whose friendship and company you can enjoy for many years. Very often, a relationship falls apart when activities aren't shared. There should be enough interests in common as a couple so that you enjoy quality time together on the weekends or in retirement.

Don't settle in this area. If you love to dance and he says "I will learn," or "sometime you can teach me," or "yes, I'll dance if I'm drunk enough" trust me, he won't dance for long. A true dancer loves to dance and usually will have been doing so for years. If you love to travel to warm island places, and he likes to snow ski on his vacations, this will become a problem. If he's a huge fan of football, and you aren't, you may feel like you've been put on the sidelines during football season. It's fine to want to learn an activity he prefers, but it's best to share many common interests from the moment you meet.

9. If you're over fifty, ask what his retirement plans and goals are. Where does he see himself in three to five years? Does he plan to retire and where would he choose to live?

If you've been making your own retirement plans, it's important that you align your retirement futures. If he seems much further behind in his planning, this might be a sign that he has yet to take financial responsibility for himself.

You must be very cautious not to make any financial mistakes. If you're close to retirement you already know that it's much harder to make up for large losses over age fifty. See this new relationship, in part, as a business relationship, and you want this business – the rest of your lives – to succeed for both of you. So no matter how nice someone is, if they have a lot of debt, no savings or investments, home or retirement plans, pension, or have costly health issues, you must protect yourself and move on. This is not a good choice for you. Allow yourself to become seriously involved only with someone extremely stable who can bring something to the table. I have found while dating that men who have their life together and a solid financial plan will share it openly and completely with me without me needing to ask. This man wants me to know he is financially secure, a quality he's quite proud of. He'll share his complete retirement plan if he's interested in a possible future with you.

Of course, when you first date you can't ask for his full financial history. If there's mutual chemistry and he starts talking about exclusivity after a while, then that's the time to discuss what a future would look like together. It's a time to be honest about your assets and credit history to evaluate if, together, you would have a solid and financially secure future. Be careful, though, if he wants to be exclusive or marry right away. Pay for a computer background check and ask about his finances.

This is the time to ask him about debts, to see credit reports and scores, discuss values of assets or pensions, and any life-time alimony obligation. From his answers, you'll get an idea of where he stands. If you're over fifty and you own a home, several retirement plans, or are expecting an inheritance, tell him you would be having a prenup drawn if you're considering marriage. A man who has his own assets will not want any of yours and will be fine with a prenup that protects you and your children! If he owns a home and his own assets equal to or more than yours, you should feel financially secure and perhaps could waive a prenup, unless he has a business where a loan or lawsuit could cause you jeopardy. Keep separate bank accounts (especially for inheritance money), and have a joint account for mutual and shared expenses. Once married, his debt and poor credit merges with yours, which can affect you in a negative way for years!

Do not fall in love with someone's potential! Either they have a retirement plan and assets, or they don't. If he honestly loves you and wants to provide you with a safe and secure future, he'll be the one to bring up financial and retirement plans early on. He'll have no problem with showing you his reports and assets if he's looking to get engaged. At that time you should prepare a solid retirement plan.

Do not overlook his flaws or unresolved baggage! A man must be totally free and healed from past relationships in all areas of his life to be a good partner for you. If you hope that things will improve or change, be wary. Men often resist change so don't expect it if you see something in him you truly don't like. He must want to change for himself, not for you. Change is very difficult, as made evident by those with addictions. Consciously they may want to change, and know that it's best for them to do so, but after staying clean for a while, they often sabotage their success. You will be disappointed if you expect him to change or stop his addictive behaviors. Be choosy and select a partner who already has the important successful characteristics and qualities you desire.

The following guidelines address dating issues for women who desire a healthy, loving partner and stable relationship.

1. A man wants to earn your love. This concept goes back to the reptilian brain and caveman days. Men like the feeling of "winning you." In the beginning, don't be sexually available, don't chase him, or initiate phone calls or texting. Let a man contact you first; he will if he's truly interested.

2. Don't talk to a man like you would a woman. Men rarely think about relationships and are more focused and goal-oriented on personal success. He won't show love the way a woman does, and you shouldn't expect the fairy-tale hero. His primary need is to feel safe with you, which allows him to share his feelings.

3. Know your own rules and guidelines in a relationship. If anything comes up that makes you feel uncomfortable, follow your intuition and stop dating. If your rule is not to date a married man and you discover that he's separated, but not divorced, stop seeing him and stop talking to him until the divorce is final. Ask him to show you the final divorce decree.

4. How you treat yourself reflects your own self-respect. Know who you are, what you want, and what you have to offer. Be a strong partner with an obviously well-balanced life (career, finances, parenting, spirituality, emotional stability, and health consciousness). Accept his compliments with gratitude and smiles. Men will treat you like a treasure if you feel that you are one. Reward his positive behavior with words and actions of appreciation. Let him know about your wants and needs and what makes you happy. Never demand or threaten. Choose your partner carefully and consciously rather than falling in love with romance.

5. Men will be at their best to win you and might act in whatever way it takes to have sex with you. The choice always remains yours. Take responsibility and pace the relationship. Guard your emotions until you're sure of who he really is. Friendship first is the best path to intimacy and trust. It also nurtures a woman's sense of sexual desire and her confidence in committing to a meaningful and lasting relationship.

6. Be your best self! How you want to be perceived is up to you. You decide whether you're seen as happy or angry, confident or insecure, negative or optimistic, hard to get or easy. When you focus on loving yourself your energy projects a positive, vibrant, sexy, romantic and alluring presence of being. You flirt because you feel poised and sexy. Keep your options open as you wait to meet your Mr. Right. When you're on a date with a man, he'll feel special and find it easy to say, "Wow, you make me look good!"

7. Your own behavior should demand the respect you deserve. Don't accept any behavior that doesn't feel right to you. Mention your disappointment if he hasn't called as promised, or do what he said he would do. Tell a man clearly what you expect, and if he doesn't want to agree to it, then stop dating him.

8. Your date will want to know about you too, and where you're going in life. Most men prefer not knowing too much about your ex and can feel uncomfortable if they think you're making comparisons. Men are goal-oriented and will want to know if you're open to a new relationship and completely done with past suitors. Be honest and tell him you're dating several people if you are. You shouldn't feel guilty about this because you're dating to enter an exclusive relationship with the right person. If he wants you exclusively, he will let you know, and at that time, you should stop dating others if you can envision a future with him. Be sure that you're at the stage in your life when you *are* ready for commitment. If you prefer only casual dating, be honest and say so.

9. Until a man speaks of exclusivity or commitment, don't choose him as "the only one" or see only him. Enjoy the new friendship without making demands or having any preconceived expectations. Remember, you want a quality friendship first that could lead to a relationship and on to commitment.

10. If you damaged the dating relationship, listen to your partner's concerns and acknowledge the full seriousness of your actions and how they affected your partner. Apologize

with sincerity and explain what you'll do differently to rebuild trust again.

11. Don't put your life on hold for a man who isn't ready for an exclusive relationship. He may have legitimate reasons for not feeling ready – such as a career change, illness or family issues, or financial pressures. Remain friends without placing demands on him. At the end of his crisis, the friendship might blossom into a more intense and wonderful relationship. When a trusting friendship turns to love, the man was likely attracted to you from the beginning. Taking things slowly allows him to get to know you as someone he can feel safe with. If, however, the attraction remains one-sided (you only), or he fails to call or write to you on a regular basis, then the relationship won't go beyond friendship for him, and you're wasting your time.

12. Don't "manage" him or the relationship. Strong career women are often problem solvers, but this approach ruins relationships. Men want to feel needed and to feel they can handle their own issues. Their egos need to feel like "the man" in the relationship. Learn to relax by doing less; stop being dominating or manipulative. "Where is this relationship going?" is one of the worst questions you can ask a man. When they're interested in a deeper relationship, they'll let you know. Just keep dating until he brings up exclusivity. Also, don't negate or play down your successes or come across as stupid or coy. Men love confident women.

13. You may not feel a huge rush of attraction when first meeting your life partner. He may not seem particularly charming,

yet there's is a gentle tug of attraction. When you build a friendship without expectations of anything more, you'll discover all you need to know as you both reveal your true selves. Fictional movie characters fall in love quickly whereas real people fall into real love slowly and live more fully ever after. Take the time needed to really get to know someone without smothering or exerting pressure.

As you get to know someone, chemistry influences different types of attraction, as noted below.

- ◆ Physical: Within the first five seconds of seeing someone, there is either physical chemistry or not. Very important to the male.

- ◆ Emotional: You're in touch with who you are, and able to positively share your feelings. You possess emotional maturity, which includes honesty and integrity, two key ingredients for a lasting relationship.

- ◆ Intellectual: You should be well matched on levels of life experience, career success and education.

- ◆ Spiritual: A person who lives a spiritual or faith-based life is kind, loving, giving, and mindful of others. Self-respect leaves you open to giving and receiving love. You're happy and successful in all life's spheres and project a positive energy.

- ◆ Go out only with singles you respect, would love to have as a friend and who inspire you to feel happy and confident.

14. Know the world is abundant. There are plenty of wonderful men to meet – just put yourself in places where healthy

men may gather: church, self-empowerment or personal growth seminars, business groups, or in recreational activities you enjoy. Be proactive and get yourself out there to meet great people. Don't settle or compromise on your requirements and wants list.

15. Don't rush into commitment based on short-term impressions and visions of romance. Don't gloss over warning signs and signals you don't want to see. Avoid letting lust blind you to the glaring signs of evident toxic behavior.

When you know the criteria for a healthy, evolved partner, it will be easier to recognize when you've found him. No one is perfect, so if you're happy and satisfied 80–85% of the time then those are good odds. Stop settling for the wrong guy, looking too hard or chasing after indifferent men.

Although you may think that some actions appear friendly, they'll be seen as chasing a man, something you want to make sure you don't do! Don't pursue or force a relationship upon a man. Such actions include:

1. Asking him why he hasn't called you.

2. Calling to invite him to go to an event, hear a band, or read something interesting you wanted to share with him.

3. Texting him that you're upset because you haven't heard from him, or wonder if he's mad at you, or what he's been doing.

4. Giving him information he hasn't asked for, or offering to buy him anything.

5. Don't contact him by email, text, phone, ask to be friends on Facebook, contact his friends to ask about him, or drop by his home or office.

6. Don't try to force the relationship to move faster by offering to cook for him, have sex, let him stay over, make plans that include him, or initiate affection (even a kiss). This also should include sending him pictures or cards, or creating things you can do together. Constantly trying to talk with him about commitment will make him anxious and he'll retreat, even if he was about to commit on his own. He needs to feel, independently, that he won you and he will initiate exclusivity when he can't stand the thought of you with another man.

7. Don't try to convince him about what a great couple you are. When he falls in love, he'll feel safe enough to share the deepest part of himself and feel confident that he can make you happy. Share specifically how he does make you happy about your time together.

8. Don't expect anything from him when you're dating. Realize that it's natural for a man to distance himself as he starts falling in love with you. He feels vulnerable and scared, so coming and going is normal. He's questioning whether he can handle the relationship, so give him space to decide without pressure. He becomes more attracted when he starts missing you so it's important to *do, say and expect nothing* as he pursues you at his own speed.

   When he does come to talk to you, be available and share your honest feelings without blame, drama or demanding anything. He wants to be the one to give to you, make you happy, and tell you he loves you first. Be open to receiving when he does come to you.

9. Anything that seems needy or desperate is a turn-off. Just be yourself, and be his friend without calling or texting him. If he tells you he's not into having a relationship with you, believe him, and brush it off and begin or keep dating others. A man respects and is attracted to a woman who knows what she wants in life and who is committed to her own goals and dreams.

10. Don't use sex or cooking to make a man fall in love with you. He'll take the sex and the food, then later see you as manipulative and desperate. Stop trying so hard; don't try at all! Don't pay for dates. Too much giving (attention, gifts, affection, time) will make him feel guilty and anxious especially if he gives less. This overdoing will appear too forward and as if you have no boundaries. Maintain your self-control and power by keeping your dating options open and your life busy and fun.

11. A man's nature is to want to serve, provide and protect. If you're the one doing those things, he won't feel inspired to be with you. No matter how powerful you are, he has to feel needed. When you do want his help, simply ask for his help and then show appreciation for his efforts.

12. When he knows you have feelings for him and loves being around you, he'll ask for commitment to ensure that another man doesn't get to you first.

How to Meet a Healthy Partner

Love will happen when you least expect it. You never have to "look for," "chase," or "work on" finding love. A loving partner will present himself when you radiate a light of self-respect and confidence. All you need to do is get busy living your life to the fullest, have faith, and know you deserve someone wonderful!

Tips to Know if He Loves You:

A gentleman I'm dating told me, "A man who is inspired by an amazing woman will never disappoint – ever!" He described his loving feelings for me as, "love is how you feel about yourself through the inspiration of who you are with." Men certainly have profound feelings of love and they know when they *feel it* for a woman. It can happen for them quite quickly. I once completed a survey involving more than ninety men for my Master's program. Eighty-five percent said they knew on the first date that they were in love and wanted to marry the woman they had just met. Then 10% said they knew they were in love by the second date, and the balance of 5% knew by the third date. Women take longer to know they're in love because they're hard wired to want safety first from a man, which takes time to develop.

Seven factors should exist when a man loves you. If five or six exist, he may be in love, but isn't confident enough to say the words. If only three or four exist, he may think you're great, but he isn't in love yet. If there are only one or two, he may be using you, so keep your options open.

1. Does he make you a priority in his life? You should be in the top three (which could fluctuate) such as, job, girlfriend, and hobby. He shows you that you're important to him through regular acts of kindness and giving occasional gifts.

2. Does he say the words, "I Love You" or other terms of endearment, like "I adore you"? If a man attaches too early, and he says those words too soon, he may be looking for a mother.

3. Does he introduce you to his family and friends? Usually he'll introduce you to his friends first, to hear their opinion. They'll judge to see if you're a "cool chick," which in guy-speak means, yes, they like you for their good buddy. When he takes you home to his parents or introduces you to his children he's serious about you. He definitely isn't hiding you from these important people in his life.

4. Does he look at you like he wants you? What he *sees* is very important. All reports on men said they'll check out other women, but a man who loves you will barely notice and look at you instead with desire.

5. He looks at you when he's making love to you because he wants to make sure he's pleasing you. When he's looking at you and concentrating on pleasing you, he isn't thinking of another woman.

6. He respects you by treating you like a lady and acts like the traditional, courting man, who "takes care" of his woman. He encourages you to have time with your friends and activities outside of the relationship. He isn't jealous of your past relationships. He treats you like an equal partner in all important decisions regarding your relationship.

7. Your friends and parents like him and how he treats you.

A man who loves you gets pleasure from making you happy. Because he's frightened of losing you to another, he sees himself committing to you. When he thinks of you, he experiences excitement and attraction and starts to crave your love and attention. This emotional hunger for only you makes no other woman attractive to him. He'll have an inner drive to fight for you and protect you. This "spell" of deep inner feelings is from the pleasure felt when he is with you.

Initially, these intense feelings may scare or intimidate him after a great few dates, or after making love to you, and he'll create distance. Usually, women get clingy at this stage, and start calling after him.

This is the worst thing to do. He has escaped into his "man cave" to wonder if he sees a future with you. Give him time and space and back off; he'll want you even more. Keep dating and enjoying your life. Believe deep within your soul that you deserve a wonderful man and stay confident to that truth. When he misses you, the flame of desire and passion continues to burn.

Chapter 20

Defining Qualities, Needs and Requirements

We learn wisdom from failure much more than from success; we often discover what will do by finding out what will not do; and probably he who never made a mistake never made a discovery. – Samuel Smiles

A<small>CCORDING TO</small> D<small>AVID</small> S<small>TEELE</small>, founder of my Relationship Coaching Certification program, *Relationship Coaching International* and author of *Conscious Dating,* every person should have a well-defined list of *Requirements, Needs and Wants* to feel a level of happiness and contentment in their love relationship. It is important to first have a vision; an internal image of your desired outcome that leads you to make certain choices in life or a partner.

When your vision is off track, you feel anxious and stressed, and when you're on track, you feel motivated and excited, yet content and peaceful. Your vision helps clarify your purpose in life, your reason for living, which in turn leads to personal power and success and the difference you make in the world. If your love partner doesn't complement this purpose or vision for your life, then you'll feel unsupported, empty and anxious. Your defined vision is important to the exact type of partner you want to include in your life; otherwise, you will not be happy in your love relationship.

Requirements

Requirements are standards that you feel you must have in a quality mate. They are necessary to fulfill your vision of an ideal life and mate. The test of a requirement is that if you feel it missing, this relationship likely will not work for you. Standards are non-negotiable, because if one is missing, the problem can become unsolvable and the relationship fails. If you don't see them within the early dating stage, stop dating and wasting your time, no matter how attracted you are to the person. Some common requirements involve lifestyle, children, financial or future goals, religion, and character traits or values.

You are looking at a person's character. Below are a few words/descriptions that should fit your own *must-have requirements* of good character. Choose your top ten in order of importance, with number one being most important to you. Feel free to add words of your own.

Able to negotiate through conflicts

Active listener

Addiction-free

Adventurous

Altruistic

Dependable

Emotionally supportive

Energy/vitality for life

Family oriented, a good parent/love of children

Financially responsible/secure

Generous/giving

Hard working

Honesty

Integrity

Intelligent/educated

Kind

Leader

Monogamous/wants a commitment or marriage

Mood management/adaptable to change/flexible

Open communicator/open with feelings

Organized/neat/picks up after himself

Patient/punctual

Respectful

Romantic/sensual

Self-confident

Sense of faith/spiritual

Sense of humor

Shared future vision and interests

Socially confident/outgoing

Successful and proud of their accomplishments

Supportive to your feelings, goals and dreams

Trustworthy

Values are sound

Now that you've identified your top ten *must-have requirements*, write a list of top ten *must-not-have personality issues*. These are the deal breakers, and if one exists, move on immediately! Some situations might be temporary, like unemployment. In such cases, and for a limited period of time, be supportive and give this person a chance to rebuild his life. However, until he's had enough time to get his life back in balance, this wouldn't be a good time for you to date him exclusively.

Risky personality traits and other issues that could be problematic include:

Abusive tendencies (emotionally, verbally, physically or financially abusive or controlling)

Active addictions

Distant/cold

History of cheating

In debt/poor credit report and scores

Defining Qualities, Needs and Requirements

Mental health problems or mood disorders (any issues listed in Section One of this book)

Narcissism

Poor parenting skills/relationships

Selfishness/stingy

Unemployed

Needs

Although *Requirements* are non-negotiable, *needs* could be somewhat flexible with a discussion of various alternatives. Issues are unmet needs and occur in all relationships. With proper communication, *needs* can be expressed and met, and the relationship can be successful. Conflict occurs when needs cannot be met or negotiated.

There are two types of *needs*:

1. **Emotional:** These needs are about being loved and accepted in the way that we need to feel secure and cherished. There are certain ways one likes to love and be loved. This is written about in *The Five Love Languages* by Gary Chapman. You can feel or give love by receiving gifts, being physically touched, spending quality time, words of affirmation, or acts of service. It's important for you to know how you want to be loved, and what your partner's love language is.

    Emotional needs are slowly uncovered with time. True quality relationships afford a mutual trust factor where each can share and meet the other's emotional needs, protect the frailty of past pain and vulnerabilities such as a childhood experience of abandonment or abuse. With respect shown and safety given to the partner's deep emotional needs, the capacity for multifaceted emotional intimacy, profound connection and love are met over the life of the relationship.

Some Emotional Needs are below:

Affection

Appreciation

Consideration

Empathy

Loyalty

Nurturing

Open with feelings

Optimistic

Patience

Thoughtfulness

Understanding

Validation

2. **Functional:** These needs are expressed as routines that must occur for your life to fit the comfort and vision you desire. There are expectations about daily events such as chores, parenting, or how to handle finances. If these events

Defining Qualities, Needs and Requirements

don't occur, you feel stress or anxiety but the relationship could still work. Issues could develop because your partner has an opposite opinion, like whether the toilet seat is left up or down. Issues can develop because you have certain habits and standards, and know how you want your life to be. To be successful, you must negotiate and work through each person's functional needs, routines and habits, so they feel their opinion is important. With these, you win some, and lose some, so try to be open-minded to your partner's needs.

Some Functional Needs are:

Cooperative

Excellent co-parent

Financially responsible

Good communicator

Good grooming/sense of style

Helpful around the house/repairs

Keep promises

Organized/neat/clean

Reliable/follows through

Shares household chores

Wants

Wants provide entertainment, pleasure, energy and enjoyment and can often change over time. They are not rigid and can often be met and satisfied with other wants. This includes how you have fun together, the type of music you enjoy, and shared hobbies and activities you both feel passionate about. These wants are still important to have an exciting and successful relationship.

Wants could include sharing the following activities:

Beach and ocean

Broadway shows

Camping

Comedy clubs

Concerts

Dancing

Drives in the country

Golfing

Gym workouts

Family holidays

Pro sports

Romantic dinner dates

Travel

Walking, biking or other specific activity

Wine tasting tours

Yoga

Defining Qualities, Needs and Requirements

When defining your *Requirements, Needs and Wants*, be careful not to be seduced by a partner's good looks or put too much value on needing "chemistry." Looks are superficial, and fade with time, and will be the least important item on the list of requirements for a happy relationship. Your perfect partner has to make you feel cherished and secure, accepted, and proud to be with him. Look for love and honor from a man through his personality, values, ability to communicate, stable moods, how he treats others, and how he makes you feel. These are the most important traits of a loving partner.

There is never a 100% perfect match; however, if your partner owns 85% of what you require, want, need and desire, very often the other 15% can be developed, changed, or accepted. Life and relationships are a compromise and require being open to another's requests as well.

Similarities and Differences

It is important to know if you and your partner share many common interests, the key to a long and satisfying relationship. There are many that could be on a list, but discuss the key topics with your dating partner to see if you're similar in these areas.

Activities: amount of TV, sports, time together

Attitudes on home environment, roles, shared chores

Finances, attitudes regarding debt, savings, investing, bill paying, sharing expenses, joint/separate accounts

Health, weight, exercise and lifestyle

In-laws, extended family time, where to spend holidays

Intelligence, educational similarities

Life goals, personal and couple goals, level of ambition

Life goals, retirement dreams

Music enjoyed, dancing, nights out – how much, where?

Openness regarding passwords, computer/phone use

Religious views, how, when and where to practice

Roles each partner plays in a relationship

Roles of parents and children

Sex drive, interest, desires, and fantasies

Shared activities, hobbies, separate interests

Sleep schedules, morning and evening routines

Social time, outside friendships, couple/family time

Socio-economic background

Traveling style and where to vacation

Views about alcohol, drugs, smoking, other addictions

Where to live, size, style and décor of home

Whether to have children, when, and how many

Create a plan for a shared vision once you feel your requirements, needs, wants and similarities are met.

Defining Qualities, Needs and Requirements

Your shared vision should include:

1. Family vision
2. Fun, interests and activities important to you
3. Lifestyle and home environment
4. Role of career or work
5. Shared purpose for your life together
6. Shared values

David Steele defines successful relationships as having a fulfilling, lifelong partnership with someone to love and be loved by. Both persons need to take full responsibility for their decisions, choices and actions by living consciously and being emotionally present.

Steele defines five elements of a successful relationship, which are summarized below:

1. Being fully committed. True intimacy is being fully emotionally present and available for each other. One's fears or defenses create the temptation to cling or seek distance. Commitment includes taking responsibility for our choices, handling our fears, being emotionally present and available to our partners.

2. Take responsibility for your own needs and be proactive in communicating those needs to others. Don't blame others for your unmet needs, expect others to take care of you, or get angry when others don't see things your way. Accept your partner as they are and be cooperative and responsive to their needs.

3. Take care of yourself and don't enable your partner. Keep a balance in life between self-partner-family, and work, relationship, and spiritual/activity time.

4. Communicate your issues, feelings, needs, wants, boundaries and desires as honestly as possible. Speak firmly but lovingly, listen to your partner's point of view on all issues, and try to reach a compromise.

5. Work to grow and learn to be a better person. Heal your past emotional issues, let go of needing to be in control, stop impulsive choices, handle fears, make your partner (not your parents) the priority, and continue to strive for unconditional love.

After the first date, you may feel turned off enough to not want to repeat the evening. I refer to this as "the one and done" date. Be polite, thank him for his company and later tell him you feel that you're not quite a match.

When unsure about someone, try a second date as sometimes during the first both people feel nervous. The third or fourth date should make clear the potential for an exclusive relationship. At this point, it's important to share at least eight to fifteen dates before becoming sexually intimate. During this period you both have the advantage of feeling comfortable together as you get to know each other. Ask all the qualifying questions to see if there are enough healthy traits and shared common interests for a lifelong relationship. By the twelfth to fifteenth date, if each is still interested in the other, there should be a strong sexual connection and feelings of love should prevail.

Within three to six months, you should be talking about exclusivity and feel fairly certain that this person meets all your

Defining Qualities, Needs and Requirements

requirements and needs for a lifetime relationship. Anything else should involve only what you feel can be easily compromised. Stop dating if you see too many fundamental differences and no future potential. Move on if he's reluctant to commit to marriage if that's what you desire. If everything goes well and he asks for an exclusive dating arrangement, an engagement should take place within six months to a year. Once engaged take at least two years to be sure this is the relationship you both want. If you break the engagement, return the ring. If he breaks the engagement, society's rule is that you keep the ring (unless you cheated or broke your promise to him).

From the beginning, stay honest and authentic. Relationships in which a person takes on a personality of pretense are destined to fail because of deception and manipulation. Build all your relationships on a foundation that is built on integrity and trust.

Preparation to enjoy love beyond your dreams begins with defining your life vision, goals and purpose, as well as knowing the type of person you want to attract. With this knowledge, you'll make better and smarter choices for a life partner. Don't settle for a good relationship – wait until you can have a great one!

One person I dated wanted an exclusive relationship the day after our first date. Considering we hadn't discussed any of that on our first evening together (and neither should you), I asked him to tell me how he envisioned our future together. Although he was very attentive, complimentary and we had enjoyed a fun date, his aggressive neediness so soon afterward was a huge red flag for me. I also learned he had been abandoned by his mother and felt angry about it. A man who hates his mother will treat you poorly. Stay away.

When I told him I wasn't ready for exclusivity, the passive-aggressive venom started to flow. This would definitely be another one and done! I ended it politely, saying we wanted different things in a relationship. When you know the rules for relationships, it's amazing how quickly and easily toxic behavior can be spotted. Successful dating begins with knowing what you want and need from your man, and he either has or doesn't have what you want or need. Lust can make you choose poorly. Know the warning signs, understand past patterns that make you choose faulty men, and if you see problems, end a relationship early in a kind way. Don't blame him, just exit so you don't have to deal with the dysfunction. When dating several men, losing one who isn't appropriate for you doesn't feel like a big deal. Know that a wonderful man does exist for you. It's simply a numbers game.

Begin by making room for a man in your life. Then make your lists, and *become everything you personally want to attract to your life*. "Like attracts like," as you'll read in the next chapter.

Chapter 21

The Law of Attraction for Love

Like attracts like. Whatever the conscious mind thinks and believes, the subconscious identically creates. – Brian Adams

---

I HAVE READ A LOT OF BOOKS on the Law of Attraction and really do believe in its lessons. This concept has been discussed throughout the book but its importance is worthy of further explanation.

Two lessons ideal for finding the healthy partner –

- Be *who* you want to attract.

If you want someone spiritually based, be spiritual. If you want someone honest, be honest. If you want someone socially confident, you also should be. If you enjoy dancing and want someone who dances, go to places where there is dancing. If you want to attract someone wealthy, be wealthy yourself.

- Be *what* you want to attract.

If you love the sunny climate, then live in a sunny climate and don't date a skier. If you want marriage, don't date someone who never has been married, or will never marry again. If you want financial security, have it already for yourself and don't date anyone without it. Find your financial match who will bring something of value into the marriage to make it a partnership. If you have a home, so should your partner. The same principle applies to any retirement plan. Salaries needn't match but should be relatively similar to what you earn. Neither party should have debt.

The Law of Attraction asks for you to pray or meditate on exactly what you want in your life. The clearer you feel about all that you want, the more you can see and then ask for it. I advise my clients, "Pray every day, twice a day. Start your prayer with your attitude of gratitude, by giving thanks for your blessings. Ask for what you want, *exactly*. You're putting the energy and confidence out there and believe you should receive it. This makes you more aware of the signs and signals that present themselves to you each day, inviting you to live in a more conscious way."

The Law says that your focused thoughts, which are backed by emotional feelings, create your reality. Like attracts like. If you resist or ignore a negative situation, or feel a sense of neediness for a mate, your state of mind will only get worse because *what you resist persists for you*.

The secret to being irresistibly attractive to your current or prospective partner is the satisfaction of your own emotional needs, purpose, life vision, and core values. Men like women who are happy and love their life. When a man feels safe with you, he will also feel that you're more special than any other woman. He wants your time, attention, affection and touch. You've connected with his deepest emotions. He'll let you know that he's interested in something more serious and lifelong. Men are attracted to a woman with a sexy, soft exterior and who is confident and resilient on the inside. Tap into your sexy feminine side and let go of the overworked, stressed-out, worried you who balances schedules and to-do lists. So take time to connect with your more feminine side, especially for your dates together.

The more you need someone, the more you're likely to repel that person. It's when you *don't need a partner* that you're more likely to attract one! People who have fulfilled their emotional and personal needs possess a manner of confidence and self-awareness. They love who they are and own their personal sense of power and purpose. They shine with an inner-light that attracts others to them. You can only attract love – you can't force someone to love you.

Live your values on a daily basis. Your core values give you purpose, whether that means inspiring others, creating, leading, managing, organizing, practicing spiritual concepts, or playing. Values are what you feel you were born to do, and you do them well. You're happily fulfilled and energized (or "in the zone") when you actively exercise a core value. Work on at least one each day and start truly living life. When you've met your own needs and are living a purpose-filled life, you will effortlessly attract loving people and plenty of dating opportunities. What repels a man is desperation, cheap drama, chasing, manipulating, or pretending to be someone other than your true, authentic self. Men appreciate an attractive woman but also like to see allure balanced with a natural and relaxed personality.

Values and passions recommended by Talane Miedaner from her book, *The Secret Laws of Attraction*, should include:

1. Cultivate beauty: let beauty surround you where you live and work by being artistic or creative. Make something beautiful, dress exquisitely, bring nature inside and have meaningful art surround you.

2. Create: write, design, build, take classes, cook, develop a business, product or service.

3. Lead: be a mentor, lead a company, coach a team, or motivate through speaking.

4. Contribute: volunteer to help children or the elderly, minister to others in your community.

5. Adventure: travel, take risks that don't hurt others, try a daring activity, or explore new territory.

6. Feel: take yoga, exercise, or dance; use any of the senses to create or explore.

7. Be spiritual: join a church or religious/spiritual group, read motivational/spiritual literature, become a minister, meditate.

8. Teach: be a teacher, trainer, public speaker, or consultant.

You can create your own value list with perhaps eight or ten values, but try to pick your top four to get started, and get busy enjoying yourself while you create a new you! You'll become, as well as feel, terrific.

To be irresistible and attract love into your life, you must not chase, convince, persuade, or seduce someone to be with you.

If the person you're dating is distant, let them go and put your energy into meeting someone else. They're not ready for love, and the relationship stops being fun. If it seems like a struggle at the beginning, it will be a nightmare later. When there is true attraction, the person will want to be with you and will do the pursuing. Love is easy when it's right.

Get involved with life and love will enter your existence. Be open to what comes your way and live consciously so you don't miss opportunities. Meanwhile, make your home your personal haven so that when a date visits he'll feel love and passion there. Your surroundings should generate an I-love-my-house sense every time you enter. Feeling peaceful, safe, content and calm in your home provides the rejuvenating time you need there.

Within the bedroom, create a setting for love with candles, aromatherapy, soft overhead lighting, luxurious silk or satin bedding, romantic music, clean and organized closets, and mess-free dresser tops. You should feel pure joy in your bed, either alone or with your partner.

An attitude of gratitude for the things you *do* have will attract more joy to your life. No matter how small, there are many things to be grateful for. Appreciate yourself and all your accomplishments.

If you are feeling anxious, bored or uneasy in your current career, the frustration in your life will be evident. Perhaps it's time to take a calculated risk and move, make a career change, go back to school, or take definite steps to change your life. This is best done while alone so that you're not responsible for bringing changes to anyone else's life. Calculated risk adds excitement, change and challenge to life, and doing something new will attract wonderful opportunities and people into your world.

Remember, attracting love is easy and effortless. You don't have to chase a love that's meant to be. You needn't seduce or work to win someone over. Just be the best, most evolved, whole, happy, and confident person you can be, and love will find you. Learn more about the laws of attraction and don't be afraid to give these techniques a try. There are many great books on how to live a spiritual life and I've recommended several in the Reference section of this book.

> *"Our soulmates seldom appeal to our personality – our ego. That's why they are called soulmates rather than egomates."*
> – Carolyn G. Miller, *Soulmates*

Chapter 22

Learning to Love Unconditionally

You must love yourself before you love another. By accepting yourself and joyfully being what you are, you fulfill your own abilities, and your simple presence can make others happy. – Jane Roberts

---

THE RENEWAL STAGE AFTER a toxic relationship or difficult breakup is marked by increased confidence due to an improved sense of self-control over one's life. When a sense of calm and acceptance of the past nonproductive relationship becomes the norm, one is ready to reinvest emotionally into a new relationship. You should experience a feeling of renewed energy, elevated self-esteem, and a sense of wholeness before starting to date.

After having been hurt by someone you trusted, it's hard to move on and love unconditionally again. But you must; otherwise, you won't know gratifying love if you never learn to love unconditionally. Here is where your spiritual study, reading and meditation become so important. Use your strongest spiritual sense to forgive your previous partner, as well as yourself, and ask for guidance to be a better partner in future relationships.

It isn't fair to imprint your past partner's injustices onto someone new. You must extend 100% trust to your new partner once you become exclusive, if that's what both of you want. Once exclusivity becomes the shared decision, then trust must be given. Exclusivity doesn't, and shouldn't, happen quickly. It should take at least 3 to 6 months before knowing that this is the only person you want to date to the point of seeing a future with this person. The decision should be made prior to any sexual activity.

If sex occurs too early, then the relationship may well be mostly about just sex rather than exclusivity or a long-term relationship. If a man shows impatience and doesn't want to wait, you'll know his intentions were primarily sexual. A man is happy to wait for sexual intimacy when he's crazy about you – being glad to have as much time with you as possible, enjoying every moment before making love. When love and friendship merge, the strongest, most lasting bonds are formed.

Trust develops and grows in the courtship phase. When you both take your time and enjoy the dating process, trust should be well established by the time you make love.

Love unconditionally until a red-flag warning appears, regarding his ability to be trusted. Have an open and loving discussion about why you are concerned over something he said or did; or didn't do. Calmly explain why this is important to you. Then come back to this book and review the importance of truth and honesty in grounding a relationship. People with a deeply spiritual faith place personal integrity first in life. It gives them personal power and a strong sense of self-esteem. They feel confident and both like and respect who they are as individuals. Therefore, they have the capacity to love their partner unconditionally as well.

The ninety-day rule of waiting for intimacy is important because within that time each of you has let down your guard enough to reveal authenticity. Yes, love and trust unconditionally, and show him that you do live with complete integrity. As time goes on, trust becomes stronger as he too continues to show levels of integrity. If you discover lies, secrets, cheating, he fails to do what he promised, he hides his phone, or you find sexy messages from other girls, get out of the relationship because he can't be trusted. Exclusive means exclusive, and you can either trust him or not.

If your integrity and trust is breached, be grateful that you discovered it early on. Don't buy into lame excuses. Trust your intuition, love yourself more and leave any relationship that doesn't have a trustworthy foundation. Let him go in friendship, wishing him well but explaining that the relationship no longer works for you because you no longer trust him.

If you choose to forgive him and want to extend another chance for him to prove his integrity, state again your boundaries for exclusivity and trust. Discuss your mutual relationship rules for emotional friendships beyond your primary relationship. This may be the one time you choose to forgive him spiritually, but if there's a second violation of trust, his true character will have been revealed and will remain unreliable.

I always advise giving someone complete trust initially because only they can betray it by acting inappropriately. Loving someone unconditionally is a spiritual-based concept you should extend to everyone when you begin to date. It adopts the notion of loving your fellow human beings in a kind and trusting way. However, you're never obligated to stay in a toxic or deceptive relationship of any kind.

Chapter 23

Relationship Rules of Success

Love is letting go of fear. – Gerald Jampolsky

THERE ARE NO GUARANTEES in love or life. What we hope for is to have a long, healthy life full of love – from family, friends, and a special partner. In a high-quality love relationship, you should feel safe emotionally and physically, as well as feel nurtured sexually, spiritually and intellectually. We aren't critical of our partner, but rather accepting of him and ourselves. We don't try to control, but instead give him supportive, unconditional love as we both focus on personal and couple growth as we build a life together.

The "norms" of relationships change over time. When I was a young girl in the 1960s there were very few divorces, parents stayed together despite being unhappy and affairs were not discussed. A couple getting divorced was a real community scandal. The majority of women stayed at home raising their children and had no financial means to move on; many lived for years in hopeless misery.

By the time I was twenty, in 1977, I was at Penn State University and expected to have a husband and career after graduation, start a family soon after marriage and college, and simply "do it all." The introduction of the "superwoman" years also was the start of much female dissatisfaction. We excelled in the job market but were underpaid, as resentment and burnout grew. We worked, raised kids, paid bills, cooked meals, and cleaned house with little or no help. The number of women engaged in affairs escalated. Not until the year 2000 did men start helping with the children and do some cleaning at home, after recognizing that women were largely unhappy in their marriages.

The best marriages today are a partnership in every way, from raising the children, to cleaning the home, to discussing and practicing a financial plan. They are about friendship and support, yet to keep the love and romance alive, balance between your love relationship, the family, and you, is imperative.

The interdependent relationship is one where two partners focus on being at their individual best and continue to strive to reach their respective dreams. At the same time, they choose to be exclusive to one, loving partner, which is different from being codependent, self-sacrificing, overly needy or controlling of your partner. Exclusivity results in two, evolved, happy and emotionally healthy people choosing each other to love and share their lives in a non-dependent way.

As couples come to my office daily for coaching, I see many putting both their relationship and themselves last, while putting their children and career first. They complain of burnout, stress, lack of sexual drive, depression, anxiety, and resentment. We look at their individual life and relationship balance, and how they can improve balance for themselves, their accountability to their partner, and improve the overall family structure. They learn that they must put themselves first, relationship second, and their children third for their marriage and family to stay together over the years.

Being accountable to the self, relationship and family means each individual partner is financially responsible, lives in truth and with integrity, are absent of any addiction, and strive to be a role model for themselves, their marriage and their children. They start each day by counting their blessings and feeling grateful for what they *do* have, and live consciously, making sure they don't dwell on what they *don't* have. They practice being positive individuals, bringing happiness into their union and the time shared together.

Knowing life is short and should be lived consciously in "the now," they lovingly kiss and hug their partner hello and goodbye, and encourage their children daily to do their best. They keep life balanced so that they can each have exercise and meditation time, dinner together, and provide a few activities for their children, but nothing is done to excess. They plan every Saturday night as a couple's date night *(their special time together)*, and look forward to dressing up for each other on their romantic date. Once a month they may meet with friends on their date night, but the majority of time, it's spent only with each other. They agree to not talk about anything negative or about chores and schedules. This is a time to let loose, have fun and romance your partner. They take turns planning and surprising their partner with the date they have in mind.

Friday night is family night, so a special outing, board game, or pizza and a movie are planned when the whole family gathers together. Computers and phones are put away, giving full attention to one's partner and children for the remainder of the day. After self, one's partner come first, children second, in-laws third, and siblings/friends fourth in priority. They have learned to say "no" so they don't over obligate themselves outside of their relationship or immediate family.

Today there is so much financial stress and fear over affairs and addiction as work hours become longer and more demanding. It's important to break your day into one-third time segments as previously advised, to live consciously and take the time to make yourself and your partner feel special. The little things are the big things: being kind, sending a random love text, picking up a card or flowers "just because," dressing attractively each day for yourself and your partner, doing the chores in a helpful, balanced way, taking the time to hold hands, hug, and kiss throughout your day. All these items combined add up to a blissful union.

The new, interdependent relationship rules for a successful, lasting evolved partnership are:

1. Live each day as if it may be your last. Don't give up your sense of self, but don't stop loving your partner and showing how much you cherish him. Carve out daily time for each other. During work hours, plan new goals for yourself. Talk with your partner about how to support one another's individual time off to exercise, go to yoga, a religious service, to study, or to visit briefly with a friend or family member.

For relationship balance, picture a three-sided equilateral triangle with the three sides for self, partner and children. Many times, with stress, the time balance given to each entity can become skewed. If you and your partner remain balanced, stress and anxiety stays down for everyone.

2. Never argue in public or discuss your private disagreements with family or friends. Family can be very judgmental – for or against you. Friends will support you, and may be upset with your partner, and if you work things out, the situation then becomes awkward for your friends in the future.

3. Both practice open and honest communication daily, with no fear, yelling, demands, control or lies. Don't hold back anger or resentment. Take a therapeutic communication break (T-break) if the discussion gets heated, but do return to it calmly so the issue can be settled.

This break can be thirty minutes to two hours, but is not an excuse to go out all night. It's fine to leave the house to run an errand or go to the gym, but tell your partner where you're going and when you're expected to return. Be respectful when you choose to take a break. While separated, each partner needs to come back to the conversation with at least two ideas on how to compromise or solve the issue. Choose to do what is best "for the team."

4. Both must live in integrity and you each must do the right thing when no one is looking! Ultimately, God is watching, and you will be found out. Lies, deceit, emotional or sexual affairs, verbal or emotional abuse, lack of maturity and emotional control, and various addictions are what ruin most marriages today.

5. Both must take care of themselves – image is important to both men and women. Eat healthy, exercise to maintain your weight, dress attractively and practice good hygiene. Try to stay as close to the image you were when you first

met. As you age and grow older together, both keeping optimum health is important for an enjoyable retirement.

6. You must put your partner first before parents, friends, in-laws, siblings or children. Make them feel loved, cherished and important every day in some small way. When you two are strong, the family unit will stay together, thus benefitting your children.

7. You must privately pledge to stay sexual – at least once to three times each week. Both partners should make advances to the other. If you're not feeling up to it one night, promise you'll make up for it soon, and do so. Keep sex exciting and playful by engaging in fantasies and romance to keep it passionate and loving with a deep emotional connection.

8. Take a partner-only vacation for at least one week, once or twice each year. Two to four times a year try an overnight out-of-town escape but keeping it close to home. Take a family vacation at least once a year. Cut back on other things for vacation time, or make it a yearly holiday tradition in lieu of a lot of gifts.

9. Both partners need to be mentally strong and emotionally healthy individuals. Neither should have an addiction. The lies, deceit, money spent, and lack of integrity surrounding addiction ruins a relationship almost immediately once it's discovered.

10. You must be an equal partner in household and child-rearing activities, balancing things around your work schedules. Do heavy cleaning for one hour together on

the weekends. Share laundry, cooking, dishes, vacuuming, yard work, and other chores as a team. Assign your children duties so they learn while young that they need to be responsible too, that you appreciate their help, and they're part of the family team.

11. You both must be open and honest about your finances and where the joint money is going. I believe it's acceptable to have your own accounts, but all credit card statements and bills must be open to each partner. If one partner spends selfishly on their own hobby, sport, or entertainment, including business travel, that leaves a lot less for the two of you as a couple.

12. There should be no secret passwords for phones, Facebook, email or anything else. These passwords encourage a secret life that can lead to the end of a relationship.

13. Have some spiritual faith or religious practice that you share together. Weekly service is strongly encouraged for you and your children. Faith in God or your higher power brings about accountability for living a life of excellence. Faith helps you believe in abundance and helps you feel your loving relationship will be blessed.

14. If you encounter trouble, seek relationship coaching or couples counseling right away – don't wait. Coaching and counseling opens the door for honest communication and trying new things. It offers a third-party opinion for issues you may be divided on, and helps you to move forward in a positive direction.

15. Don't go to bed mad or upset over unresolved issues. You can ask your partner to "take a break" or to think things over by "sleeping on it" and then agree to discuss things again in the morning when you both can approach it with a new perspective. Tell him you love him and that you have the intension of wanting to work things out. Don't run away from the issues or your partner, don't leave the house angry or without saying where you're going, and don't shut down, refusing to talk for days. Immature, passive-aggressive and toxic behavior will kill the love within most relationships.

16. Don't give up. If things are volatile, a few hours of quiet thinking, or an overnight stay at a parent's or friend's house to decompress may help. Think of why you fell in love and married your spouse, and practice some soul searching on what you can personally do better. Avoid the blame game, and take responsibility for what mistakes you made and changes you need to put into place. Then return to your partner with an open heart and mind, and a rededication to making your relationship work.

Remember, it always takes two people to make a relationship work. If both dedicate themselves to the relationship rules of success with 150% effort from each, your loving, evolved relationship can last forever, creating for both of you, love beyond your dreams!

Conclusion

Love Yourself More! Facing Your Future Boldly

We all cling to the past, and because we cling to the past we become unavailable to the present.

– Bhagwan Shree Rajneesh

THIS BOOK IS ABOUT FINDING the love you deserve, that meets your desires and needs and that is mutually loving and satisfying for both partners. It won't always be easy, and it isn't always smooth sailing. When one partner breaks wedding vows or promises made, consistently lies, engages in an addiction, or has other destructive personality traits, they must apologize sincerely, show remorse and be willing to get individual therapy and couples coaching. If you're the only one willing to work on the relationship and there is neither an apology nor any effort from your partner to change destructive habits, then you must love yourself more and move on. Face your future boldly and with faith that you *can* achieve and attract love beyond your dreams.

Know that God has a plan to bring healthy love into your life. Doing your daily goals toward personal transformation and saying your prayers of gratitude should include thanking God for lining up and providing a new, evolved partner to enter your life. Thank Him for sending this new love your way. Use the law of attraction to feel and believe a new love is coming into your life. Prepare yourself and every aspect of your life to receive him. Keep an open mind and give unconditional love to all those you meet. One of those people will be your new love. You are now looking beyond exterior packaging, faulty love maps and the instant rush of chemical attraction. You're taking the time to get to know the real heart and soul of a person as you become friends first, not rushing into sexual intimacy. You now clearly know the positive character traits and qualities that encompass an evolved partner and those toxic behaviors that are warning signs not to get involved. You will be confident to quickly eliminate any dysfunctional dates because you won't settle for less until you receive the loving partner you deserve!

Make a goal for you and your new partner to live each day practicing the relationship rules of success. Discuss the sections of this book that define an evolved person and partnership so that your relationship stands the best success of life-long love.

If you are with a current partner who has recently caused you pain by lies or deception, it's the best spiritual practice to forgive him his infraction – the first time, and only if he will commit to individual counseling and couples coaching. However, you must clearly explain your boundary. If there is ever *one* more infraction, you will love yourself more and leave the relationship. You now know the second time a partner has an affair, or lies about or engages in an addiction, that this is a clear signal he has selfish, toxic personality flaws and loves "it" more than you or the relationship. Whatever "it" may be – alcohol, drugs, pornography, gambling, another person (real or in cyberspace), the hurtful actions and choices he had promised never would happen again he clearly repeated without remorse or concern for you. Recognize that the trust is now shattered and you must boldly move on to save yourself and attract a healthy love into your life.

You should see with this second incident signs of a deeper personality disorder that you may not have noticed before, such as sociopathy, narcissism, borderline, bipolar, or other toxic traits described in the first section of this book.

Leaving someone you still love is indescribably emotionally difficult, especially when so much of your love relationship was fun and exciting. But living on the edge, waiting for another toxic episode, another relapse into his addiction, or needing to become his "mother" to watch after his childish impulsivity, will keep you in a state of anxiety and depression. His dysfunction can make you physically sick, exhausted, moody, and codependent. You will lose yourself as you are trying to fix him and keep the pieces of this toxic relationship together. You know your own behavior is evolved, honest and in integrity, so why isn't his? He's probably not capable of giving it; he's a donkey and not a thoroughbred. You now know that you deserve better!

Gather up your courage and ask him to get help, or leave. If he refuses to get help or to work on the relationship, you must know keep down that this relationship is over. Look at it as a blessing as you prepare for change. You are now free of all the toxic pain you've likely endured for years!

Now your work will be to find "you" again. Time will pass slowly as you mourn the loss of your partner and the dreamed vision of your future together, along with the expectation that he would responsibly protect you and your love relationship. Take the time you need to heal. Arrange time off to relax, travel, spend time with children and friends and set new goals. Begin to dream, plan and prepare a new future vision and define the goals needed to achieve your amazing, exciting life and future evolved relationship. You can do this – and have faith it will work!

Don't jump into another relationship when you still feel sad or angry. It could take at least six months to a year or more until your heart may be ready for someone new. Know that when you're truly ready to date you won't be comparing your ex to anyone. You know that your past relationship had been unhealthy, and it has long ago been forgiven. Be sure to give the new person in your life a chance and extend full trust. Don't punish your new man for your ex's actions. If you begin to miss your ex at any time, pull out that journal list of all his deceptions and lies, and the toxic ways he treated you, and realize that you did the best thing to save yourself, your children and your future. Then write in your journal that you proudly had enough self-esteem not to contact him, because you chose to love yourself more!

The world is abundant, so trust that love will come to you when you pray on it and are open to receiving it. Successful relationships happen when two people take responsibility for their respective roles in the partnership, resulting in smart choices and decisions. Both need to ask four questions before making a choice:

1. Will this choice or action hurt me in any way?
2. Will it hurt the partner I love?
3. Will it hurt my children or extended family?
4. Will it hurt my reputation on the job or in the community?

Every choice you and your partner make affects the other and should be made to create happiness and a better life for the both of you. Well-informed choices make life easier and dating less traumatic. Your level of peace, bliss and happiness and your ability to be completely authentic confirms whether you're in the right relationship. If not, you'll feel anxious, depressed, exhausted, resentful and angry. It's time to set up a better life. Move on confidently, my friend, and without fear!

Osho, a great spiritual teacher, explained, "love brings freedom; it does not come out of duty, but out of your own experience of joy and your desire to share it. Love is not controllable, once it is gone, there is no way to bring it back." He wrote that, "love is wild, its whole beauty is in its wildness. It comes like a breeze with great

Conclusion: Love Yourself More! Facing Your Future Boldly

fragrance, fills your heart, and suddenly where there was desert there is a garden full of flowers. And just as it had come one day, as a guest, suddenly one day it is gone. There is no way to cling to it, no way to hold it."

He believed that marriage is about loyalty and created by a society wanting guarantees and securities, which removes love from life completely. He felt that loyalty is a form of slavery, and "only out of your freedom is your love, and out of your dignity is your trust." Here is his idea of a new humanity: "People will love from pure joy, but will not allow love to be ordered. Love is its own joy, by living in one's own sense of spirituality. Trust and loyalty will not be ordered from another, trust can only come from one's own sense of self. Love starts with self-love. Don't be selfish but be self-full. Don't be narcissistic or obsessed with yourself, but natural self-love and deep acceptance of oneself is a must. Only then out of it can you love somebody else. Love is only possible when you start seeing the uniqueness and beauty of others and the world."

Fear and lack of security arises when we become dependent on another for our happiness. Freedom to give and have love and be one's genuine self occurs without controlling, possessing or depending on another. This is the ultimate goal. Love can never possess or be possessed. Remember the old adage, "if you love someone, set them free." Learn to love something in every human being you meet. If you've loved someone and they've mistreated you in an exclusive relationship, you must recognize that you had given away too much of your personal power and freedom "out of duty or love." Love is never about duty put upon you or control over another. Set yourself free to have the love you deserve so that you will begin to transform and feel unconditional love for yourself and others. Once you understand this concept, you have the freedom and strength to leave a person who doesn't live in an emotionally healthy, loving way.

When you choose to date several people, the one person who tries to hurt you with toxic actions, words or abuse makes it easy to leave and continue to love many. Relationships should exist with numerous people – your children, friends, siblings, parents, and those whom you've come to love over a long period of time. Continue to seek consciously-aware people who understand that love is a treasure to share and not a conquest or ownership.

Like the rivers that flow, love will rush upon you, surround you and lift your spirits to the highest heights and fill the depths of your soul. But water flows on; you can't stop it, or possess it, or grasp it in your hand. If a love relationship ends by flowing out of your life, feel grateful for the love you shared. By becoming angry, fearful, revengeful, cynical, and emotionally closed off, love cannot flow back into your life. Forgiveness is essential, both for yourself and your toxic partner. The healthier self-love you possess, the easier it is to heal and experience other loving relationships. Before dating again, take the time you need to become the best you, and to feel confident, calm and open to new experiences by examining your life spheres to make sure you're really ready to get involved with someone exclusively.

Keep dating many until the natural flow of love progresses to a deeper state of friendship and connection with another. As you date, remember the warning signs of an emotional manipulator and keep your personal power strong to decide if this person is truly for you before becoming intimately or sexually involved and exclusive. Real love takes time. You may not recognize your true soul-mate right away – closeness usually comes from a treasured, long-term, trusting friendship. Be at peace – in calmness comes great light and insight. Meditate to quiet the mind. Take on new challenges to continue your personal growth toward self-love and confidence. Live life consciously in "the now" and find joy and laughter in the simple things presented each day. Don't wait until you have a new life partner to enjoy all of life's blessings. Start today!

Do not look for love, be love. Only then will it flow to you from many sources and it will surround you in all its essence.

I wish you a happy, evolved, peaceful and healthy love and life!

In Love and Light,
Riana

Every end is a new beginning – Unknown

Poems of Love and Emotion

Selections from Riana's High School Journal written at ages 13 through 18.

Relationships
I am
  You are
    We are.
I am not…if you are not.
And We cannot be.

Lonely Memories…
Love may come, and love may go
but it is always remembered.

The times you shared, cared, and understood
will never be forgotten.

When we laughed together, cried together
and loved together –
I never thought this would become a thing of the past.
A beautiful memory.

Your Key...
Talking is the key that opens the lock to understanding
For without conversation
A compromise cannot be met
A relationship cannot exist –
Without talking to me, I feel that is the key
to setting me Free...

Salad of my Mind
The indecision of what to do
Combined with the wanting to be with You
Mixed with feelings of Love and Hate
Tossed with dreams which I create.
Sprinkled with both the good and bad
Topped with all the great times we had.
Served with feelings of uncertainty
And with the knowledge that I've gotta be Free!

I Love You
My dear friend of age and old,
I wish you would say the words – so often told
Don't be afraid to say them to me
Don't worry my friend, you can still be free.
It's just a good feeling to know that you care
It's such a pleasure knowing you'll be there
Why do these words seem to frighten you?
Is it because of the time you were left lonely and blue?

Love is a Rose
Love, like a wilting flower, trying to stay alive –
   Wanting to survive, but knowing better.
It can't last, it's too beautiful to be true
   I'm dying with thoughts and memories of you.
Bent out of shape, and looking sad
   Holding knowledge that love is bad.

Il n'y a pas de rose sans épine

There is no rose without a thorn, just like the title said,

I found a thorn in you my love, and now Utopia is dead.

I found the "u" in Human, or should I say – the human that's in you,

With myths and Gods you don't belong, and the Devil owns you too.

My eyes were blind for half a year, my mind up in a cloud,

I dared to see for just one day, and now I'm not so proud.

My white rose wilted and has turned to black,

Yet how I fear to discard it, for I just might want it back.

Desperately Alone
Here today, gone tomorrow
   And I am left with such sweet sorrow.
He touched my heart, and then my soul
   And my Love he easily stole.
Not complete, and unfulfilled
   My mind and body are lonely, still.

Dream On...
My eyes are tired, my mind is weary
Yet I must not lie motionless, I cannot waste time
For it is precious and going rapidly...
I must find my dream and share it with others
For sharing many dreams is always more powerful than owning one
I hope to have the time to share mine...
The Dream of Love, Peace, and Understanding...
I hope others will join my dream;
   And perhaps, it will become reality!

Time's Running Out
When will the time come for complete happiness?
It wasn't in the past
   It's not in the present
      Will it come in the future?
Only the future is left
If we strive, we will reach it....
   If we do not try – it will never come.

Look Up!
Forget the past
   Forget the present
      Focus on the future...
It will come tomorrow – a brand new start
Your beginning...
   Your chance to try again!

Once Again –

   Thank you my Love, for being You,
     Thanks again, for all the things that you do.
   I think you know exactly how I feel,
     I'm sure you know my Love is Real.
   So far all my dreams have come true –
     The desire of sharing my life with you.

Hiku

   It's the way he is

     That makes him special to me

       To love only him.

Selections from Riana's daughter, Stephana Ferrell:

   Your fingers through my hair carry my heart through the wild storm of emotions; your presence adds to my day.

Limitations

   Carry me far from this heated fire, show me the way through the wild valley of untamed hearts, leave me standing at the gates of love, so that I may decide when to cross them.

Selection from Riana's daughter, Alexi Panos:

Commit to turning

Hurt into Hope.

Competition into collaboration,

Resentment into compassion.

Fear into determination.

And hate into love.

You choose which emotion rules the situation.

Choose wisely.

References and Recommended Reading

Al-Anon Family Groups: *Courage to Change, One Day at a Time in Al-Anon II: For Families & Friends of Alcoholics*. NY: Al-Anon Family Group Headquarters Inc, 1992.

Altalida, Lisa. *Dating Boot Camp. Conquering the Dating Obstacle Course*. NY: Alpha Books, 2004.

American Psychiatric Association. *Quick Reference to the Diagnostic and Statistical Manual of Mental Disorders, Fourth Edition*, Text Revision. Washington, DC, American Psychiatric Association, 2000.

Argov, Sherry. *Why Men Love Bitches: From Doormat to Dreamgirl – A Woman's Guide to Holding Her Own in a Relationship*. MA: Adams Media Corporation, 2002.

Assaraf, John, and Smith, Murray. *The Answer: Grow Any Business, Achieve Financial Freedom, and Live an Extraordinary Life*. NY: Simon & Schuster, 2008.

Bagarozzi, Dennis A. *Enhancing Intimacy in Marriage, A Clincan's Guide*. MI: Sheridan Books, 2001.

Ban Breathnach, Sarah. *Something More: Excavating Your Authentic Self* (audio recording). NY: Time Warner Audio Books, 1998.

Beattie, Melody. *Codependent No More. How to Stop Controlling Others and Start Caring for Yourself.* San Francisco, CA: Harper, 1987.

Behrendt, Greg, and Tuccillo, Liz. *He's Just Not That Into You: The No-excuses Truth to Understanding Guys.* NY: Simon Spotlight Entertainment, 2004.

Behrendt, Greg, and Ruotola-Behrendt, Amiira. *It's Called a Breakup Because It's Broken: The Smart Girl's Breakup Buddy.* NY: Broadway Books, 2005.

Brafman, Ori, and Brafman, Rom. *SWAY: The Irresistible Pull of Irrational Behavior.* NY: Doubleday Publishing, 2008.

Britten, Rhonda. *Fearless Loving: 8 Simple Truths That Will Change the Way You Date, Mate and Relate.* NY: Dutton Press, 2003.

Brown, Elizabeth B. *Living with Screwed-Up People.* MI: Revell, 1999.

Browne, Sylvia. *Lessons for Life and Blessings from the Other Side.* www.SylviaBrowne.com.

Butler, Gillian, and Hope, Tony. *Managing Your Mind: The Mental Fitness Guide.* NY: Oxford University Press, 1995.

Byrne, Rhonda. *The Secret.* (DVD movie). TS Productions LLC, 2006.

Carnes, Patrick, Ph.D. *Out of the Shadows, Understanding Sexual Addiction.* MN: Hazelton, 2001.

Carnes, Stefanie, Ph.D. *Mending a Shattered Heart, A Guide for Partners of Sex Addicts.* Carefree AZ: Gentle Path Press, 2011.

Carter, Steven and Sokol, Julia. *Men Who Can't Love: How to Recognize a Commitmentphobic Man Before He Breaks Your Heart.* New York: M. Evans and Company, 1996.

Chopra, Deepak. *The Book of Secrets: Unlocking the Hidden Dimensions of Your Life.* NY: Random House, 2004.

References and Recommended Reading

Chopra, Deepak. *The Seven Spiritual Laws of Success: A Practical Guide to the Fulfillment of Your Dreams* (audio recording). San Rafael, CA: New World Library, 1994.

Chopra, Deepak. *Ageless Body, Timeless Mind: The Quantum Alternative to Growing Old.* NY: Harmony Books, 1993.

Cohan, Beatty & Elliot. *For Better, For Worse, Forever: 10 Lasting Steps for Building a Lasting Relationship with the Man You Love.* MA: Chandler House Press, 1999.

Coles, Robert. *The Moral Intelligence of Children: How to Raise a Moral Child* (audio recording). Los Angeles, CA: Audio Renaissance Tapes, 1997.

Collins, Paldrom, and Collins, George N. *A Couple's Guide to Sexual Addiction: A Step-by-Step Plan to Rebuild Trust & Restore Intimacy.* MA: Adams Media, 2012.

Covey, Stephen. *Beyond the 7 Habits* (audio recording). NY: Simon & Schuster, 2003.

Covey, Stephen. *Living the 7 Habits: Stories of Courage and Inspiration* (audio recording). NY: Simon & Schuster Audio, 1999.

Dattilio, Frank M., and Bevilacqua, Louis J. (Editors). *Comparative Treatments for Relationship Dysfunction.* NY: Springer Publishing, 2000.

Daniels, Dawn Marie, and Sandy, Candace. *Tears to Triumph: Women Learn to Live, Love and Thrive.* NY: Kensington Publishing, 2009.

DeAngelis, Barbara, Ph.D. *Are You the One for Me? Real Moments.* NY: MJF Books, 1994.

DeAngelis, Barbara, Ph.D. *Secrets About Men Every Woman Should Know.* NY: Dell Publishing, 1990.

Doman, Glen, *The Institutes for the Achievement of Human Potential,* www.laph.org.

Dooley, Mike. *Manifesting Change: It Couldn't Be Easier.* NY: Simon & Schuster, 2010.

Dyer, Dr. Wayne. *Inspiration: Your Ultimate Calling* (audio recording) Hay House Inc. 2006.

Dyer, Dr. Wayne. *Staying on the Path.* Carisbad, CA: Hay House Inc. 2004.

Edward, John. *One Last Time. A psychic medium talks to those we have loved and lost.* www.JohnEdward.net.

Ellison, Sheila. *The Courage to Love Again: Creating Happy, Healthy Relationships after Divorce.* CA: HarperOne, 2002.

Erickson, Erik. *Psychological Stages of Development Summary Chart.* www.psychology.about.com/library/bl_psycholsocial_summary.htm.

Fein, Ellen, and Schneider, Sherri. *Not Your Mother's Rules – the New Secrets for Dating.* NY: Grand Central Publishing, 2013.

Ford, Debbie. *Why Good People Do Bad Things: How to Stop Being Your Own Worst Enemy.* NY: HarperOne, 2008.

Friends in Recovery. *The 12 Steps for Adult Children.* Centralia, WA: RPI Publishing, 1996.

Gafni, Marc. *Soul Prints: Your Path to Fulfillment* (audio recording). NY: Simon & Schuster Audio, 2001.

Glass, Lillian, Ph.D. *Toxic Men: 10 Ways to Identify, Deal with, and Heal from the Men who Make Your Life Miserable.* Avon, MA: Adams Media, 2010.

Gravitz, Herbert L., and Bowden, Julie D. *Recovery: A Guide for Adult Children of Alcoholics: Questions and Answers to Help you Understand your Past…Overcome your Fears.* NY: A Fireside/Learning Publication, 1985.

Gottman, John M. Ph.D., and DeClaire, Joan. *The Relationship Cure: A 5 Step Guide to Strengthening Your Marriage, Family and Friendships.* NY: Three Rivers Press, 2001.

Gottman, John, Ph.D, *Why Marriages Succeed or Fail...and How You Can Make Yours Last.* NY: Simon & Schuster, 1994.

Gray, John, Ph.D. *Mars and Venus Starting Over: A Practical Guide for Finding Love Again After a Painful Breakup, Divorce, or the Loss of a Loved One.* NY: Quill Publishing, 2002.

Gray, John, Ph.D. *Men, Women and Relationships: Making Peace with the Opposite Sex.* OR: Beyond Words Publishing, 1993.

Greenspon, T.S. *Making Sense of Error: A view of the origins and treatment of perfectionism.* American Journal of Psychotherapy, 62 (3) 263–282. 2008.

Greenspon, T.S. *What to do when good enough is not good enough: The real deal on perfectionism.* Minneapolis: Free Spirit Publishing. 2007.

Hallowell, Edward M.D., and Hallowell, Sue G., LCSW. *Married to Distraction: Restoring Intimacy and Strengthening your Marriage in an Age of Interruption.* (audio book). Random House. 2010.

Halpren, Howard, Ph.D. *Finally Getting it Right: From Addictive Love to The Real Thing.* NY: Bantam Books, 1995.

Hamachek, D. E., "Psychodynamics of normal and neurotic perfectionism", Psychology 15: 27–33, 1978.

Harris, Blase, MD. *How to Get Your Lover Back: Successful Strategies for Starting Over and Making it Better than it was Before!* NY: Dell Publishing, 1989.

Harvey, Steve. *Act Like a Lady, Think Like a Man: What Men Really Think about Love, Relationships, Intimacy and Commitment.* NY: HarperCollins Publishers, 2009.

Hawkins, David, Ph.D. *When Pleasing Others is Hurting You.* OR: Harvest House Publishers, 2004.

Haywood, Susan. *A Guide for the Advanced Soul: A Book of Insight.* NY: Little, Brown and Company, 1984.

Hendrix, Harville. Ph.D. *Getting the Love You Want: A Guide for Couples.* NY: Owl Books, 1988.

Hetherington, E. Mavis, and Kelly, John. *For Better or For Worse, Divorce Reconsidered.* NY: W.W. Norton & Company, 2002.

Hicks, Esther and Jerry. *The Astonishing Power of Emotions: Let Feelings Be Your Guide.* Carlsbad, CA: Hay House; 2007.

Hill, Napoleon. *Think and Grow Rich.* NY: Penguin Group, 2005.

Hussey, Matthew. *Get the Guy – Learn Secrets of the Male Mind to Find the Man you Want and the Love You Deserve.* New York, NY: Harper Collins Publishers, 2013.

Ilardi, Stephen. *The Depression Cure: The 6-Step Program to Beat Depression without Drugs.* Philadelphia, PA: Da Capo Press, 2009.

Katz, Stan J. Ph.D, and Liu, Aimee E. *False Love and other Romantic Illusions: Why Love Goes Wrong and How to Make it Right.* NY: Pocket Books, 1988.

Kendrick, Stephen, and Kendrick, Alex. *The Love Dare.* TN: B & H Publishing Group, 2008.

Kiley, Dan, Ph.D. *The Peter Pan Syndrome: Men who have never grown up.* NY: Dodd, Mead & Co. 1983.

Kirshenbaum, Mira. *Too Good to Leave, Too Bad to Stay: A Step by Step Guide to Help you Decide Whether to Stay In or Get Out of Your Relationship.* NY: Penguin Group, 1996.

Lerner, Harriet G., Ph.D. *On Mothers & Daughters: Breaking the Patterns that Keep You Stuck* (audio recording) Boulder, CO: Sounds True Audio, 1995.

Lerner, Harriet G., Ph.D. *The Dance of Intimacy: A Woman's Guide to Courageous Acts of Change in Key Relationships.* NY: Perennial Library, 1990.

Levine, Amir, MD and Heller, Rachel: *Attached. The New Science of Adult Attachment and How it Can Help you Find and Keep Love.* NY: Penguin Group, 2010.

Lieberman, David. *Instant Analysis: How You Can Understand and Change Self-Defeating Behaviors & Habits.* NY: Martin's Press, 1997.

Lluch, Alex A. *Simple Principles for a Happy and Healthy Marriage.* CA: WS Publishing Group, 2008.

Mackay, Harvey. *Pushing the Envelope: All the Way to the Top* (audio recording). NY: Random House Audio Books, 1999.

Markman, Howard J., Scott, Stanley M., and Blumberg, Susan L. *Fighting for your Marriage.* CA: Jossey-Bass, 2010.

McGibbon, Amalia, Vogel, Lara, and Williams, Claire A. *The Choice Effect: Love and Commitment in an Age of Too Many Options.* CA: Seal Press, 2010.

McGraw, Phil C., Ph.D. *Life Code – The New Rules for Winning in the Real World.* CA: Bird Street Books, 2013.

McGraw, Phil C., Ph.D. *Love Smart – Find the One You Want – Fix the One You Got.* NY: Free Press, 2005.

McGraw, Phillip C., Ph.D. *The Relationship Rescue Workbook – Exercises and Self-Tests to Help you Reconnect with your Partner.* NY: Hyperion, 2000.

McNeilly, Robert. *Healing the Whole Person.* NY: John Wiley & Sons, 2000.

Martin, Stephen, MFT. *The Everything Guide to a Happy Marriage: Expert Advice and Information for a Happy Life Together.* MA: F & W Media, Inc., 2009.

Mataix-Cols, D., Frost, R.O., Pertusa, A., Clark, L.A., Saxena, S., Leckman, J.F., Stein, D.J., Matsunaga, H., and Wilhelm, S. (2010). *Hoarding disorder: A new diagnosis for DSM-V? Depression and Anxiety,* Vol. 27, pp. 556–572.

Mellody, Pia, Miller, Andrea Wells, and Miller, J. Keith. *Facing Love Addiction: Giving Yourself the Power to Change the Way You Love.* CA: HarperOne, 1992.

Mellody, Pia. *The Intimacy Factor: The Ground Rules for Overcoming the Obstacles to Truth, Respect and Lasting Love.* NY: HarperOne, 2004.

Meyers, Seth, PsyD. *Dr. Seth's Love Prescription.* MA: Adams Media, 2011.

Miedaner, Talane. *The Secret Laws of Attraction: The Effortless Way to Get the Relationship You Want.* NY: McGraw Hill, 2008.

Miedaner, Talane. *Coach Yourself to Success: 101 Tips from a Personal Coach for Reaching your Goals at Work and in Life.* Chicago, IL: Contemporary Books, 2000.

Milne, Riana, LMHC, LPC, LCADC, and Panos, Alexi. *Live Beyond Your Dreams: From Fear and Doubt to Personal Power, Purpose and Success.* NJ: By the Sea Books LLC, 2013.

Milne, Riana, LMHC, LPC, LCADC, and Panos, Alexi. *Watch Me! The Bold New Motivational Attitude for Personal Success.* NJ: By the Sea Books LLC, 2006.

Mims, Ana. *Keeping the Faith: How Applying Spiritual Purpose to Your Work Can Lead to Extraordinary Success.* NY: HarperCollins, 2007.

Moore, Thomas. *Care of the Soul: A Guide for Cultivating Depth and Sacredness in Everyday Life* (audio recording). NY: Harper Audio, 1992.

Orbuch, Terri L., Ph.D. *5 Simple Steps to Take Your Marriage from Good to Great.* NY: Delacorte Press, 2009.

References and Recommended Reading

Orman, Suze. *Women & Money*. NY. Random House, 2007.

Osho. *Intimacy – Trusting Oneself and the Other*. NY: St. Martin's Griffin, 2001.

Osteen, Joel. *Become a Better You: 7 Keys to Improving Your Life Every Day*. NY: Free Press, 2007.

Osteen, Joel. *Good, Better, Blessed: Living with Purpose, Power and Passion* (audio recording). NY: Simon & Schuster, 2008.

Osteen, Joel. *Your Best Life Now: 7 Steps to Living at your Full Potential*. NY: Hachette Books Group, 2004.

Papp, Peggy. *Couples on the Fault Line: New Directions for Therapists*. NY: The Guildford Press, 2000.

Pinto, Anthony, Eisen, Jane, Mancebo, Maria and Rasmussen, Steven. *Obsessive Compulsive Personality Disorders*. Rhode Island: Elsevier Ltd. Wikipedia.com. 2008.

Prochaska, James, Norcross, John, and Diclemente, Carlo. *Changing for Good: A Revolutionary Six-stage Program for Overcoming Bad Habits and Moving Your Life Positively Forward*. NY: Avon Books, 1994.

Robbins, Anthony with Gray, Dr. John: *Powertalk! On Creating Extraordinary Relationships;* Audio Renaissance Tapes; Los Angeles, CA, 1996.

Robbins, Anthony with Madanes, Cloe, and Peysha, Mark. *Love & Passion – The Ultimate Relationship Program (audios and videos);* Robbins Research International, Inc.; CA, 2007.

Robbins, Anthony: *Giant Steps: Small Changes to Make a Big Difference;* Fireside Publishing, NY, 1994.

Robbins, Anthony: *Ultimate Edge Program: A 3-part System for Creating an Extraordinary Life in any Environment (audios and videos)*, Robbins Research International, Inc.; CA, 2009.

Rock, Joseph W. Psy.D, and Duncan, Barry L., Psy.D. *Let's Face it, All Men are @$$#%\¢$": What Women Can Do About It.* FL: Health Communications, Inc. 1998.

Roger, John, and Kaye, Paul. *Momentum – Letting Love Lead: Simple Practices for Spiritual Living.* CA: Manderville Press, 2003.

Rosenberg, Ross A. *Emotional Manipulators & Codependents: Understanding the Attraction.* CMI Education Institute, 2012.

Rouse, Linda P. *You are Not Alone: A Guide for Battered Women.* FL: Learning Publications, 1986.

Salzberg, Sharon. *Faith: Trusting Your Own Deepest Experience.* London: Element Books, 2002.

Sanena, S., and Maidment, K. *Treatment for compulsive hoarding.* Journal of Clinical Psychology, Vol. 60, No. 11, pp.1143–1154. 2004.

Schlessinger, Laura, Ph.D. *10 Stupid Things Men Do to Mess Up their Lives.* NY: HarperCollins Publishers, 2002.

www.saa-recovery.org: Sex Addicts Anonymous; Sexual Addictions Recovery website.

Sha, Dr., and Master Zhi Gang. *Divine Transformation: The Divine Way to Self-clear Karma to Transform Your Health, Relationships, Finances and More.* NY: Simon & Schuster, 2010.

Shumsky, Susan. *Divine Revelation.* NY: Simon & Schuster, 1996.

Sotile, Wayne M., Ph.D., and Sotile, Mary O. *Supercouple Syndrome: How Overworked Couples can Beat Stress Together.* NY: John Wiley & Sons, 1998.

St. James, Elaine. *Inner Simplicity: Regain Peace and Spirituality* (audio recording). NY: Bantam Doubleday Dell Audio Publishing, 1998.

Steele, David, LMFT. *Conscious Dating: Finding the Love of Your Life in Today's World.* CA: RCN Press, 2006.

Steele, David, LMFT. *Conscious Mating: A Program for Pre-Committed and Pre-Marital Couples.* www.RelationshipCoachingInstitute.com, 2007.

Steele, David, LMFT. *Relationship Coaching: New Approaches for Helping Singles and Couples Achieve their Relationship Goals,* and – *The Communication Map,* www.RelationshipCoachingInstitute.com, 2005.

Steffens, Barbara, Ph.D., and Means, Marsha. *Your Sexually Addicted Spouse: How Partners Can Cope and Heal.* NJ: New Horizon Press, 2009.

Stoeber, Joachim, and Otto, Kathleen. "Positive Conceptions of Perfectionism: Approaches, Evidence, Challenges." *Personality and Social Psychology Review* 10 (4): 295–319, 2006.

Stout, Martha, Ph.D. *The Sociopath Next Door: The Ruthless Versus the Rest of Us.* NY: Three Rivers Press, 2005.

Tallis, Frank, Ph.D. *Love Sick: Love as a Mental Illness.* NY: Thunder's Mouth Press, 2004.

Taylor, John Maxwell. *The Power of I Am: Creating a New World of Enlightened Personal Interaction.* CA: Frog Publishing, 2006.

Thomas, Katherine Woodward. *Calling in "The One"* – *7 Weeks to Attract the Love of Your Life.* NY: Three Rivers Press, 2004.

Tolle, Eckhart. *A New Earth: Awaking to Your Life's Purpose.* NY: Penguin Group, 2005.

Tolle, Eckhart. *The Power of Now: A Guide to Spiritual Enlightenment.* CA: New World Library, 1999.

Urban, Hal. *Choices that Change Lives: 15 Ways to Find More Purpose, Meaning and Joy.* NY: Simon & Schuster, 2006.

Van Praagh, James. *Tuning into Healing/Forgiveness* (audio recording). NY: Penguin Audio Books, 1998.

Vitale, Dr. Joe. *Expect Miracles: The Missing Secret to Astounding Success* (audio recording). Gildan Media Corp. 2009.

Warren, Neil C., Ph.D. *Falling in Love for all the Right Reasons.* NY: Center Street, 2005.

Weeks, Gerald R., Ph.D; Fife, Stephen T. *Couples in Treatment: Techniques and Approaches for Effective Practice.* NY: Brunner/Mazel, Publishers. 1992.

Wetzler, Scott, Ph.D. *Living with the Passive Aggressive Man: Coping with Hidden Aggression – from the Bedroom to the Boardroom.* NY: Simon & Schuster, 1992.

Wikipedia, The Free Encyclopedia. http://en.wikipedia.org.

Williamson, Marianne. *The Gift of Change: Spiritual Guidance for a Radically New Life* (audio recording). CA: Harper Audio, 2004.

Williamson, Marianne. *On Intimacy* (audio recording). www.marianne.com/books.

Wilson, Beth. *He's Just No Good for You: A Guide to Getting Out of a Destructive Relationship.* CT: The Globe Pequot Press, 2009.

Wilson, James Q. *The Marriage Problem: How Our Culture Has Weakened Families.* NY: HarperCollinsPublishers, 2002.

Woititz, Janet G., Ed.D. *The Complete ACOA Sourcebook, Adult Children of Alcoholics at Home, at Work and in Love.* FL: Health Communications, Inc. 2002.

Wolf, Sharyn, CSW. *How to Stay Lovers for Life: Discover a Marriage Counselor's Tricks of the Trade.* NY: Dutton Books, 1997.

Woods, Len. *Handbook of World Religions.* OH: Barbour Publishing, 2008.

Zukav, Gary. *Soul to Soul: Communications from the Heart.* NY: Free Press, 2007.

Great Websites to Visit:

www.healthy-exchange.com/online – Breaking Up is Hard to Do, Relationships: Secrets of Happy Couples (7/2003)

www.Drphil.com/articles: The Character of Him, Stop Excusing Inexcusable Behavior, The Marriage Checklist (11/2012)

www.RianaMilne.com. Free articles for Couples and Singles, on creating wonderful and loving relationships in your life.

www.Transformationnation.podbean.com – with Alexi Panos. Host Alexi interviews personal transformation leaders to inspire change in your life.

www.Webmd.com. Web resource for herbal and holistic vitamins, remedies, and medicines.

App: *My Relationship Coach,* by Riana Milne, MA, LPC, LMHC, Cert. Relationship & Life Coach. Free Downloadable app for Droid and Apple Smart phones/iPads. Launched 12/2012.

Life & Relationship Coaching provided by Riana Milne
Coaching Life Transformation & Successful Relationships

For details, pricing information and to register for any coaching program, go to the website http://www.rianamilne.com/ or email: RianaMilne@gmail.com.

Coaching services for those:

Single, Dating, Engaged, Married, in Painful Relationships, or Surviving the loss of a loved one or relationship; Healing from affairs, Addictions, Abuse/Toxic relationships, Separation, Divorce, in Difficult transitions, Troubled teens, and Parenting/family/sibling issues; Adult Business/career and Teen college prep coaching

- Individuals & Couples
- Dating Success Strategies for Singles
- Pre-Marital Relationship Coaching/Workshops
- Marriage/Couples Coaching/Retreats
- Gay/Lesbian Relationships
- Strategies to Stay Together; Keeping Love Alive
- Healthy Communication Skills
- Are you in an Abusive Relationship?

- How to Identify a Toxic Person
- Breaking Free from Toxic Relationships
- Surviving Divorce, Breakups & Toxic Relationships
- Are You Addicted to Love or a Person?
- After the Loss – Transition at any age
- Re-entering the Dating World
- Choosing an Emotionally Healthy Life Partner
- Midlife Changes and Goals
- Finding Balance in Life/Relationships
- Life and Career Coaching
- Resume and college prep for Teens
- Finding Motivation to Change
- Spirituality & Success – the Essential Connection
- Spiritual Healing and Wellness – Life Coaching for Conscious Living
- Be a Positive, Powerful Woman
- Mighty Men – the Evolved Male Partner
- De-Stress! Personal Time Management
- Sexuality and Intimacy Issues
- Stop Anxiety and Depression
- Raising Self Esteem
- Bereavement, Loss of a Loved One
- Overcoming Post Traumatic Stress, Grief
- Coaching for Parents of difficult children and teens
- Raising Successful Children and Teens

- Teen and Children's Anxiety, Depression, and Anger
- Addictions in Relationships (Alcohol, Drugs, Gambling, Sexual Addiction and Eating Disorders)
- Life Coaching for the ACOA (Adult Child of an Alcoholic, or other trauma)
- Are you Codependent?
- Entertainment Industry Coach (Modeling/Acting/Singing)

Personal Coaching with Riana available:
Monday through Thursday 12–7 pm EST (day rate) or 8 pm–11pm EST (night rate); sessions held by phone, Skype, Face Time, email, or within Riana's office in Delray Beach, Florida:

>Therapy by the Sea, LLC
>15300 Jog Road, Suite 109
>Delray Beach, FL 33446
>Ph: (201) 281-7887

MC, Visa, PayPal available through www.RianaMilne.com.

Ask about Coaching package discounts and bonuses. See website for other offers, seminars, speaking events, book signings and retreats.

Group Coaching–Relationship Success Training for Singles ©

For finding the Love of your Life & Living the Life that you Love!

Riana Milne, MA, LMHC, LPC, LCADC, CAP
Certified Relationship & Life Coach

Phone: 201-281-7887   RianaMilne@gmail.com

http://www.rianamilne.com/

App: My Relationship Coach

Link for Apple phones and iPads: https://itunes.apple.com/us/app/my-relationship-coach/id589020215?mt=8

Link for Google play and Droid Smart phones: https://play.google.com/store/apps/details?id=com.app_mycoach.layout&hl=en%C3%82%C2%A0%C3%82

Section ONE – Establishing my Relationship Vision: Requirements, Wants and Needs; Preparing myself to be the best I can be for a quality Relationship

Section One Classes can include

1. Mind maps, vision board, my values and life purpose, what I want to do, be and have

2. My Relationship history, childhood patterns, Needs, Wants, Requirements, Personality traits
3. Perfecting my image – for myself and to attract the partner I really want
4. My Relationship Plan: Self and partner profile, setting goals for meeting your vision, my Attraction plan, venues, Dating plan, Life sphere goals and timelines
5. Summary, Review, Questions and answers

Part Two – Starts at Conclusion of Part One; a Total of 4 weeks
Same times, place, and same limit of Group participants

Section TWO – My Relationship Plan: Navigating the Attraction Stage, getting what you want in a relationship, Dating traps, sorting and screening, being partners for Life

Section Two Classes can include
1. The Attraction Stage – Who I am, what I want, and how to get it; Relationship Readiness assessment
2. Avoiding the Dating Traps, 10 Principals of Conscious dating, What you believe you can achieve, Discussion of actual dating/meeting experiences
3. Understanding and using the Laws of Attraction and "The 10 Love Secrets"
4. Summary, Review, Questions and answers

Group Coaching–Relationship Success Training for Singles

Dates & Times – go to App Calendar, website or email Riana to get start dates.

Coaching Groups limited to 15 participants
*The Professional, Singles workbook is required; $40 extra; used for workbook in both sections

For details, pricing information and to register for any coaching program, go to http://www.rianamilne.com/ or email: RianaMilne@gmail.com

Private Coaching packages available!

BONUS: For those booking a PRIVATE Coaching package, for a total of 8 sessions; you will receive a FREE 15 minute individual Coaching session with Riana for your Personal goal setting, both of the *Beyond Your Dreams* series books for free, and receive a $100 savings off your package price! – A $200 value!

Group Coaching – Relationship Success Training for Couples ©
Re-Kindle the Love You Once Knew

Riana Milne, MA, LPC, LMHC, LCADC, CAP
Certified Relationship & Life Coach

Phone: 201-281-7887   Email: RianaMilne@gmail.com

http://www.rianamilne.com/

App: My Relationship Coach

Link for Apple phones and iPads: https://itunes.apple.com/us/app/my-relationship-coach/id589020215?mt=8

Link for Google play and Droid Smart phones:
https://play.google.com/store/apps/details?id=com.app_mycoach.layout&hl=en%C3%82%C2%A0%C3%82

Section ONE – Reclaiming the Relationship Vision; An Action plan for Couples

1. **Qualities of the ideal, Evolved Relationship:** Relationship status, Assessment, Rating form, feeding your Emotional bank account, understanding Interdependence
2. **Addressing your Individual Requirements, Wants and Needs:** Personal needs shared, Discovering the Couples Love language, Building integrity and trust

3. **Balance and Daily Life Management:** Finding Balance together for household chores, Money/finances, children, work, Couple time/intimacy and sexual desires
4. **Facing my Relationship Competencies and Dysfunctional Behavior:** Admitting our faults, Creating an Action plan for behavior change and a new vision

Section TWO – Our Relationship Plan

Starts at Conclusion of Part One; a Total of 4 weeks for each section

Same times, place, and same limit of Group participants

1. **Discussing Key Relationship Topics:** Money, sex, children, home, faith, lifestyle, extended family, and creating a plan for a happy balance of all the above
2. **Communication and Conflict Resolution:** Communication Map, a process for better, loving communication, Behavior change requests, working through issues
3. **Ten new Laws of Love:** Discussing Fears, Fantasies, Love and Appreciation to have the Love relationship you always wanted
4. **Rebuilding our Vision:** My ideal Love, Life, Future, Purpose, Relationship values, setting new Relationship goals, Rituals, and plans for your future

Group Coaching—Relationship Success Training for Couples

Dates & Times – go to App Calendar, website, or email Riana to get start dates.

Coaching Groups limited to 8 couples,
*The Professional, Training for Couples workbook is required; $40 extra; used for workbook in both sections.

For details, pricing information and to register for any coaching program, go to the web site http://www.rianamilne.com/ or email: RianaMilne@gmail.com

Private Couples Coaching package available!

BONUS: For those booking a PRIVATE Couples Coaching package For a total of 8 sessions; you will receive a FREE 15 minute individual Coaching session with Riana for *each partner* for Personal goal setting, both of the *Beyond Your Dreams* series books for free, and receive a $100 savings off your package price! – A $250 value!

ORDERING INFORMATION

Love Beyond Your Dreams: *Break Free of Toxic Relationships to Have the Love You Deserve*

Please see Riana's Web site, http://www.rianamilne.com/, for other products available, and get information on other books, how to receive Relationship or Life Coaching, set therapy appointments, attend speaking events/seminars, and to join her mailing list.

Get Riana's free app, **My Relationship Coach,** *for your smart phone.*

Link for Apple phones and iPads: https://itunes.apple.com/us/app/my-relationship-coach/id589020215?mt=8

Link for Google play and Droid Smart phones: https://play.google.com/store/apps/details?id=com.app_mycoach.layout&hl=en%C3%82%C2%A0%C3%82

E-mail orders:	BytheSeaBookPublishingCompany@gmail.com
Phone orders:	201-281-7887 (please have credit card ready)
Postal orders:	By the Sea Books Publishing Company c/o Riana Milne, 15300 Jog Rd., Suite 109, Delray Beach, FL 33446

Name _____

Address _____

City _____ State/Province ____ Zip/Postal Code _____

Telephone _____ E-mail _____

Per book cost: $16.95 US; $20.95 CAN and other countries
$4.00 US shipping, $6.00 outside of USA
Volume discounts available – please call for information

Payment: ☐ Check   ☐ Credit Card: ☐ Visa ☐ MasterCard

Card Number _____ Expiration _____

Exact name on card _____

_____ **check here if you would like to order – Live Beyond Your Dreams –** *from Fear and Doubt to Personal Power, Purpose and Success;* Riana's first book in the series. The same ordering and price information applies.

Please state here – *Book Dedication to* – Riana will be glad to sign your book!

_____

eBook versions available at www.amazon.com, www.barnesandnoble.com, and on many other platforms.

Thank you for your order! Satisfaction guaranteed.

*Success is a journey not a destination –
half the fun is getting there.*
- Gita Bellin

Notes

Notes

Notes

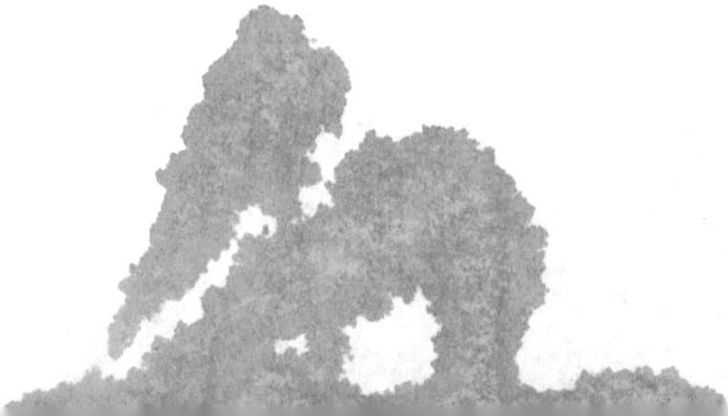

CPSIA information can be obtained
at www.ICGtesting.com
Printed in the USA
BVHW041030160519
548477BV00015B/1011/P